Housing Law in Scotland

Housing Law in Scotland

CMG Himsworth

Fourth edition

Butterworths/The Planning Exchange
Edinburgh
1994

United Kingdom	Butterworths a Division of Reed Elsevier (UK) Ltd, 4 Hill Street, EDINBURGH EH2 3JZ and Halsbury House, 35 Chancery Lane, LONDON WC2A 1EL
Australia	Butterworths, SYDNEY, MELBOURNE, BRISBANE, ADELAIDE, PERTH, CANBERRA
Canada	Butterworths Canada Ltd, TORONTO and VANCOUVER
Ireland	Butterworth (Ireland) Ltd, DUBLIN
Malaysia	Malayan Law Journal Sdn Bhd. KUALA LUMPUR
New Zealand	Butterworths of New Zealand Ltd, WELLINGTON and AUCKLAND
Singapore	Butterworths, Asia, SINGAPORE
South Africa	Butterworths Publishers (Pty) Ltd, DURBAN
USA	Michie, CHARLOTTESVILLE, Virginia

A CIP Catalogue record for this book is available from the British Library

First published 1994

Reprinted 1996, 1998

ISBN 0406 02979 2

Typeset by Phoenix Photosetting, Chatham, Kent
Printed by Antony Rowe Ltd, Chippenham, Wiltshire

Preface

Although this book is a successor to the three editions of my *Public Sector Housing Law in Scotland*, it also contains much new material. In particular, the attention given to the statutory landlord and tenant regimes in the private sector is intended to produce a more rounded picture of housing law as a whole. Original material has also been adapted and expanded as necessary to take account of recent changes in the law, including those contained in the Leasehold Reform, Housing and Urban Development Act 1993. As far as possible, the book has been updated to be accurate at the end of 1993 although some later developments have been incorporated.

At the time of writing, few legislative changes affecting Scottish housing law are in the pipeline which makes this a good moment for the book to appear. Hanging over the whole of Scottish public administration, however, are the changes, fully effective from April 1996, to be made to Scottish local government by the current Local Government etc (Scotland) Bill which will probably reach the statute book soon after this book is published. That legislation does not greatly affect housing law as such but its principal effects are anticipated in Chapter 1. As in the past, my hope is that the efforts (including those of the publisher whose great help is acknowledged) taken to produce accurate up-to-date material and, at the same time, to exclude unnecessary detail in a notoriously complex field will sustain this book as a useful guide for the non-specialist (and a first point of reference for the specialist) during the next few years.

I am very grateful for their help in the preparation of this book to Tom Duncan, Margaret Lindley and Neil Walker.

C M G Himsworth
March 1994

Contents

Table of cases

Table of statutes

Table of statutory instruments

Scottish Office circulars

The following list of circulars issued by the Scottish Development Department (usually in the style eg 'SDD No 28/1974') and then, since 1991, by the Scottish Office Environment Department (in the style eg 'Env Circular No 2/1994') is taken from an index of extant housing circulars as at 31 August 1993 (issued as Env Circular No 23/1993) with the addition of housing circulars issued since that date.

28/1974	Housing (Financial Provisions) (Scotland) Act 1968 and Housing (Scotland) Act 1969. Improvement of houses. (Amended by SDD 35/1978.)
79/1974	Housing (Scotland) Act 1974.
94/1974	Housing (Scotland) Act 1974: Housing (Forms) (Scotland) Regulations 1974.
67/1975	Housing (Scotland) Act 1974—Houses Below the Tolerable Standard: Housing Action Areas.
108/1975	Housing Act 1974—Housing Rents and Subsidies (Scotland) Act 1975. Retention of property subject to demolition etc: consent to demolition of buildings subsequently listed: Rehabilitation Orders.
120/1975	Housing for the Elderly.
14/1977	Tenant Participation and Housing Co-operatives.
35/1978	Housing (Financial Provisions) (Scotland) Act 1978—Housing Improvement and slum clearance. (Amends SDD 28/1974.)
23/1980	Tenants Rights Etc (Scotland) Act 1980. (Amended by SDD 17/1984 and SDD 34/1986.)
29/1980	Tenants Rights Etc (Scotland) Act 1980: local authority home loans. (Amends Circular SDD 23/1980.)
30/1980	Tenants Rights Etc (Scotland) Act 1980: Sale of local authority houses. (Amended by Circular SDD 23/1983.)
31/1980	Tenants Rights Etc (Scotland) Act 1980 Part II. (Amends Circular SDD 23/1980.)
32/1980	Sale of houses by public bodies other than housing authorities. (Amended by SDD 14/1983 and SDD 22/1983.)
33/1980	Tenants Rights Etc (Scotland) Act 1980: Housing Improvement Grants under the Housing (Scotland) Act 1974.
3/1981	Housing (Scotland) Act 1974: Housing (Percentage of Approved Expense for Improvement Grants) (Scotland) Order 1978: Housing (Forms) (Scotland) Regulations 1980.
17/1981	HRA: service charges.
19/1981	Local Government (Miscellaneous Provisions) (Scotland) Act 1981: housing provisions.
20/1981	Improvement Grants.
25/1981	Part I: Housing Plans (Superseded by SDD 16/1989). Part II: Demolition of Local Authority Houses.

Abbreviations

Because frequent reference is made in the text and footnotes to the Housing (Scotland) Act 1987 and the Housing (Scotland) Act 1988, they are often referred to as the '1987 Act', and the '1988 Act' respectively. The Housing Act 1988 is always referred to as such. Other abbreviated names of statutes used in the book are:

1973 Act	Local Government (Scotland) Act 1973
1980 Act	Tenants' Rights, Etc (Scotland) Act 1980
1984 Act	Rent (Scotland) Act 1984
1989 Act	Local Government and Housing Act 1989
1993 Act	Leasehold Reform, Housing and Urban Development Act 1993

Other abbreviations appearing in the book include:

All ER	All England Law Reports
Cmnd, Cm	Command Paper
COSLA	Convention of Scottish Local Authorities
GFC	General fund contribution
HAA	Housing action area
HC	House of Commons paper
HRA	Housing revenue account
HSG	Housing support grant
JLS	Journal of the Law Society of Scotland
SC	Session Cases
SCLR	Scottish Civil Law Reports
SCOLAG	Bulletin of the Scottish Legal Action Group
SDD	Scottish Development Department
SI	Statutory Instrument
SLT	Scots Law Times

CHAPTER 1

Local housing authorities and their functions

1. INTRODUCTION

In November 1987, the Government launched its proposals for the reform of housing policy in Scotland and, when it came to discuss the future role of local housing authorities, it said:

'. . . the Government will encourage public sector housing authorities to change and develop their role. The scale of provision by housing authorities as landlords should gradually diminish through the availability to tenants of a greater choice of alternatives. Some authorities will want to move in this direction themselves, and the Government will assist them. Some tenants will want to take the initiative and the Government will give them new rights to do so. This will enable them to improve their housing conditions and to have a say in their own future. Although local authorities will remain substantial landlords, they should increasingly see themselves as enablers who ensure that everyone in their area is adequately housed; but not necessarily by them. Their strategic role has been neglected and should now receive greater attention, as the choice of alternative providers of housing increases.'[1]

The years since 1987 have seen the enactment of much of the legislation which will 'change and develop', for better or worse, the housing role of local authorities and it may be that, in the years to come, further changes will remove local authorities from the centre stage of housing practice. There remains no doubt today, however, where any account of the law and practice of housing in Scotland must begin and that is with the powers and responsibilities of local authorities. They dominate the housing statute book, as they have in the whole of this century.

2. STRUCTURE

When Scottish local government was reorganised on 16 May 1975 in consequence of the report of the Wheatley Royal Commission[2] and the

1 *Housing: The Government's Proposals for Scotland*, Cm 242 (1987) para 1.22.
2 Cmnd 4150 (1969).

Local Government (Scotland) Act 1973, primary responsibility for local housing functions was transferred from the old cities, burghs and counties to the 53 mainland district councils and the 3 islands councils of Orkney, Shetland and the Western Isles.[1] Housing became, for the districts, their most important function.

The 1973 Act gave these authorities a general power (but they were not required) to arrange for the discharge of their functions by a committee or sub-committee; an officer of the authority; or even another local authority.[2] Whilst most authorities do in practice delegate functions to a housing committee, this is not a statutory requirement. Functions are also routinely delegated internally to council officials on a formal or informal basis.

Collectively the interests of local housing authorities are represented on the Housing Committee of the Convention of Scottish Local Authorities (COSLA). The committee considers a wide range of housing matters affecting the work of local authorities on the initiative of either member councils or, more usually, the Secretary of State or national Scottish or UK bodies with housing interests. Frequently the outcome of its deliberations is simply an expression of opinion representative of housing authorities and the committee becomes particularly active in this way as it responds to major legislative proposals from the Secretary of State. In recent years, COSLA has given publicity to many of its views on housing issues as part of a wider campaign to attract support for them—see eg *Scottish Housing Manifesto* (1987) and *By Popular Demand—Scotland's Council Housing* (1987) (produced jointly with Shelter). It is also involved in the annual statutory consultations on the housing support grant[3] and the co-ordination of the performance of housing duties (eg in relation to homeless persons under Part II of the 1987 Act).[4]

The Scotland Act 1978 brought with it the prospect of an adjustment of local authority functions including housing, but that possibility of a major change receded with the repeal of the Act in 1979.[5] The allocation of functions was examined by the Stodart Committee appointed in 1980 to review the reorganised system of local government with a view to improving the effective discharge of local authority functions. Dealing with housing, the Committee reported that, in spite of arguments favouring its removal to the regional councils, the function should remain with the districts: 'The core of

1 1987 Act, s 338(1) and 1973 Act, s 130.
2 Section 56.
3 See p 12 below.
4 See Chap 10 below.
5 SI 1979/928.

that case is that the loss of housing would seriously impair the viability of district councils and deprive them of a function which gives coherence and substance to their present range of duties.'[1]

More recently the Government has embarked on a complete restructuring of local government designed to come fully into operation in 1996. Its proposals derive from a belief (strongly opposed by its critics) that the role of local government has changed greatly since the 1960s and 1970s when authorities were major service providers and when the regions in particular had a comprehensive planning function in their areas; that the need for the large regional authorities has disappeared; and that a single-tier system of local government should be established.[2] As far as the housing role of local authorities is concerned, the Government has reaffirmed that, in its view the present functions will continue to be the main concerns of local authorities in the future. The council housing sector is expected to continue to diminish but it will remain a large and important part of the total housing stock for the foreseeable future. The wider enabling role of local authorities will, the Government says, become more important and a particular advantage claimed for a single-tier system of authorities will be the opportunity for co-ordination of the housing and social work functions by unitary authorities responsible for both. Improved co-ordination may also be expected with other functions such as education, roads and transport.[3]

The Local Government Etc (Scotland) Bill (1993–94) provides for the setting up of 28 local authorities with elections to be held early in 1995 to produce 'shadow authorities' which will take over full control from 1 April 1996. They will have all the housing functions of the existing district and islands councils.

3. FUNCTIONS, PLANS AND FINANCE

Functions

Although the capacity to carry it out varies considerably according to the political and financial climate for the time being, the most

---

1 *Report of the Committee of Inquiry into Local Government in Scotland*, Cmnd 8115, para 84.
2 See consultation papers *The Structure of Local Government in Scotland: The Case for Change* (1991) and *The Structure of Local Government in Scotland: Shaping the New Councils* (1992) and the White Paper *Shaping the Future—The New Councils* Cm 2267 (1993).
3 See *Shaping the New Councils* Chap 22 and *Shaping the Future* paras 3.25–3.26.

important historical and continuing function of a housing authority is the provision of housing accommodation. It is the duty of every authority to consider the housing conditions in its area and the needs of the area for further housing accommodation.[1] Provision of accommodation may be by the erection of new houses; the conversion of buildings into houses; the acquisition of houses; and the altering, enlarging, repairing or improving of houses or other buildings. They may also provide hostels.[2] Ancillary powers include the power to provide shops and recreational and other amenities in association with housing developments.[3] In providing houses and other facilities, authorities are expected to have regard to 'artistic quality' in the lay-out and planning of houses, the beauty of the landscape or countryside and the desirability of preserving existing works of architectural, historic or artistic interest.[4] To enable them to carry out these functions, authorities have the power to acquire the necessary land and buildings either by agreement or, with the consent of the Secretary of State, compulsorily under the Acquisition of Land (Authorisation Procedure) (Scotland) Act 1947.[5]

The next important housing authority function is to manage its housing stock as landlord. This landlord and tenant relationship is the subject of Chapter 7. In some circumstances, an authority will wish to dispose of its houses by sale and, under Part III of the 1987 Act, it may be compelled to sell to its own tenants. These matters are dealt with in Chapters 8 and 9 which are followed by a chapter on the duties of authorities in relation to homelessness. Following uncertainty created by a decision of the English Court of Appeal,[6] specific powers were given (retrospectively) to local authorities by the 1993 Act to provide 'services for promoting the welfare' of the people for whom housing accommodation is provided.[7] The nature of such services is not spelled out but it may be assumed to include wardening for sheltered accommodation and advice work. Charges may be made.[8] Joining the power to provide the welfare services is a power for the Secretary of

---

1 1987 Act, s 1(1).
2 Ibid, s 2. But nb s 2(6) (inserted by the Local Government and Housing Act 1989) which declares that there is no obligation on authorities to own houses or land in order to discharge their housing responsibilities.
3 Ibid, ss 3–5.
4 Ibid, s 6.
5 Ibid, ss 9–10. For sales, see Chaps 8 and 9 below.
6 *R v London Borough of Ealing, ex p Lewis* (1992) 24 HLR 484.
7 Leasehold Reform, Housing and Urban Development Act 1993, s 149 inserting a new s 5A into the 1987 Act.
8 1987 Act, s 5A(2). Accounting for housing welfare services may be handled through the housing revenue account or another account of the authority—s 5A(3) and Sch 15, para 4A.

State to repeal the relevant provisions by order.[1] It is likely that repeal will follow local government reorganisation when housing authorities will also acquire social work responsibilities which, in the Government's view, are a more appropriate source of powers to provide housing welfare services.

In addition to these functions concerned principally with their own housing stock, councils have important responsibilities in relation to the demolition, repair and improvement of substandard houses of all types in their areas. These are discussed in Chapters 11 and 12 which are followed by a concluding chapter on financial assistance for housing. It should also be remembered, however, that an authority's housing functions do not exist in a vacuum. Most housing authorities have planning, public health and building control responsibilities which all overlap with housing powers and duties. One particularly close cousin is the responsibility (shared with regional councils) for travelling people. Scottish local authorities are not under a statutory duty to provide sites but they are strongly urged to do so and may receive grants from the Secretary of State of up to 75% of approved capital costs.[2] The Secretary of State has an Advisory Committee on Scotland's Travelling People.

Considered together, these functions cover a wide range. They have accumulated in housing authority hands in a somewhat haphazard manner as successive pieces of legislation have reflected different priorities of central government. As a result, there is little in the Housing Acts to ensure that powers are used to achieve any sort of comprehensive housing policy at the local level whether in response to central guidelines or in accordance with a local authority's own choice although, in practice, housing powers have not been deployed in widely divergent ways largely because of the imposition of control by the Secretary of State. Of various forms of control, much the most important has been in relation to finance. Councils have undertaken nationally prescribed housebuilding programmes because they have been given the authority to borrow the money to do so; they have distributed more improvement grants because the cash was forthcoming in line with a central priority. In the past, the tendency was to impose financial controls by very specific subsidies or capital consents attached to particular projects but more recently the tendency has been away from such detailed financial control and towards the allocation of funds to councils on a block basis (for both capital and revenue expenditure) leaving greater discretion to the councils themselves on

1 Ibid, s 5B.
2 Previously 100% grants. See SDD Circular No 5/1989.

spending within the total sums. To these financial arrangements we shall return in a moment.

Housing plans

First, however, we should look at another development which, though not strictly of a legal nature, was made with a view to achieving a more co-ordinated approach to housing policy at the local level (including better integration with the work of other agencies) as well as imposing a new and broader system of central oversight. This was the introduction and operation of housing plans.

The history of the process which led to the launching of the system of housing plans began with the publication in 1972 of a report entitled *Planning for Housing Needs: Pointers Towards a Comprehensive Approach*, HMSO 1972. A sub-committee of the Scottish Housing Advisory Committee recommended the adoption of comprehensive assessment of housing needs for each area as the basis for the formulation of housing policy. In support of this approach there was published in 1976 the report of a Scottish Office research group *Local Housing Needs and Strategies—A Case Study of Dundee Sub-Region*, HMSO 1976, but already the Secretary of State had indicated his wish to see the adoption by local authorities of comprehensive housing strategies.[1] On the basis of the interim report of a joint working party of Scottish Office and local authority officials which received the support of both the Secretary of State and COSLA, notice was given to housing authorities that a new system of housing plans was to be adopted with effect from 1977 when authorities would need to prepare their first five-year plans for the period beginning 1978–79.[2] Authorities were urged to take preliminary steps in preparation. By the time authorities were actually requested to submit their first plans[3] the joint working party had issued its final report and the plans were to be prepared in accordance with their recommendations. Later further guidance was published in the form of Part 1 of the *Scottish Housing Handbook* under the title *Assessing Housing Needs—a Manual of Guidance* and by the issue of circulars concerned with financial aspects of the plans. (It is this link with the statutory rules governing consent to capital expenditure which provides the legal force underpinning the merely administrative request from the Secretary of State to conduct their housing policies in accordance with housing plans.) Arrangements for

1 SDD Circulars No 50/1975 and 100/1975.
2 SDD Circular No 76/1976.
3 SDD Circular No 6/1977.

the submission of plans were adjusted in 1989[1] and further revisions were made in 1993[2] with effect from 1994–95.

As originally described in 1976 but reaffirmed in guidance issued since then, the essential purpose of housing plans is:

(i) to provide local authorities with an opportunity to assess fully the housing requirements of their areas and formulate appropriate policies to meet these requirements;

(ii) to establish expenditure programmes which are consistent with available resources and contributions of other agencies to implement these policies; and

(iii) to inform the Government of locally assessed housing needs and strategies which should be taken into account in making capital allocations to local authorities and other agencies.

Housing plans are prepared, on a 'rolling' basis, for minimum periods of five years to set out authorities' medium term strategic views. They are supposed to reflect the 'strategic and enabling role' of the local authorities themselves but also take full account of the contributions of other agencies (especially Scottish Homes) and the private sector in meeting housing needs. Those needs are to be assessed primarily in terms of an analysis of housing demand and supply in the area of the authority (taking into account population and household projections, economic indicators, housing waiting lists) and then of information on the condition of local housing stock.[3]

In the light of their assessment of local housing needs but then bearing in mind 'resource planning assumptions' supplied to them by the Scottish Office, authorities are required to produce realistic strategies and to set quantified targets at which they are to aim. They have been instructed to give priority to the three strategic issues of dealing with housing which is below the tolerable standard;[4] dealing with condensation and damp; and reducing homelessness. Other strategic priority issues may, however, be identified (the Government's suggestions include energy efficiency improvements and dealing with lead plumbing) and authorities are urged to formulate their strategies in the manner of a business plan, adopting a corporate approach. They should, in particular, liaise with other bodies such as health boards and housing associations and, above all, with Scottish Homes.[5]

---

1 SDD Circular No 16/1989.
2 SO Env D Circular No 12/1993 and accompanying guidance.
3 Guidance on the preparation of house condition surveys is contained in Part 2 of the *Scottish Housing Handbook*.
4 See p 181 below.
5 For strategic agreements with local authorities made by Scottish Homes, see p 30.

Consultation is, in this last case, institutionalised in the form of tripartite meetings involving Scottish Homes, Scottish Office officials and the local authority.

Authorities are also encouraged to ensure that the process of preparing housing plans should be related to that of making the new housing management plans.[1]

According to the original proposals, revision of housing plans was to be on an annual basis. Each year each authority was expected to resubmit its plan to the Secretary of State and this was indeed the practice in the early years of the new system. However, a procedural change was made which removed the need for annual resubmission and substituting instead a normal four-year gap between submissions. Thus, apart from Glasgow which is expected to submit a plan in alternate years, authorities are on a rota for the four-yearly preparation of full plans. They are, however, required to submit an annual policy statement together with a capital programme identifying proposed capital expenditure in order of priority. (For the system of approval of capital spending, see below.)

Despite what some people see as an official reduction of emphasis on the housing plan system as a result of the shift away from annual submission[2] and despite the discouraging financial and economic climate in which it was introduced, it seems likely that it will continue to operate. It has some attractions for housing authorities in the relaxation of detailed central controls that it brings with it and its encouragement of a comprehensive and corporate approach to housing policy. Housing plans, which are expected to be sent to regional councils for comment prior to their submission assist with inter-authority relationships. The regions have to produce structure plans which include housing proposals and some compatibility between the strategies adopted at both levels is clearly important. The housing plan system also assumes fruitful communication between local housing authorities and Scottish Homes, the new towns and housing associations. Another beneficiary should be the general public and voluntary housing organisations since there is official encouragement for the publication of housing plans which should enable a wider and more informed debate of housing policies. Finally, of course, the system has attractions for central government. It is in line with the general tendency in central-local relationships towards less central

---

1 See p 67.
2 See, for instance, discussion in Committee on Scottish Affairs: Housing Capital Allocations (HC 112) (1980–81), and the Shelter memorandum appended thereto. See also SDD Circular 16/1989.

interference with detailed projects but coupled with a continuing interest both in being kept informed of local authority activities and in maintaining a firm control over spending.

Finance

We should now turn to the question of the financing of housing authority activities and to the Secretary of State's control over it and, as we do so, we have to distinguish immediately between capital expenditure on the one hand and revenue expenditure on the other. In common with that on other local authority activities, housing expenditure has to be divided between spending on capital works such as building, improvement and clearance which are financed by borrowing and the repayment of principal and interest over a period of years, and, on the other hand, works such as routine management, repair and maintenance which are financed on a recurrent basis primarily out of rents but also from the council tax, rates and central grant. What distinguishes housing from other local authority functions is that it receives separate treatment. Approval for capital expenditure is hived off from the general system of financial plans covering other functions and housing is not included within the general revenue support grant but is subsidised by a housing support grant.

Capital expenditure

When an authority undertakes capital works such as new building, it borrows the necessary money. The source of the funds and the terms on which the loan is made are matters for the local authority and not things which directly concern the Secretary of State. He does, however, share the concern of central government as a whole for the overall level of public borrowing since this is an important factor in national economic policy and this concern is given legal force by section 94 of the Local Government (Scotland) Act 1973 which provides that any local authority liability to meet capital expenses requires the prior consent of the Secretary of State. This section (and the earlier 'borrowing consent' provisions which it replaced) would enable the Secretary of State to grant or withhold consent to capital expenditure on an *ad hoc* basis and in the past approval for individual capital projects was indeed required. This, in turn, permitted the Secretary of State to influence housing standards and design at the same time as policing the limits of public sector borrowing.

Latterly, however, the central power of control has been used not on an individual project basis but to allocate to authorities annual 'blocks' of capital within which they have some freedom to decide on its disposal.[1] Thus, as one aspect of the wider system of housing plans, authorities produce assessments of their capital requirements as a reflection of their housing needs. These assessments are made not only for the financial year immediately following but also for future years as an indication of likely need and in response to these local authority assessments or 'bids' the Secretary of State, following his own consideration of the needs of authorities and bearing in mind limits on public sector borrowing imposed on all services, makes his allocations—firm for the coming year but with an indication of the level for the following year also.

One complication is that bids and allocations are not made in respect of a single block but instead there are two. The first relates to spending on an authority's own housing stock which, for this and other purposes, is attached to the authority's housing revenue account (HRA). Taken into account in this block are the estimated receipts from the sale of council houses in the coming year and, in some cases, sales have fallen below expected levels leaving the authorities short of capital for building and improvement works. In such cases, however, there is the possibility of renegotiation of the year's allocation.[2] Since 1989–90, some authorities have been given a negative 'net allocation' of capital funding which reflects an assumption by the Secretary of State that an authority's receipts from sales will exceed the amount of the authority's gross consent. This in turn means that the 'excess' capital receipts may have to be surrendered for use by other authorities. The other block (the non-HRA block) relates to spending on private sector housing principally in the shape of improvement grants, loans for house purchase, and environmental improvement. The reason for the continued operation of the two blocks rather than their merger into one is that it allows the Secretary of State specifically to designate funds as available in the private sector and, therefore, to provide home loans or improvement grants.[3] They have freedom within each block although this freedom may sometimes be quite strongly circumscribed. Thus, in those years in which 90% improvement grants were made

---

1 An excellent summary of capital allocation practice as it then operated is contained in the SDD Memorandum appended to the above Report (HC 112) (1980–81). The central principles continue to apply.
2 The Secretary of State has the power to vary (or withdraw) a consent under s 94(1B) of the 1973 Act.
3 Until 1989–90 authorities were permitted to transfer a limited percentage between blocks but general permission to transfer from the non-HRA block to the HRA block was then withdrawn.

available,[1] more funds from non-HRA blocks had necessarily to be devoted to that purpose—with some reduction of allocations to home loans.

A final point on capital allocations is of interest. It was mentioned above that the purpose of capital expenditure control has changed over the years from the wish to control individual projects to a wish to keep overall capital expenditure within limits. The division into the two allocation blocks is the only remaining explicit policy control of importance (although it may also be said that the linking of council house sales with capital allocation is designed to encourage sales). For a time, however, control over capital allocations was used for an additional purpose—that of controlling levels of revenue expenditure. During the years 1981–82 to 1984–85, capital allocations were linked in a system known as housing expenditure limits (HEL) to amounts of rate fund contribution (RFC) to authorities' HRAs. An authority which did not hold down its RFC to a level indicated in Scottish Office guidelines was penalised by a reduction of its capital allocation.[2] This was an indirect sanction (designed to reduce rate-borne and increase rent-borne housing expenditure) and, since it did not work sufficiently well in practice, it was replaced by the statutory power created in the Rating and Valuation (Amendment) (Scotland) Act 1984 (discussed below) enabling the Secretary of State to prescribe specific maximum levels of RFC.[3] The sanction based on restriction of capital allocations, however, remains in the background.

Revenue expenditure

Arrangements for financing the revenue expenditure of local housing authorities have also been the subject of periodic alteration. The only sector left relatively unscathed has been that outside an authority's housing revenue account (HRA) which is, in any event, very small. Outside the HRA (which relates to all income and expenditure affecting each council's own housing stock) councils maintain separate accounts for their private sector and other activities. The most important examples of these are the rent rebate and rent allowance

---

1 For improvement grants and the system of exchequer funding, see Chap 12 below.
2 For criticisms of the system, see the evidence published with Report (HC 112) (1980–81) above.
3 See p 14 below.

accounts.[1] The income to these accounts derives from specific subsidies from the Secretary of State and the outgoings are the rebates and allowances themselves plus administrative costs. The deficit is made up out of the authority's general fund.

It is, however, the HRA itself which handles the bulk of housing authority income and expenditure since it relates to all the land and buildings forming the council's own housing stock. Into it is paid the entire rent income (before rebate) as well as grant provided by the Secretary of State (if any) and contributions from the general fund (GFC) if necessary and permitted. On the debit side are the loan charges payable on capital expenditure liabilities together with the cost of repairs, maintenance and management.[2] Since, for large urban authorities in particular, annual expenditure charged to the HRA is very high and relatively inflexible from year to year (throughout Scotland about two-thirds of HRA expenditure is on loan charges) and since income from (historically low) rents supplemented by a reasonable GFC would not balance the account, the subsidy forthcoming from the Secretary of State was, in the past, crucial to the financing of council housing.

Until 1979–80, central assistance came to authorities not as a single HRA subsidy but as several, based on different measures of local need, but the big change brought about by the Housing (Financial Provisions) (Scotland) Act 1978 was the complete replacement of these separate subsidies by a single annual housing support grant (HSG). In the formula for its calculation and distribution and the procedure involved, the HSG very much resembles the revenue support grant (and its predecessor the rate support grant). There is a process of annual determination of the grant by the Secretary of State; it involves fixing first an aggregate amount for all authorities followed by the apportionment within that aggregate; there is a statutory duty to consult with COSLA ('such associations of local authorities as appear to him to be concerned'); the formal making of the grants is by order requiring an affirmative resolution of the House of Commons; and there is provision for the subsequent variation of orders.[3]

The way in which the aggregate amount of grant is established by the Secretary of State is by his estimating the 'aggregate amount of eligible expenditure which it is reasonable for local authorities to incur for that year.' 'Eligible expenditure' is what is spent from the HRA.

1 1987 Act, ss 205–206. For these rebates and allowances under the housing benefit scheme, see p 96 below.
2 1987 Act, Sch 15.
3 Ibid, ss 191–193.

He then estimates the 'aggregate amount of relevant income which local authorities could reasonably be expected to receive.' 'Relevant income' is income (except HSG) and GFC credited to the HRA. The total relevant income is then deducted from the total eligible expenditure to produce the aggregate amount of HSG to be paid. In making his estimates of expenditure and income, the Secretary of State has to consult COSLA and to take into account latest information available as to the level of each; the level of interest rates, remuneration, costs and prices which would affect eligible expenditure; and latest information on changes in the general level of earnings which would affect relevant income.[1] It becomes, in other words, a process of looking at existing patterns of income and expenditure and adjusting them in the light of assumed future trends. Revised estimates made later in the same year or subsequently can take care of unforeseen changes.

It is then for the Secretary of State (in a process of continuous consultation with COSLA by means of a standing Housing Finance Working Party) to prescribe the way in which the aggregate amount of HSG is to be distributed among authorities. The Secretary of State has a wide discretion including the power to award a specific proportion to a particular authority and indeed to award no grant at all to authorities which appear to him not to need any.[2] In recent years many authorities have been awarded no grant—in 1989–90 only 23 out of the 56 authorities received HSG and in 1993–94, only 17.[3]

Like his control over capital spending, the Secretary of State's power to determine the aggregate and individual amounts of HSG is a potentially powerful means of determining Scottish housing policy. Although the HSG is distributed (to those authorities which receive it) as a general grant without strings attached, the dominance of unavoidable loan charge expenditure has tended to leave authorities with little room to manoeuvre. With effect from 1984–85, this freedom was further constrained. Until then (the capital allocation restraint under HEL apart) authorities were theoretically able under the HSG system to decide for themselves the relative size of rent and rate contributions to their HRAs. This led the Government to conclude that some authorities were holding down rents and correspondingly raising the contribution from rates to an unacceptable degree. Their response in 1984 was to enact the provision now contained in section 204 of the

---

1 1987 Act, s 191. But there can be left out of account expenditure and income of authorities which will receive no HSG.
2 Ibid, s 192.
3 For details of the HSG for 1989–90 see SI 1989/181 and for 1993–94, SI 1993/497.

1987 Act. This section requires every authority to submit to the Secretary of State an estimate of income and expenditure in relation to its HRA for the following year. More importantly, the Secretary of State is authorised to prescribe by order upper limits to the general fund contribution (GFC) which an individual authority or class of authorities may propose to make to their HRA. The authority or class of authorities is then obliged not to exceed the prescribed maximum. The overall result is that the Secretary of State is in a position to maintain a very strict control over GFCs and thus, less directly, over rent levels too. Since statutory limits on GFCs were introduced, the permitted levels have declined sharply. By 1989–90 only 8 out of the 56 housing authorities were allowed to make any contribution at all from the general fund to the HRA and this has since declined to none at all.[1] Seen alongside the generally reduced levels of HSG, this produces a situation in which most authorities are required to fund all HRA expenditure out of rents.

In the first year in which GFC (then RFC) limits were imposed, Edinburgh District Council initially refused to comply with its limit. The council started proceedings to challenge the validity of the Secretary of State's order in so far as it affected it. Its main complaint related to the fairness of the procedure used but it was rejected first in the Outer and then in the Inner House of the Court of Session.[2] Then, following a public inquiry, the Secretary of State made a default order against the council requiring compliance with his RFC limit and, after an order of specific performance from the Court of Session, the council did so comply.[3] More recently Stirling District Council exceeded the RFC prescribed for it for 1985–86. That too resulted in default proceedings against the council requiring both a reduction in its RFC and a reduction in the rate level for that year. These proceedings were followed by an investigation by the council's auditor into certain costs (some £31,420) incurred as a result of the council's non-compliance with the statutory limits. This led, following reports by the Controller of Audit and the Commission for Local Authority Accounts, to the first imposition by the Secretary of State of surcharges on councillors after local government reorganisation in 1975.[4]

1 See SI 1988/2081 (for 1989–90) and SI 1993/75 (for 1993–94).
2 *City of Edinburgh District Council v Secretary of State for Scotland* 1985 SLT 551. For a note on this case see Himsworth 1985 SLT (News) 369.
3 The default procedure is that contained in the Local Government (Scotland) Act 1973, s 211.
4 See Report of Accounts Commission 1988.

4. ACCOUNTABILITY, SUPERVISION AND CONTROL

It is already apparent from the discussion of the financial controls on housing authorities that they are not able to discharge their functions in a wholly autonomous manner, independent of external controls. This is a point which can be made much more broadly. As they are democratically elected bodies, there is a very strong sense in which control over decision-making by local authorities is, and should be, seen to be imposed through the processes of political accountability. This is the accountability achieved by the discipline of the ballot box, as moderated, in modern local government practice, by the operation of political parties. Local authorities are expected, on this democratic model, to be constrained by the wishes of their electorates.

It is not, however, the local electorate which determines the level of capital finance to be made available to housing authorities. This is one of the many controls imposed by the Secretary of State in the exercise of his own statutory powers. As will be seen in the next chapter, his powers extend much more widely than controls over local expenditure. They range from the power to determine the content of primary legislation and, therefore, the statutory powers of local authorities down to the power to withhold the consent necessary for the exercise of many of their functions.

The Secretary of State is not the only external source of control and supervision over housing authorities. Others appear in the powers of tribunals and courts, the local ombudsman, and the audit system.[1] Thus, many of the functions of local authorities (and other public sector landlords) under the 'right to buy' and 'change of landlord' provisions can be the subject of appeal to the Lands Tribunal for Scotland;[2] and housing benefit decisions are reviewed by the review boards established by authorities.[3]

It is, on the other hand, to the sheriff that many other disputes between local authorities and their tenants are referred. It is the sheriff who, in particular, presides over proceedings for recovery of possession of houses subject to both secure and assured (and protected) tenancies.[4] In addition, appeals against loan decisions under

---

1 A useful review of these different forms of supervision and control appears in Chap 9 'Public challenge' of the Widdicombe Report on *The Conduct of Local Authority Business*, 1986, Cmnd 9797.
2 See pp 124 and 146 below.
3 See p 97 below.
4 See pp 79 and 62 below.

the right to buy[1] and against closing and demolition orders and many other decisions affecting sub-standard housing all go to the sheriff.[2] They constitute only a small part of a wide jurisdiction exercised by the sheriff over the administrative activities of local authorities.[3]

Many local authority decisions are not, however, made subject to any statutory form of appeal or review. These include decisions about homelessness and also, for instance, decisions on applications for improvement or repairs grants. This does not mean that such decisions are not subject to supervision by the courts at all but that it is restricted to the process of judicial review in the Court of Session.[4] Many important decisions on homelessness have been made by the Court of Session and its English equivalent—the High Court and the Court of Appeal—and, on appeal from both, the House of Lords.[5] A more general form of review, extending over the whole range of local authority housing functions, is exercised by the commissioner for local administration, the local ombudsman.[6] He has the task of investigating and reporting on the complaints of individuals (or, in some cases, groups) who claim to have suffered 'injustice in consequence of maladministration.' The ombudsman enjoys the advantages of ease of access, relative informality and cheapness and the ability to extend well beyond complaints about illegality alone. Other forms of unfairness, administrative malpractice and delay are subject to investigation and, as a result, housing complaints have dominated the local ombudsman's workload since the creation of the office in 1975.[7] They have included complaints about the treatment of homeless people and the refusal of improvement grants (thus, in both cases, demonstrating an alternative to judicial review), the allocation and also the sale of council houses. The main drawback frequently ascribed to investigation by the local ombudsman is that he has no power to enforce a remedy. Actual refusals by local authorities to implement recommendations made by the ombudsman have been infrequent but there was sufficient criticism of non-implementation

---

1 See p 132 below.
2 See p 190 below and other examples in Chap 11.
3 See ID McPhail, *Sheriff Court Practice* (1988), Part VI.
4 For a full discussion of the grounds of judicial review and the procedure under Rule of Court 260B see A W Bradley 'Administrative Law' in 1 *Stair Memorial Encyclopaedia* paras 213–302. See also C M G Himsworth 'Judicial Review in Scotland' in M Supperstone and J Goudie (eds) *Judicial Review* (1992).
5 See p 178 below.
6 Local Government (Scotland) Act 1975, Pt II.
7 See statistics accompanying the annual reports of the Commissioner.

during the 1980s[1] to prompt the procedural amendments made by the Local Government and Housing Act 1989. These enable the ombudsman to require authorities who decide not to implement his recommendations to give publicity to the ombudsman's case against them as well as a statement of reasons for non-implementation if they so wish.[2]

A final mention should be made of the audit system, already referred to in connection with limitations on general fund contributions to housing revenue accounts. Local authority accounts are required to be kept and audited under rules in the Local Government (Scotland) Act 1973.[3] One special aspect of the audit arrangements lies in the power of the Controller of Audit to report to the Accounts Commission on certain types of irregularity and illegality he has discovered not only in an authority's preparation of accounts but also in the exercise of its functions at all. Whilst this power has been of some significance in local authority practice in general, its impact on housing functions has not been very great. It has been, however, in the past, an important factor affecting the fixing of rent levels and has produced significant additional consequences for authorities held, in other proceedings, to have neglected their legal obligations.[4] In addition to its formal audit powers, the Accounts Commission undertakes studies of selected aspects of local authority financial management. An important example of this was the Commission's publication in 1991 of *Tenants' Rent Arrears—A Problem?*—a study of local authority procedures on rent arrears and recommendations for future improvements. More recently the Commission has been given new *Citizen's Charter* powers.[5]

---

1 See eg HC Select Committee Report 'Local Government Cases: Enforcement of Remedies' HC 448 (1985–86) and also the Widdicombe Committee Report (Cmnd 9797) above.
2 See amendments to the 1975 Act made by ss 27 and 29 of the 1989 Act.
3 Sections 96–106.
4 See p 14 above.
5 See p 21 below.

CHAPTER 2

The Secretary of State for Scotland and the Scottish Office

At the level of central government, responsibility for Scottish housing is vested in the Secretary of State for Scotland. He is assisted in discharging this responsibility by a junior minister and together they give political leadership to that part of the Scottish Office Environment Department (SOEnvD) concerned with housing matters. The Secretary of State and the SOEnvD do not, of course, provide and manage housing in Scotland. That is for the local authorities and the other agencies described in the next two chapters, as well as for the private sector. On the other hand, the general direction and also the cost of housing policies are matters of national concern and the powers of the Secretary of State are of the greatest significance in housing law. The Secretary of State's power and influence is evident at many levels. At the highest level, he is able, as a senior member of the Government and Cabinet, to use with his colleagues the power which derives from their majority in the House of Commons to determine the statutory framework within which housing will be conducted. New legislation can greatly affect the powers and indeed the very existence of the different housing agencies and the ways in which they discharge their functions. Developments in the last 15 years have provided many examples of this. The major initiatives in the Tenants' Rights, Etc (Scotland) Act 1980 and, in particular, the right to buy greatly changed the relationships between landlords and tenants in the public sector, the balance between owner-occupied and tenanted houses in Scotland, the role of local housing authorities and indeed the role of the public sector in housing provision at all. More recently, the Housing (Scotland) Act 1988 set out further to redraw the map of housing policy and provision in Scotland with the creation of Scottish Homes and related changes. Restructuring of the statute book has been an integral part of the restructuring of housing. The Secretary of State and the Scottish Office have been central to this process although it should, at the same time, be acknowledged that changes in the law and policy of housing have been closely linked with other aspects of the Government's social, economic and financial policies and that, in very large measure, developments in Scotland have paralleled similar changes in England and Wales. The Secretary of

State does not, in this aspect of his role, operate wholly independently of his counterparts at the Department of the Environment (and Welsh Office) or of the Treasury.

Statutory change apart, there are many other ways in which the Secretary of State exerts influence on housing policy. In the laws he proposes to Parliament, the Secretary of State reserves to himself substantial powers, including wide powers to control the activities of other agencies. He has quite explicit powers to control the financing and policies of Scottish Homes[1] and we have already seen that the Secretary of State exercises very significant powers over local authorities. General financial controls may be the most important but they are joined by others. Either by the issue of regulations governing the general exercise of local authority powers or by the granting or withholding of consent to specific actions, his influence affects most areas of activity. In relation to the right to buy,[2] for instance, the Secretary of State can make regulations to vary levels of discount, to add to the list of public sector tenancies for discount purposes, and to prescribe forms. He can make determinations governing the application of the 'cost floor' rules and to modify conditions of sale. He can authorise the refusal to sell a house provided for special purposes; by designation of a rural area, permit the insertion of a right of pre-emption, and give financial assistance to tenants in proceedings. He can make a default order to compel a local authority to carry out its statutory duties.[3] In other areas, he prescribes levels of improvement grant;[4] he issues guidance under the homelessness provisions of the 1987 Act;[5] and he is required to supervise the procedures (in particular, consultation with tenants) for 'voluntary sales' of public sector housing stock.[6]

In addition to the exercise of his formal powers, the Secretary of State is frequently involved, through his officials, in more informal processes of consultation, usually by way of COSLA, with local authorities and in the supply of information and guidance in circulars. Information on a more structured basis is supplied in the volumes of the *Scottish Housing Handbook*. The *Handbook* now includes sections dealing with *Assessing Housing Needs, Housing Development, Housing*

1 See especially 1988 Act, s 2(10) (directions) and ss 5–10 (finance). See Chap 3 below.
2 See Chap 8 below. The powers referred to are all discussed in that chapter.
3 Local Government (Scotland) Act 1973, s 211 as strengthened by s 159 of the Local Government and Housing Act 1989.
4 See Chap 12.
5 See Chap 10.
6 See Chap 9.

for the Elderly, *Housing for the Disabled*, and *Housing for Single People, Shared Accommodation and Hostels* and more recently *Local House Condition Surveys: A Manual of Guidance*. In addition the SOEnvD publishes a series called *Statistical Bulletin* (until 1986 also the annual *Scottish Housing Statistics*) which contains many of the statistical returns from local authorities on eg housing stock, sales, housing action areas and improvement grants.

One particular Scottish Office initiative which has had some impact on the law and practice of housing in Scotland has been the introduction of the Citizen's Charter[1] in the shape of the *Tenant's Charter for Scotland* (1991).[2] This had the declared aim of assuring for public sector tenants a high quality of service from their landlords based on the five principles of strengthening rights, increasing choice, improving standards and quality of housing service, making landlords more responsive and more accountable, and achieving better value for money in housing management. In addition to cataloguing improvements claimed to have been achieved in the previous decade, the *Charter* contained a wide range of proposals for further changes. These included the strengthening of the right to buy by introducing penalties for landlord delay,[3] the rent to mortgage scheme,[4] and a new right to repair scheme.[5] Also proposed was an obligation to be placed on local authority landlords to provide information on the standards of service they undertake to provide (eg speed of repairs, answering letters, and completing sales under the right to buy) and on their performance in meeting those standards. This proposal was later enacted in the 1993 Act[6] and local authorities are, from April 1994, required to publish information on the management of their housing which is specified in regulations made by the Secretary of State as well as information which they themselves decide to publish. Tenants must be consulted on the information to be published and authorities must take account of the need to publish different information in relation to different parts of their district. If the Secretary of State considers that published information is unsatisfactory, he may direct that it be published differently. In addition the Secretary of State may, by

1 The original framework document was Cm 1599 (1991).
2 The *Charter* is not to be confused with an earlier document of the same name which heralded the changes introduced by the 1980 Act.
3 See p 128 below.
4 See p 136 below.
5 See p 93 below.
6 Section 153 inserting new ss 17A–C in the 1987 Act.

notice to any authority, require the preparation of a plan for the management of its houses.[1] The *Charter* went on to refer to a new role for the Accounts Commission. It would 'be able to publish league tables of performance by local authorities showing what standard of performance they provide and what cost'. The machinery for achieving this was put in place by Part I of the Local Government Act 1992 which gives the Accounts Commission the power to give directions to local authorities requiring them to provide the information necessary to produce the tables of comparative performance. The first direction, requiring *inter alia* information on housing repair response times, amounts of rent arrears and times for completion of council house sales was issued in respect of 1993–94.[2]

---

1 These last two powers of the Secretary of State are contained in ss 17B and 17C of the 1987 Act which are very poorly drafted. Section 17B does not specify what information it concerns, and s 17C gives no indication what a 'plan for the management of . . . houses' means.
2 See also 'The Citizen's Charter' and 'Housing Standards of Performance' in the Accounts Commission *Report and Accounts 1993* pp 18–19.

CHAPTER 3

Scottish Homes

1. ORIGINS

The most recent institutional arrival on the housing scene has been Scottish Homes. This new body formally came into existence on 1 April 1989 and is the new 'third force' in housing provision. It assumed the mantle of two predecessor organisations—the Scottish Special Housing Association (SSHA) and that part of the Housing Corporation based in Scotland. Scottish Homes has, however, been given additional new powers and it by no means merely continues their work.

The SSHA was originally established in 1937 as the Scottish Special Areas Housing Association Ltd and was, in law, a company limited by guarantee and without share capital. It had a council of management consisting of members appointed by the Secretary of State and operated under its own memorandum and articles of association with powers exercised in terms of an agreement with the Secretary of State. Originally its function had been to build houses for 'distressed' areas but this had changed over the years to the provision of houses for other special needs (most recently, for instance, in areas of development for oil) and to supplement the efforts of local authorities.[1] In some cases it managed houses on its own account (having become the second largest public sector landlord in Scotland) and in others it acted on an agency basis for local authorities. The Housing Corporation is of more recent origin than the SSHA. It was created by the Housing Act 1964 as a new agency to make a contribution to housing provision complementing that of local authorities. It was established to operate in Great Britain as a whole and during the first 10 years of its life concentrated upon the promotion and encouragement of cost rent housing and co-ownership schemes. From 1972 it was able to lend money to housing

---

1 For descriptions of the work of the SSHA see its *Annual Reports* and *A Chronicle of Forty Years 1937–77*. See also Hogan and Al-Qaddo, *Scottish Government Yearbook*, 1985, p 171.

associations to provide housing at 'fair rents'.[1] The Housing Act 1974 suddenly changed things. It introduced a completely new policy designed to channel very large amounts of government money into the hands of housing associations which, by building new houses or improving old ones, would supplement the work of local authorities but also provide a range of new housing services. Housing associations would be able to attract substantial publicly funded loans coupled with grants to enable them to carry out projects approved by the Secretary of State. A necessary condition of this new financial assistance, however, was that housing associations would have to be subject to supervision and control and it was to achieve this that the Housing Corporation was revitalised and given extensive new powers. The provisions of the Housing Act 1974 together with provisions scattered elsewhere were consolidated in the Housing Associations Act 1985.

Although the Housing Corporation was established on a Great Britain basis, it was subject to the direction of all three relevant Secretaries of State (for the Environment, Scotland and Wales) and its funding similarly divided. As a body corporate it was (and is) managed by an appointed board.[2] During the period to March 1989, appointments to the board were made by the three Secretaries of State. There were two 'Scottish' members and, with the Chairman and Chief Executive, they constituted an extra-statutory Scottish Committee of the corporation. Administratively, the Housing Corporation maintained a Scottish Head Office in Edinburgh under the Director–Scotland, and two regional offices in Glasgow and Edinburgh.[3]

Proposals for the creation of a new body to replace the SSHA and the work of the Housing Corporation in Scotland were launched by the Secretary of State in a consultation paper called *Scottish Homes: A New Agency for Housing in Scotland* in May 1987. It followed earlier discussions about merger promoted by the Secretary of State who, in his Foreword to the document, saw 'the creation of Scottish Homes as a unique and exciting opportunity to improve Scottish housing over the next decade.' There had been 'welcome changes' in Scottish housing. Good quality rented accommodation and greater choice in housing tenure had been provided by local authorities, the SSHA and

1 Housing (Financial Provisions) (Scotland) Act 1972, Pt VI.
2 Housing Associations Act 1985, s 74 and Sch 6.
3 For recent descriptions of the organisation and work of the Corporation in Scotland see the 24th Annual Report (for 1987–88) with its accompanying Scottish Statistical Supplement and other material. See too *Scottish Homes: A New Agency for Housing in Scotland*, 1987, pp 23–24.

housing associations. Many former public sector tenants had bene-
fited from the right to buy under the scheme introduced by the
Tenants' Rights, Etc (Scotland) Act 1980; and, in the private sector,
the number of houses below the tolerable standard had been halved.
On the other hand, there was the 'continuing challenge' of the
demand for better quality housing, for special kinds of housing to
meet special needs, and for the rehabilitation of older houses. There
was, in particular, the need, in the Government's view, to respond to
the problem of the large peripheral estates. They had been built to
rescue people from the intolerable living conditions but 'today, in
many cases, these monolithic local authority estates are themselves
areas of deprivation.'[1] Essential to the process of regenerating these
estates was the 'introduction of a range of housing tenures to develop
balanced communities.'[2]

To achieve these housing purposes a radical approach was
required—in the shape of a unified agency. 'Scottish Homes would be
primarily an enabling and funding body with wide powers and a wide
remit.'[3] It would need to act in partnership with local authorities,
other public bodies and with the private and voluntary sectors. A
flexible financial framework would be required to enable investment
from the private market and joint funding. Comparisons were to be
drawn with the flexible methods used by the development agencies
operating outside housing, such as the Scottish Development Agency
and the Highlands and Islands Development Board.[4] Direct financial
assistance to 'bridge the gap' between the costs and income of those
providing housing would probably be the most commonly used
power.[5] In addition, Scottish Homes might offer, in parallel with local
authorities, grants for the improvement and repair of individual
owner occupied houses. Other possibilities would include environmental improvement.[6]

Scottish Homes would, it was proposed, inherit the housing stock
of the SSHA although the need for the 85,000 houses then owned by
the SSHA to be in public ownership had, in the Government's view,
'progressively reduced.'[7] Some houses would, however, have to be
transferred to a new 'landlord' division of Scottish Homes.[8] These
arrangements would be 'essentially transitional . . . At the end of the

1 *Scottish Homes*, para 11.
2 Ibid, para 12.
3 Ibid, para 15.
4 Subsequently Scottish Enterprise and Highlands and Islands Enterprise.
5 *Scottish Homes*, para 20.
6 Ibid, paras 25–26.
7 Ibid, para 33.
8 Ibid, para 34.

day, a number of solutions might emerge, such as co-operatives or registered housing associations, reflecting the wishes of tenants in each area.'[1]

Alongside the establishment of Scottish Homes itself, other related changes were anticipated. In particular, under the heading of 'Partnership with Local Authorities', the paper suggested that although 'district councils have a responsibility to identify and take action on housing issues in their areas', increasingly that responsibility 'need not extend to direct action on the part of local authorities as providers of housing or as landlords.' Scottish Homes would be expected to be 'ready to form a partnership with [a] local authority to bring expertise, knowledge and ultimately the right provider to [a] project.'[2]

This theme of the future relationship between Scottish Homes and local authorities was further developed in the Government's wider review of housing policy published in November 1987 as a White Paper, *Housing: The Government's Proposals for Scotland.*[3] That paper noted 'widespread approval' for the wide remit proposed for Scottish Homes—both in relation to its direct activities and its role in partnership with others.[4] There had, however, also been the 'misapprehension that there was an intention for Scottish Homes to displace local authorities from their housing role.' The White Paper also responded to a number of concerns expressed about the role of Scottish Homes in urban regeneration;[5] it denied suggestions that the problems of rural areas might be ignored;[6] and offered reassurance on the relationship of Scottish Homes with the private sector. The role of Scottish Homes would be promotional. Its own powers to give direct financial assistance in the private sector would normally only be as lender of last resort but grant assistance would also be a possibility and, in some cases, investment would be secured by taking equity in a project.[7] The proposed power to give improvement grants to house owners should not produce conflict between the continuing role of local authorities as the main providers of grants and the much more limited powers of Scottish Homes.[8]

Overall, responses to its consultation paper had confirmed the Government's judgment that 'a new development agency would make

1 Ibid, para 35.
2 Ibid, paras 41–42.
3 Cm 242.
4 Ibid, para 2.9.
5 Ibid, para 2.11.
6 Ibid, para 2.12.
7 Ibid, para 2.14.
8 Ibid, para 2.16.

a substantial contribution to the housing needs of Scotland and enhance the success of the housing policies' also proposed by the Government in the White Paper.[1] Despite the doubts of external critics already mentioned and others (including some resistance to the incorporation of the SSHA into the new agency),[2] the Government was committed to its plans for Scottish Homes as the centre-piece of new reforming legislation.

The publication of a Bill followed immediately and, with Scottish Homes as the flagship in Part 1, the Housing (Scotland) Act 1988 duly reached the statute book on 2 November 1988. Although the Bill had been amended in important respects during its Parliamentary passage and, on enactment, further amended by the Housing Act 1988, the Scottish Homes provisions emerged substantially unscathed. Part 1 of the Housing (Scotland) Act 1988 supplemented by Schedule 1 (constitution and proceedings) and Schedule 2 (consequential amendments of enactments) contained the new law relating to Scottish Homes although, for a full understanding of its functions in relation to housing associations, those provisions have to be read with the Housing Associations Act 1985.[3]

2. STRUCTURE

Scottish Homes was created with effect from 1 April 1989.[4] Its status is that of a body corporate whose members are not more than nine persons appointed by the Secretary of State plus its chief executive.[5] The Secretary of State must also appoint one of the members to be chairman and may appoint another deputy chairman.[6] Before appointing any member the Secretary of State must satisfy himself that the person will not have a financial or other interest likely to affect prejudicially the performance of his own functions. This must be repeated in relation to each member of Scottish Homes from time to time thereafter.[7]

---

1 Ibid, para 2.3.
2 Ibid, para 2.4.
3 See s 59 of the Housing Act 1988. Pt 1 of Sch 6 to the Act contains amendments to the Housing Associations Act 1985 which include amendments originally contained in Sch 3 to the Housing (Scotland) Act 1988. That Schedule is deemed not to have come into force.
4 Housing (Scotland) Act 1988, s 1 and SI 1988/2038. Guidance on Scottish Homes and its relationship with local authorities was given in SDD Circular No 13/1989.
5 Ibid, Sch 1, paras 1, 4(1).
6 Ibid, para 6(1).
7 Ibid, para 4(2).

The tenure of office of a member (except the chief executive) ends on the expiry of the term for which he or she was appointed or on resignation.[1]

The Secretary of State is empowered to remove a member if satisfied that the member has been adjudged bankrupt; or is incapacitated by physical or mental illness; or has been absent from meetings for over three months without the permission of Scottish Homes; or is otherwise unable or unfit to discharge the functions of a member or unsuitable to continue as a member.[2]

The Secretary of State is empowered, with Treasury approval, to remunerate the chairman, deputy chairman and members. Scottish Homes may pay further allowances for expenses incurred.[3]

The first chief executive of Scottish Homes was required to be appointed by the Secretary of State after consultation with the chairman and deputy chairman designate. His successors are appointed by Scottish Homes, with the approval of the Secretary of State.[4] Other staff are appointed by Scottish Homes, on terms and conditions approved by the Secretary of State.[5] Few statutory provisions govern the manner in which Scottish Homes must conduct its business. The most important are aimed at preventing conflicts of interest when members attend meetings and vote.[6] There is a general authority to establish committees, which may include non-members.[7] Scottish Homes has adopted a structure of organisation which relies upon the management of service delivery (especially the development funding and housing management functions) on a decentralised basis with many area offices throughout the country. A management group of senior officials headed by the chief executive makes decisions delegated to it by the board of Scottish Homes itself. Scottish Homes is subject to the jurisdiction of the Parliamentary Commissioner for Administration (the ombudsman)[8] except in relation to its actions as a landlord when it is subject to the Commissioner for Local Administration (the local ombudsman).[9]

1 Ibid, para 5(1)–(2).
2 Ibid, para 5(3).
3 Ibid, para 7.
4 Ibid, para 9.
5 Ibid, para 10.
6 Ibid, para 15.
7 Ibid, para 17.
8 Parliamentary Commissioner Act 1967, Sch 2 (as amended by Housing (Scotland) Act 1988, Sch 2, para 2).
9 Local Government (Scotland) Act 1975, s 23 (as amended by Housing (Scotland) Act 1988, Sch 2, para 4).

3. POWERS

As a statutorily created body Scottish Homes may do only those things authorised by statute—whether the Housing (Scotland) Act 1988 itself or other Acts of Parliament. The 1988 Act starts off by listing a number of general functions. These are:

(a) providing, and assisting in the provision of, finance to persons or bodies intending to provide, improve, repair, maintain or manage housing;

(b) providing, improving, repairing, maintaining and managing housing (whether solely or in conjunction with any other person or body);

(c) promoting owner-occupation (especially by those seeking to purchase for the first time), the wider ownership of housing by its occupants and a greater choice of tenancy arrangements;

(d) promoting the provision and improvement of housing and the improvement of management of housing (whether by its occupants or otherwise);

(e) promoting and assisting the development of housing associations, maintaining a register of housing associations and exercising supervision and control over registered housing associations;

(f) undertaking, and assisting the undertaking of, the development, redevelopment and improvement of the physical, social, economic and recreational environment related to housing;

(g) such other general functions as are conferred upon Scottish Homes by or under the 1988 Act or any other enactment.[1]

That list of functions is immediately supplemented first by the authority to 'do anything, whether in Scotland or elsewhere, which is calculated to facilitate or is incidental or conducive to the discharge of its general functions'[2] and then, without prejudice to the generality of that authority, by a further list of more specific functions. Scottish Homes may:

(a) make grants;

(b) make loans;

(c) acquire, hold and dispose of securities;

1 Housing (Scotland) Act 1988, s 1(3).
2 Ibid, s 2(1).

(d) guarantee obligations (arising out of loans or otherwise) incurred by other persons, or grant indemnities;

(e) provide or assist in the provision of advisory or other services or facilities for any person;

(f) acquire land by agreement or gift;

(g) acquire land (including servitudes or other rights in or over land by the creation of new rights) compulsorily;

(h) hold and manage land and dispose of, or otherwise deal with, land held by it;

(j) acquire and dispose of plant, machinery, equipment and other property;

(k) develop land or carry out works on land, and maintain or assist in the maintenance of any such works;

(l) make land, plant, machinery, equipment and other property available for use by other persons;

(m) appoint other persons to act as its agents;

(n) act as agents for other persons;

(o) form companies within the meaning of the Companies Act 1985;

(p) form partnerships with other persons;

(q) promote, provide or assist in the provision of, training in matters relating to housing;

(r) carry out, commission or assist in the provision of, research and development;

(s) promote, or assist in the promotion of, publicity relating to its general functions and powers and to matters relating to housing;

(t) make such charge as it thinks fit for any of its services;

(u) accept any gift or grant made to it for the purposes of any of its general functions and powers and, subject to the terms of the gift or grant and to the provisions of the 1988 Act, apply it for those purposes;

(v) turn its resources to account so far as they are not required for the exercise of any of its general functions and powers.[1]

The powers (a) to (d), (m) and (o) are exercisable by Scottish Homes only with the approval of the Secretary of State or in accordance with a general authority given by him and, in either case, with Treasury consent. Powers (e) to (l) are to be exercised only in accordance with arrangements made with the Secretary of State[2] save that the exercise of the power under (h) to dispose of land requires the Secretary of State's consent.[3]

1 Ibid, s 2(2).
2 Ibid, s 2(3).
3 Ibid, s 2(3A) inserted by the 1989 Act.

These lists of powers clearly equip Scottish Homes with the authority to achieve most of the general purposes intended for it. Thus its powers to acquire and hold land and then to provide and manage housing enable it to act as a landlord in succession to the SSHA.[1] The powers and duties of Scottish Homes as a landlord of its secure tenants;[2] the rights of those tenants to buy their own houses;[3] and the lead role of Scottish Homes in the 'change of landlord' provisions[4] are dealt with at appropriate stages of this book—as is the power of Scottish Homes to join local authorities in making improvement and repairs grants.[5]

The main responsibilities of Scottish Homes (as successor to the Housing Corporation) for housing associations are separately treated below. Other powers to assist in the provision of housing, the promotion of owner-occupation and of wider home ownership are all in the lists above, together with the necessary financial and administrative powers—to make grants and loans; to make guarantees; to form companies and partnerships. The actual use of these powers is organised under the umbrella of a strategic plan—currently the plan for 1993–1996, *Towards our Housing Future*. It is a plan which adopts as its objectives: contributing to improved quality in housing and its management (using the 1993 report on the Scottish House Condition Survey as a baseline); enabling home ownership and promoting the development of a more diverse rented sector; making an effective contribution to community regeneration strategies; assisting those with particular housing needs; and making an effective contribution to the reduction of homelessness. Emphasis is placed upon the need for Scottish Homes as 'The National Housing Agency' to work in partnership with local housing authorities and other housing agencies.[6] Scottish Homes has also adopted other more specific policy documents on issues such as homelessness;[7] housing elderly persons[8] and care in the community.[9]

1 Except where explicit alternative provision has been made, references to the SSHA in earlier legislation have become references to Scottish Homes: 1988 Act, Sch 2, para 1.
2 See Chap 7.
3 See Chap 8.
4 See Chap 9.
5 See Chap 12.
6 See eg the contribution to housing plans, p 7 above.
7 *Homelessness: A Scottish Homes Perspective*, 1992.
8 *Housing the Elderly in the 1990s*, 1993.
9 *Scottish Homes and Care in the Community*, 1993. In a variety of further documents, Scottish Homes sets out its investment strategies. See also the agency's annual reports.

It should be observed that, in addition to the specific ministerial consents already noted, the Secretary of State may give Scottish Homes directions of a general or specific character as to the exercise of its general functions and powers. It is the duty of Scottish Homes to comply with such directions.[1] In addition to such powers of general policy control, the Secretary of State has important powers to regulate the finances of Scottish Homes. These take a number of different forms:

1. With the approval of the Treasury, the Secretary of State may 'determine the financial duties of Scottish Homes.' Such determinations may relate to different general functions, powers and activities of Scottish Homes. Notice of determinations must be given to Scottish Homes; determinations may be varied.[2]

2. The Secretary of State may, with the consent of the Treasury, give grants to Scottish Homes and these grants may be made subject to conditions. They are Scottish Homes' principal source of income.[3]

3. In addition, the Secretary of State (with approval of the Treasury) is empowered to lend to, and control borrowing by, Scottish Homes.[4] The Treasury may guarantee loans to Scottish Homes by persons other than the Secretary of State.[5] Aggregate amounts of sums borrowed (and any sums issued in fulfilment of guarantees) are statutorily restricted to £1,000 m, which sum may be increased by the Secretary of State by order to a maximum figure of £1,500 m.[6]

4. The Secretary of State has powers to regulate the financial reserves of Scottish Homes.[7]

5. Each year, Scottish Homes must submit to the Secretary of State a statement of account which is to be transmitted by him to the Comptroller and Auditor General. An annual report dealing with the activities of Scottish Homes must also be submitted to the Secretary of State and laid by him before both Houses of Parliament.[8]

---

1 Housing (Scotland) Act 1988, s 2(10).
2 Ibid, s 5.
3 Ibid, s 6.
4 Ibid, s 7(1). Section 7(2) permits Scottish Homes to borrow from a wholly owned subsidiary without the consent of the Secretary of State.
5 Ibid, s 8.
6 Ibid, s 9.
7 Ibid, s 10.
8 Ibid, s 11.

4. SCOTTISH HOMES AND HOUSING ASSOCIATIONS

The principal functions inherited on 1 April 1989 by Scottish Homes from the Housing Corporation in Scotland were those which related to housing associations. Thus Scottish Homes has the function of 'promoting and assisting the development of housing associations, maintaining a register of housing associations and exercising supervision and control over registered housing associations.'[1] Every housing association registered with the Housing Corporation and having its registered office (for the purposes of the Industrial and Provident Societies Act 1965), in Scotland immediately prior to 1 April 1989 was transferred to a register maintained by Scottish Homes.[2] Provision was also made for the transfer to Scottish Homes of all heritable and moveable property held in Scotland by the Housing Corporation and its rights and liabilities relating to transferred housing associations and land in Scotland held by unregistered housing associations.[3] At the same time, parallel arrangements were made for the transfer of the Housing Corporation's responsibilities in Wales to a new body called Housing for Wales.[4] In each case, however, it should be noted that, in addition to retaining responsibilities for associations, registered and active in England, the Housing Corporation remained responsible for all other associations whose registered offices were in England— including a handful of associations whose activities extended to Scotland. That qualification apart, general provision has been made for the principal functions conferred on the Housing Corporation by the Housing Associations Act 1985 to be split between the Housing Corporation, Scottish Homes and Housing for Wales—all of which are recognised as 'the Corporation' for the purposes of the Act in relation to their own responsibilities.[5]

Thus the primary concern of Scottish Homes is with the registration and subsequent supervision and control of housing associations. A housing association is defined in section 1 of the 1985 Act as a society, body of trustees or company which is established for the purpose (in part at least) of 'providing, constructing, improving or managing, or facilitating or encouraging the construction or improvement of housing accommodation' and which does not trade for profit. Scottish Homes (which, for the avoidance of doubt, is specifically declared

1 Ibid, s 1(3)(e).
2 Ibid, s 4(1).
3 Ibid, s 4(5).
4 Housing Act 1988, ss 46–47.
5 Housing Associations Act 1985, s 2A (inserted by Housing Act 1988).

not to be a housing association) may register only societies already registered under the Industrial and Provident Societies Act 1965 and satisfying the statutory conditions laid down including (1) that an association does not trade for profit and (2) that it is established for the provision of housing for letting or for occupation by members of the association only or for hostels.[1] Although an association must, if it is to be eligible for registration, have these required purposes, additional purposes or objects are permissible. These include the ancillary powers of providing land, amenities, services or buildings for the benefit of the association's residents; the acquisition, or repairing and improving, of houses to be sold or leased; and encouraging and advising on the formation and running of other housing associations and other voluntary organisations concerned with housing. The Housing Act 1988 further provided that an association is not ineligible for registration by reason only that its powers include the power to acquire commercial premises or businesses (and, for a limited period, carry on the business) as an incidental part of an authorised housing purpose; or the power to repair or improve houses after the exercise by tenants of their right to purchase.[2] The lists of powers may be amended by statutory instrument by the Secretary of State, but not in such a way as to restrict the permissible purposes or powers.[3]

Scottish Homes may register any association eligible in terms of its purposes and powers but it must also establish criteria (which it may vary and which need not be the same as those adopted by the Housing Corporation or Housing for Wales) which should be satisfied by an association seeking registration. Scottish Homes must have regard to these criteria when deciding whether to register an association.[4] Once registered, associations fall under the financial and general supervision of Scottish Homes. Associations must submit copies of their accounts; Scottish Homes may order an extraordinary audit; Scottish Homes' consent is required for a change in the rules of an association and for disposals of land; it may appoint a person to conduct an inquiry into the affairs of an association; it may act for the protection of an association by the removal of a committee member; Scottish Homes may petition for the winding up of an association from the

---

1 Ibid, s 4(1)–(2). For some purposes (eg exclusion from secure tenancy and right to buy), a co-operative 'fully mutual' association which restricts membership to tenants (and vice versa) is differently treated.
2 Ibid, s 4(3)–(5) inserted by Housing Act 1988, s 48(1).
3 Housing Act 1988, s 48(2)–(4) which, oddly, was not itself incorporated into the 1985 Act.
4 Housing Associations Act 1985, s 5, as amended.

register if it appears to be no longer eligible for registration or has ceased to exist.[1] With effect from the beginning of 1994 there has been an ombudsman appointed by Scottish Homes, to investigate complaints against housing associations.

In the period prior to April 1989, a number of general promotional functions were vested in the Housing Corporation but these were secondary to the corporation's involvement in the funding of housing associations. Registration and supervision by the corporation were for housing associations the means of access to the vital central government funds and this continued under Scottish Homes except that the inception of the new body happened alongside a restructuring of the system of housing association financing. This is reflected in a much more radical recasting of the rules in the Housing Associations Act 1985 dealing with the financing of associations than was the case for their registration and regulation. Indeed, the core of Part II of the Act 'Housing Association Finance' dealing with housing association grants and deficit grants was repealed[2] and replaced, for Scotland, by the power of Scottish Homes contained in the Housing (Scotland) Act 1988 to 'make grants' and, to a lesser degree, the power to 'make loans'—powers exercisable only 'with the approval of the Secretary of State given with the consent of the Treasury or in accordance with a general authority given by him with such consent.'[3]

Within this scant legislative framework (augmented by certain provisions in Part II of the Housing Act 1988 and the general accounting and audit provisions already referred to) was established the 'New Financial Regime for Housing Associations in Scotland'— the title of the Housing Corporation (Scotland) Circular in which it was launched.[4] In the past and, on a limited continuing transitional basis, the general purpose of government funding of housing associations was to enable projects for the provision of housing to produce rented accommodation to let at 'fair rents.'[5] This necessarily implied a substantial public subsidy which took the form of capital grants— housing association grant—augmented by loans; together with a system of adjustment for revenue imbalances—revenue deficit grants and, in the case of surpluses, payments into the grant redemption fund.

---

1 Ibid, s 24 (and the accounting rules contained in SI 1993/487) ss 29, 19, 8–9, 28, 16, 22 and 6 respectively.
2 Housing Act 1988, Sch 18.
3 Housing (Scotland) Act 1988, s 2(2)(a), (b) and 2(3)(a).
4 Housing Corporation (Scotland) Circular 3/89.
5 For housing association tenancies, see Chap 5.

In moves heralded in consultation papers issued in September 1987,[1] however, the Government radically altered the rules and assumptions underpinning the pre-1989 funding system. In the first place, all new housing association tenancies created after 2 January 1989 have been assured tenancies which are not let at 'fair rents.'[2] This gives associations the responsibility for setting their own rent levels and, although the Government has said that rents should be 'significantly below free market level'[3] and at 'levels which are affordable to those who can be expected to look to the movement for their housing requirements',[4] the deregulated financial regime based on assured tenancies makes housing association projects better able to attract private investors. This links directly with the Government's commitment to mixed private and public funding as the principal method of housing association capital funding.[5] The former presumption of substantial public sector subsidy has been displaced but with an undertaking that some schemes unable to attract private finance despite efforts to do so may still continue to be wholly funded by the public sector. A further purpose clearly present in the Government's thinking has been the creation of what it has called 'greater responsibility' on the part of associations for their financial affairs and an accompanying emphasis upon greater value for money, stronger cost controls and a more disciplined financial regime.[5]

The result of these changes of approach and emphasis is a system of capital grants dispensed by Scottish Homes but, in the normal case, in support of projects also attracting long-term private finance on a low-start basis, with repayment obligations increasing over time in parallel with increasing rental income.[6] Grants are, therefore, based on an agreed percentage of costs and paid 'up front', with only limited scope for additional financing through grant for 'legitimate overruns'

---

1 DOE, *Finance for Housing Associations: the Government's Proposals*; and SDD, *Finance for Housing Associations—Government Proposals: Scotland* ('Scottish Proposals').
2 See p 52 below.
3 'Scottish Proposals', para 13.
4 Circular 3/89, para 3.
5 Ibid, para 4.
6 The principles laid down in Circular 3/89 were restated and supplemented in a Guidance Note issued by Scottish Homes (SHGN 90/28) in 1990 and have continued to be applied—though not without criticism. See, in particular, the SFHA's *Making it Work* (1991) which recommended *inter alia* greater freedom for associations in dealing with accumulated surpluses and A More *The New Financial Regime for Housing Associations* Centre for Housing Research (1991). Details of the grant rules are contained in Scottish Homes' *Housing Association Grant Procedures Manual*.

in anticipated expenditure.[1] In some circumstances, on the other hand, levels of grants paid may be reduced. Specific powers are conferred upon Scottish Homes, acting in accordance with such principles as it may from time to time determine, (a) to reduce the amount of grant payable; (b) to suspend or cancel an instalment of grant; or (c) to direct an association to repay the whole or a proportion of a grant. These powers are exercisable on the occurrence of such 'relevant events' (including the failure to comply with grant conditions) as may be determined by Scottish Homes.[2] 'Determinations', whether of 'principles' or of 'relevant events' as above, may be general (ie not relating solely to a particular case) and may make the same provision for all cases covered or the provision may vary. No determination may be made without the approval of the Secretary of State (given, if the determination is general, with the consent of the Treasury). A general determination may be made only after consultation with bodies representative of housing associations and appropriate publication of the determination.[3] The new financial regime also brought with it consequential adjustments to revenue arrangements. In line with their new 'independence', revenue deficit grant was effectively phased out. Any surpluses may be paid into a sinking fund known as the rent surplus fund, which is generally directed towards future major repairs.[4] The statutory machinery for establishing and operating rent surplus funds is provided by section 55 of the Housing Act 1988. This requires that a separate account be maintained by all associations in receipt of grant for any period from Scottish Homes showing 'surpluses arising from increased rental income during that period from such housing activities to which the grant relates as the Secretary of State may from time to time determine.'[5] It is then open to the Secretary of State from time to time to give notice to an association requiring it to pay to him (with interest if demanded) or to apply or appropriate for purposes he specifies any sums standing in its rent surplus fund.[6]

Collectively, the interests of housing associations are represented by the Scottish Federation of Housing Associations. The SFHA is a source of much written guidance for associations on matters such as model constitutions as well as Scottish Homes registration and financial procedures. The Federation campaigns on behalf of housing

1 Circular 3/89, Annex I and SHGN 90/28, para 3 'Principles of Capital System'.
2 Housing Act 1988, s 52(1)–(2). Interest may also be payable.
3 Ibid, s 53.
4 Circular 3/89, Annex II and SHGN 90/28, para 4 'Principles of Revenue System'.
5 Housing Act 1988, s 55(1).
6 Ibid, s 55(6).

associations and makes representations to the Government and Scottish Homes. It has, however, joined with Scottish Homes to produce the best practice manual *Raising Standards in Housing*.[1]

5. LOCAL AUTHORITIES AND HOUSING ASSOCIATIONS

Local authorities—regional councils as well as district and islands councils—have a general power to promote the formation (or extension) of housing associations and to give them assistance. This includes the power to assist financially by making grants and loans to registered associations. The exercise of this power is, however, conditional upon the consent of the Secretary of State (and subject to other regulations made or conditions imposed by him).[2] In the past, local authorities were used as an additional means of channelling grant to housing associations but this is no longer the case. District and islands councils do, however, have a separate power to supply furniture to the tenants of housing associations.[3]

These are not the only ways in which local authorities can become involved in housing association activities. They are encouraged and expected to work closely together. In particular, their tenant selection procedures should be co-ordinated, with associations accepting as a proportion of their tenants people nominated to them by local authorities from their waiting lists;[4] and the role of housing associations in the work of house improvement in housing action areas declared by local authorities has been of great importance. Taking full advantage of the normal financial assistance available to the occupants of houses in those areas as well as housing association grant, housing associations are then able to provide an efficient and co-ordinated service coupled with a degree of tenant participation which a local authority might not be able to achieve.[5]

---

1 1992. This looseleaf manual contains valuable and detailed sections on tenancy selection and allocation, factoring and rent arrears.
2 Housing Act 1988, ss 59–60.
3 Housing Associations Act 1985, s 61.
4 SDD Circular No 10/1975.
5 See Maclennan, Brailey and Lawrie, *Effectiveness of Housing Associations in Scotland*, Scottish Office CRU, 1983. Also Scottish Federation of Housing Associations, *Who do we house?—a survey of tenants of housing associations in Scotland*, 1988. For housing action areas generally, see Chap 11.

CHAPTER 4

Other housing bodies in the public sector

1. INTRODUCTION

The housing functions of district and islands councils, of the Secretary of State and the Scottish Office, and of Scottish Homes (and residually the Housing Corporation) very nearly provide a comprehensive picture of the public sector of housing in Scotland. Depending, however, on how the 'public sector' is defined and on what are to be regarded as housing functions, it is necessary to embrace a further range of authorities.

Probably the longest statutorily approved list of bodies with housing responsibilities in the public sector appears in section 61(11) of the 1987 Act. These are bodies whose tenancies rank as qualifying tenancies for the purposes of eligibility and discount in relation to the right to buy. The list is set out in Chapter 8.[1] However, these tenancies are not all secure tenancies and do not themselves confer the right to buy. Moreover, the landlords concerned are not in any real sense housing bodies[2] carrying out housing functions.

A narrower list of public sector bodies may be derived from the list of landlords which do have secure tenants who have the right to buy. These are listed in section 61(2) of the 1987 Act and set out in Chapter 8.[3] Recently, for the purposes of redefining secure tenancies, that list has been modified and, in related provisions, the term 'public body' has been introduced[4] and for the purposes of the 'change of landlord' provisions, the term 'public sector landlord' has been statutorily

---

1 See p 108 below.
2 The term 'housing body' has, in another context, been given a different meaning of its own. Schedule 2 to the Abolition of Domestic Rates Etc (Scotland) Act 1987 used the term to include district councils, new town corporations and Scottish Homes to which regional councils could delegate their duties as community charge levying authorities and this usage has been retained (for council tax purposes) in s 99 of the Local Government Finance Act 1992.
3 See p 101 below.
4 See 1988 Act, s 45(4) (and also s 43(3)) and p 53 below.

endorsed.[1] In yet another context, the term 'public sector authority' has been employed.[2] These provisions are discussed in subsequent chapters. At this stage, however, three important types of landlord in the public sector should be mentioned briefly: regional councils (and police and fire authorities when not regional councils); new town development corporations; and 'section 22' housing co-operatives.

2. REGIONAL COUNCILS

It has already been noted that the structural changes to be made to local government with effect from 1 April 1996 will see the end of a two-tier system and, therefore, of the division of responsibilities between the different levels.[3]

Until that date arrives, however, some recognition must be given to the role of the nine existing mainland regional councils. They do not have general housing responsibilities but limited powers were conferred by the Local Government (Scotland) Act 1973 upon regional councils which wish, with the consent of the Secretary of State, to promote the provision of housing accommodation by either district councils or housing associations[4] and further housing responsibilities were conferred on regions as social work authorities by the Housing (Homeless Persons) Act 1977.[5] It should be borne in mind, too, that many regional functions overlap considerably with the district housing functions. Housing cannot be considered in isolation from the provision of educational and social work services or roads and transportation, and the possible consequences of the separation of some of these functions have been the cause of some concern. The divide between housing and social work was seen as a problem at the time of local government re-organisation in 1975 and was considered first by the Morris Committee[6] and later by the Stodart Committee.[7] The continued division between the functions produced the need for a close co-ordination of the services of authorities with related responsibilities for homeless people, poor housing conditions and family stress,

---

1 Ibid; s 56 and p 143 below.
2 See 1987 Act, ss 300–301 (relating to defective housing). See p 134 below.
3 See p 3 above.
4 Local Government (Scotland) Act 1973, s 131 and the Housing Associations Act 1985, s 59.
5 See now 1987 Act, Pt II.
6 *Housing and Social Work: a Joint Approach*, HMSO (1975).
7 *Report of the Committee of Inquiry into Local Government in Scotland*, Cmnd 8115 (1980).

and some emphasis has been placed upon the development of appropriate interlocking relationships at both member and officer level to try to ensure a satisfactory service overall. Another area where a significant co-ordination of responsibilities is called for is in relation to the planning function. In their preparation of regional reports and structure plans, regional councils have to take into account the housing needs of the districts within their areas.[1]

Although they do not have general powers to provide housing or to undertake other housing responsibilities, regional councils (sometimes separately recognised when acting in amalgamation with each other or with islands councils as police and fire authorities[2]) are landlords of the houses they hold for other statutory purposes. The tenancies of these houses have never received Rent Act protection[3] but they were, from the start of the right to buy in 1980, recognised as qualifying tenancies in the public sector for the purposes of eligibility to purchase and the calculation of discount.[4] Initially, however, regional council tenancies were not themselves secure tenancies carrying directly the right to buy. This was changed by the Housing (Scotland) Act 1986.[5] Since then, regional councils have been included as 'public bodies' for the purposes of the 1988 Act.[6] As local authorities, regional councils are subject to investigation by the local ombudsman.[7]

3. NEW TOWN DEVELOPMENT CORPORATIONS

The five new town corporations designated under the New Towns (Scotland) Act 1968 (Cumbernauld, East Kilbride, Glenrothes, Irvine and Livingston)[8] have been substantial providers of housing. The corporations, which receive grants from the Secretary of State,[9] are empowered to provide housing within their areas both to rent and for sale.[10]

---

1 Local Government (Scotland) Act 1973, s 173.
2 Ibid, ss 146–147.
3 See now Rent (Scotland) Act 1984, s 5.
4 1980 Act, s 1(10).
5 See now 1987 Act, s 61(2).
6 Sections 43(3) and 45(4).
7 Local Government (Scotland) Act 1975, Pt II.
8 A sixth new town, Stonehouse, was designated in 1973 but subsequently dedesignated in 1977.
9 1987 Act, s 194.
10 New Towns (Scotland) Act 1968, s 3 contains the general powers of the corporations. Their housing functions are subject to investigation by the local ombudsman.

More recently added by the 1988 Act was the power to improve the amenities of predominantly residential areas, whether by works carried out by the corporation itself or by financial assistance given to others.[1] However, another provision of the 1988 Act gave a clearer indication of the future of the new towns. A new section inserted into the New Towns (Scotland) Act 1968 reinforced and clarified the powers of new towns to dispose of their interest in land held for housing purposes. Sales require the consent of the Secretary of State and must, without further consent, be on the best terms that can be reasonably obtained.[2]

It has always been intended that the life-time of the new town corporations should be finite. They should be wound up when each town's expansion was completed and the corporation's job is done. As far as the housing stock is concerned, it was once assumed that this would be transferred to the district councils.[3] More recently, however, the Government issued a Green Paper, followed by a White Paper in mid 1989,[4] in which revised proposals were made. The process of winding up the new towns was to begin shortly with each wind-up taking about three years.[5] Since 1989, a firmer time-table has been established. East Kilbride and Glenrothes will wind up finally on 31 December 1995[6] and it is expected that the other three will wind up on 31 December 1996.

On housing in particular, the 1989 White Paper noted a considerable diversification of tenure in the new towns. The promotion of private house-building and also of sales to tenants in the public sector had produced towns in which more than 50 per cent of houses were owner-occupied and it was plainly the Government's wish that diversification should continue until wind-up, with increased activity by housing associations and housing co-operatives.[7] On wind-up itself, 'Ministers have made it clear that they do not now see the district councils as the automatic inheritors of new town housing at wind-up, although the councils might remain as one option among a number of other possibilities, such as home ownership, housing associations, tenants' co-operatives and Scottish Homes.'[8]

---

1 See 1987 Act, s 23 substituted by the 1988 Act.
2 New Towns (Scotland) Act 1968, s 18AA.
3 See, eg *Scottish Housing*, Cmnd 6852, para 9.28 (1977).
4 Industry Department for Scotland, October 1988 and July 1989.
5 *The Scottish New Towns*, paras 3.6–3.10.
6 See Winding Up Orders in SIs 1992/355 and 354 respectively under s 36 of the New Towns (Scotland) Act 1968, as substituted by the Enterprise and New Towns (Scotland) Act 1990.
7 *The Scottish New Towns*, paras 4.1–4.8.
8 Ibid, para 4.9.

More recently the Government has issued detailed guidance to corporations about how their objectives should be achieved, including advice on the ballotting of tenants on their preferred arrangements for landlords after wind-up, criteria for determining the acceptability of private landlords and the financial consequences of transfer of stock to local authorities.[1]

4. 'SECTION 22' HOUSING CO-OPERATIVES

Since the powers were first introduced in 1975,[2] district and islands councils have been able to make an agreement with a society, company or body of trustees, known as a 'housing co-operative' (but not to be confused with a 'co-operative housing association'), under which the co-operative may assume some of the powers of the local authority.[3] The co-operative takes over the landlord functions of the authority in relation to the land and houses covered by the agreement, for which the Secretary of State's consent is required.[4] Little advantage has been taken of this facility and only a small number of co-operatives have ever been established.[5] Houses included in the co-operative agreement continue to be held on the authority's housing revenue account[6] but, since the introduction of secure tenancies and the right to buy in 1980, housing co-operatives have been separately recognised as the landlord of their secure tenants.[7] The 1988 Act provided, however, that, with effect from 2 January 1989, no new secure tenancies could be created by housing co-operatives.[8]

1 *Guidance on Wind-Up* (1993) Scottish Office Industry Department, Chap 5 'Disposal of Housing Stock'.
2 Housing (Rents and Subsidies) (Scotland) Act 1975, s 5.
3 1987 Act, s 22.
4 Ibid, s 22(1)–(3).
5 See Scottish Office research publications, *Options for Housing Co-operatives in Scotland* (1979) and *Monitoring the Summerston Housing Co-operative* (1977 and 1979). On the new s 22A and the creation as co-operatives of Tenant Management Organisations, see p 66.
6 1987 Act, s 22(5).
7 See now 1987 Act, s 61(2).
8 Section 43(3).

CHAPTER 5

Landlords and tenants

1. INTRODUCTION

The main purpose of this chapter is to serve as a preface to Chapters 6 and 7. Those deal with the rules which determine the legal relationship between the major categories of tenants of housing accommodation and their landlords. It will be found that, in the modern law, these tenants fall into two main statutorily defined groups—'secure' tenants in what we may still appropriately call the 'public sector' and the tenants under 'regulated' and 'assured' tenancies in the 'private sector' (including many tenants of housing associations). Most of the important rules which govern these tenancies derive from statutory sources rather than the common law and are of recent origin. They are, for the most part, contained in self-standing codes.

It is, however, helpful to be reminded that the statute law in this area does, in many ways, build on the common law rules of landlord and tenant and that there are some aspects of the law which are little affected by statute at all and where, therefore, the common law retains its importance. It is also useful to be aware of the more recent legislative developments which have produced the different types of tenancy in the modern law and the policy considerations which have required substantial modification of the common law landlord and tenant relationship.

2. COMMON LAW FOUNDATIONS

At the core of landlord and tenant law is a simple agreement, a contract, made between the two parties. As a contract, it must be entered into by parties who have the legal capacity to do so—the parties may be 'natural' persons ie individual human beings provided they are of age or they may be 'artificial' persons such as companies, firms or public authorities (provided that it is within their legal powers)—and who consent to the terms of the contract. Neither party can, for instance, be bound by an arrangement made under duress.[1] In addition to general legal capacity a landlord must also, of course, be a person who, whether as owner or as a tenant (who would then create a sub-tenancy), has a sufficient legal relationship with the property concerned.

Thus the first two essential elements[2] of any lease are that the parties to it and the subjects (the land, house or other property) must be identified. In addition the amount of the rent must be stated. An agreement for the occupation of property rent free is not a lease. The fourth 'essential element' is that the period for which a lease is to last must be stated (or be capable of being inferred from its terms). In addition to these rules as to the content of a lease there is a common law requirement that a lease (unlike many other forms of contract) must be in writing.

Although these characteristics may constitute the principal common law requirements of a lease, they are, in most accounts of the law, conventionally joined by the further requirements imposed by a very early Act of the Scottish Parliament, the Leases Act 1449, which must be observed if it is to be ensured that the terms of a properly formed contract of lease are binding on and enforceable by not only the immediate parties to the original document but also (as a real right) by the tenant against someone who has purchased the house or other property from the original landlord. This is an important guarantee of the continuity of the legal relationship between the tenant and the new landlord. It does not, of course, bind the landlord to anything more than is specified in the lease itself and the lease may be brought to an end under its original terms. It has been the more recent statutory guarantees of security of tenure capable of overriding the terms of a lease itself which have made a much more substantial contribution to modern tenant security. What the 1449 Act did was to ensure a real right for tenants by (a) reinforcing the common law requirements of writing and that the subject of the lease be heritable property let for a continuing rent subject to an ish (expiry date); and (b) adding further requirements that the tenant has 'entered into

1 For modern works on the general law of contract, see eg A B Wilkinson and W A Wilson (eds) W M Gloag and R C Henderson *Introduction to the Law of Scotland* (9th edn, 1987) Chap 4 ff; W McBryde *The Law of Contract in Scotland* (1987); S E Woolman *An Introduction to the Scots Law of Contract* (2nd edn, 1994).
2 For specialised works on the modern law of landlord and tenant on which much of the following account relies, see the 'Landlord and Tenant' title in volume 13 of the *Stair Memorial Encyclopaedia*; Paton and Cameron *The Law of Landlord and Tenant in Scotland* (1967); *Gloag and Henderson* above Chap 33 and A McAllister *Scottish Law of Leases* (1989).

possession' and that the landlord, if letting as owner rather than as tenant to a sub-tenant, is infeft ie has the legal title formally vested in him or her.[1] The same consequence, a real right enforceable by the tenant against a successor landlord, is created by the recording of the lease in the Register of Sasines (or the Land Register), although this is of little significance to general housing law since recording applies only to leases for 20 years or more.[2] It is unnecessary here to consider the consequences of the failure, in any respect, of an agreement to satisfy the formal requirements of a lease or tenancy except to observe that in the modern law, landlords have sometimes found it to be in their interests to claim that a tenancy does not formally exist in order to avoid some of the statutory consequences (in terms of security of tenure or rent control) which flow from the creation of certain tenancies.

Apart from providing the core rules on the formation of the contract of lease and then, in principle, the freedom of the parties (the landlord and tenant) to agree upon the terms of their lease, the common law also provides some of the terms which will be assumed to apply under any lease unless they are explicitly modified or excluded. Because modern housing tenancy agreements are, in practice, quite comprehensively drawn and because, in any event, mandatory statutory terms have in many cases displaced the common law rules, there is little remaining significance in these implied terms although, as we shall see, they are still of importance in some areas. The terms implied into a contract of lease take the form of a number of rights and obligations of the tenant and the landlord. From the point of view of the tenant, these may be briefly listed as, on the one hand, obligations to occupy the house or land, to use the property for its proper purpose, to take reasonable care of the property, to pay the rent when due and to 'plenish the subjects' ie keep within the property which is let sufficient moveable property to provide security for the rent; and, on the other hand, rights to full possession of the property, to be given property which is reasonably fit for the purpose for which it is let and to have repairs carried out by the landlord. Of these, the most important in the context of housing law are probably the rights to the fitness of the property and to have it maintained in repair.[3]

Another important contribution of the common law, with some continuing consequences, is the provision of remedies for one party to

---

1 Although these rules are stated to derive from the 1449 Act, they do so only very indirectly and as a result of creative judicial interpretation of the very sparse fifteenth century text. For a full account, see *McAllister* above.
2 As amended.
3 See p 88 below.

a lease if the other party is in breach of one of its terms. These are, in the main, the remedies available for any breach of contract and include specific implement (a court order requiring compliance with a legal obligation), interdict (an order requiring a person not to act in breach of an obligation or to refrain from further breach), an action for debt followed by enforcement by diligence in the form of poinding and sale or arrestment, rescission of the contract (ie declaring the contract to be at an end because of a material breach) and damages. In addition, it may be possible for one party to hold back payments to the other against non-performance of another obligation under the lease. Most obviously, this facility of retention is available to the tenant where rent is withheld pending performance by the landlord of, for instance, obligations to repair.[1] On the other side, it is open to a landlord to invoke the remedies of enforcement of an irritancy (termination for breach of a specification) of hypothec and summary diligence.

3. SECURITY FOR PRIVATE TENANTS

It is apparent from the outline above that the common law contract of lease, the basis of the landlord and tenant relationship, was able to provide an adequate foundation upon which the two consenting parties to the contract could arrange their affairs. What the formal rules of contract could take no account of, however, was the great inequality of bargaining power which almost inevitably builds up between landlords and tenants in housing tenancies. Especially in conditions of housing shortage, property-owning landlords are more powerful than their tenants, better placed to insert their preferred terms into leases and to exploit tenants by the oppressive abuse of the legal relationship. Mainly, but not exclusively, in the private sector, landlords have sufficient common law powers to oppress with terms which limit security of tenure and threaten increased rents and which, despite their formal legal equality to contract, tenants may be powerless to resist. It is this situation which came to be addressed first in the Rent and Mortgage Interest (War Restrictions) Act 1915, and then in successive versions of the 'Rent Acts' thereafter.

The exact nature of the restrictions imposed by the Rent Acts has varied over the years since 1915. A number of different regimes of control have operated, often simultaneously, with some tenancies

---

1 See p 90 below.

governed by one set of rules and some by another depending on the date at which each tenancy was created. Until recently, however, the principal ingredients of regulation have been a restriction on the rents chargeable by landlords coupled with a restriction on the circumstances in which a landlord can end a tenancy by service of a notice to quit. Necessarily, these statutory restrictions operate in relation to all tenancies they are defined to cover regardless of the terms of the tenancies themselves. The terms originally agreed are overridden by the statutory guarantees of security of tenure or of rent restriction or both. Tenancies known as controlled tenancies dominated the scene until the introduction of regulated tenancies by the Rent Act 1965 and were wound up as a separate category in 1980.[1] Those that remained were converted into regulated tenancies. 'Regulated tenancy' is the term used to describe tenancies subject to the 1965 Act (and now the Rent (Scotland) Act 1984) both at their contractual 'protected' stage before they have been affected by any notice to quit and also their 'statutory' stage when the tenant's status comes to be guaranteed not by the original contract but by the Act's own provisions.

As will be explained, the era of regulated tenancies has itself been brought to a close. The 1988 Act provided that, with certain very limited exceptions, no *new* regulated tenancies could be created from 2 January 1989 and they are, therefore, frozen as a category containing those tenancies which were created up to that date and which satisfied certain statutory conditions.[2] The number of regulated tenancies cannot grow but many tenants continue to occupy their houses under the terms which were laid down by the 1965 Act. The relevant provisions are now contained in the 1984 Act as amended.

The principal defining characteristics of regulated tenancies were that they applied to houses let as separate dwellings[3] and which had a rateable value lower than a prescribed maximum.[4] The prescribed figure started at a 1965 level of £200 and then rose by way of £600 for houses entered on the valuation roll between 1978 and 1985 to £1,600 for houses entered on the roll after 1 April 1985.

Some tenancies which satisfied the rateable value criterion were, however, specifically excluded from protection. These are tenancies:

1 1980 Act, s 46.
2 1988 Act, s 42.
3 1984 Act, s 1(1). The term 'separate dwelling' is not one directly defined in the Act. See 13 *Stair Memorial Encyclopaedia* para 607.
4 1984 Act, s 1(1)(a), (2); Protected Tenancies and Part VII Contracts (Rateable Value Limits) (Scotland) Order 1985, SI 1985/314.

1. Where, under the tenancy, no rent was payable (or the rent was less than two-thirds of the rateable value);
2. Where the house was 'bona fide' let at a rent including payments for board or attendance.[1]
3. Where the landlord was an educational establishment and the tenant a student.
4. Where the tenancy was a 'holiday let'.[2]
5. Where the house was let with agricultural land exceeding two acres.[3]
6. Where the house was let by a public body (local authority development corporation etc).[4]
7. Where the landlord was 'resident' in the building.[5]
8. Where the landlord was the Crown.[6]
9. Where the house was used exclusively for certain business purposes.[7]

4. TENANCIES IN THE PUBLIC SECTOR

Prior to 1980, the relationship between local authorities (and other landlords in the 'public sector', such as the SSHA) and their tenants did not attract much attention in legal commentaries because it was not subject to much special regulation by the law. Rules of the common law relating to such matters as the creation of the landlord and tenant relationship itself, general repairing obligations and the termination of tenancies applied but some of the most important areas of concern to the council tenant or potential tenant were unaffected by direct legal intervention. Some matters such as rent levels were subject to special rules,[8] although the regime of 'fair rents' which

---

1 In the case of payments for attendance, this exclusion applied only if the amount attributable to attendance, having regard to the value of the attendance to the tenant, formed a substantial part of the whole rent.
2 This (and some others in the list of exclusions) has no continuing significance since the effective bar on new regulated tenancies, but is retained for the sake of completeness.
3 But there is protection under the Agricultural Holdings Acts.
4 But see 'Tenancies in the Public Sector' below.
5 But see p 56 below.
6 An exclusion which did not apply where the landlord's interest was under the management of the Crown Estate Commissioners.
7 1984 Act, s 10.
8 See p 94 below.

governed the private rented sector did not extend to public authorities. It was also argued that the status of public authorities as creatures of statute subjected them in some respects to enforceable constraints on the manner in which they exercised their powers as landlords. The circumstances in which an authority might terminate a tenancy were in some measure controlled in ways which would not be applicable to a private landlord.[1] But many matters such as access to housing waiting lists and house allocation itself were not the subject of statutory regulation. Rules tended to evolve simply through the local practice of authorities. Because of their exclusion from Rent Act protection, there was little to be said even about the tenure enjoyed by tenants in the public sector.

In this same period (up to 1980), the position of tenants of housing associations was rather different. Housing association tenancies, like local authority tenancies, could not be regulated tenancies.[2] Tenants did not, therefore, have the security of tenure afforded to tenants with private landlords. On the other hand, housing association tenants were able to take advantage of the 'fair rents' provisions of the Rent Acts.[3]

Two major legislative innovations in the 1980s radically changed the position just described—the Tenants' Rights Etc (Scotland) Act 1980 and the Housing (Scotland) Act 1988. These have affected both public authority and housing association tenancies. In the first place, Parts I and II of the 1980 Act (since consolidated in Part III of the 1987 Act) contained new rules which greatly strengthened the position of public sector tenants. Although eventually included within the Conservative Government's legislation of 1980, many of the changes had already been proposed by the previous Labour Government, especially in its 1977 Green Paper *Scottish Housing*.[4] The chapter in that paper on 'Housing Authorities and their Tenants' made proposals for more sensitive housing management policies and also for the granting of security of tenure to council tenants and the extension of the 'freedom' and 'rights' of tenants. It was this theme of conferring 'rights' on tenants which was given legislative form in the 'tenants' charter'[5] incorporated into the 1980 Act. The most radical and most controversial of the rights conferred was the tenant's right to purchase his or her own house—a right leading to the end of the landlord and tenant relationship.

---

1 See p 73 below.
2 Rent (Scotland) Act 1971, s 5 as amended and consolidated in the Rent (Scotland) Act 1984, s 5.
3 Housing (Financial Provisions) (Scotland) Act 1972 as amended and consolidated in the Rent (Scotland) Act 1984, Pt VI.
4 Cmnd 6852 (1977).
5 Not to be confused with the *Tenant's Charter* (1991).

The key concept, introduced by the 1980 Act, was that of the 'secure tenancy.' The 'secure tenant' was given some statutory protection from termination of the tenancy by the landlord but this was accompanied by rights of succession to tenancies and other rights to be enjoyed during a tenancy. With some exceptions, it was 'secure tenants' who were given the right to purchase[1] and 'secure tenants' have since become the 'qualifying tenants' for the purpose of the 'choice of landlord' provisions introduced by the 1988 Act.[2] It therefore became very important, after the 1980 Act, to be able to identify which tenancies were secure tenancies.

Now re-enacted (with amendments explained below) in section 44(1) of the 1987 Act, the conditions a tenancy must satisfy to be a secure tenancy are as follows:

1. The house must be let as a separate dwelling.[3] Hostel accommodation does not, therefore, qualify.[4]
2. The tenant must be an individual (and not, for instance, a company[5]) and the house must be his or her only or principal home. Where the tenancy is joint, this condition is satisfied provided that all the joint tenants are individuals and at least one of them occupies the house as his or her only or principal residence. Furthermore, a tenancy which has become a secure tenancy will continue to be a secure tenancy despite the fact that this condition has ceased to be fulfilled.[6]
3. The landlord must be one of the following bodies:

   (a) an islands or district council;[7]
   (b) a regional council;[8]
   (c) a new town development corporation;[9]
   (d) Scottish Homes;[10]
   (e) the Housing Corporation;

---

1 See Chap 8.
2 See Chap 9.
3 1987 Act, s 44(1)(a).
4 See *Thomson v City of Glasgow District Council* 1986 SLT (Lands Tr) 6.
5 Nor a partnership. See *Lamont v Glenrothes Development Corporation* 1993 SLT (Lands Tr) 2.
6 1987 Act, s 44(1)(b), (2) and (6).
7 Ibid, s 44(1)(c), (2) and s 61(2)(a). This designation includes a joint board or joint committee of an islands or district council, or the common good of either, or any trust under the control of either.
8 Ibid. Includes joint boards, committees and controlled trusts. Regional councils were added by the Housing (Scotland) Act 1986.
9 Ibid. Also any urban development corporation.
10 Ibid. Prior to 1 April 1989, the SSHA was the equivalent landlord.

(f) a registered housing association (except co-operative housing associations);[1]

(g) a housing co-operative under section 22 of the 1987 Act;[2]

(h) a police authority in Scotland;[3]

(i) a fire authority in Scotland;[4]

(j) certain housing trusts.[5]

Even if a tenancy satisfies these conditions it will still not be a secure tenancy if it is one of the following types:[6]

1. A tenancy of a house required to be occupied by the tenant under the terms of a contract of employment with the landlord or with a local authority or development corporation for the better performance of his or her duties. A number of difficulties have arisen with this exclusion in relation to the right to purchase. They are discussed below.[7]

2. A temporary letting to a person who has moved into an area for employment reasons seeking permanent accommodation;[8]

3. A temporary letting pending developments;[8]

4. A temporary letting of accommodation during works affecting a house normally occupied by the tenant;

5. A temporary letting of accommodation to a homeless person under Part II of the 1987 Act;[9]

6. A tenancy of agricultural or business (including the sale of liquor) premises;

7. A tenancy granted by a police or fire authority where, in the case of a police force, the house is let rent free to a constable; and, in the case of a fire brigade, the house is let to a member of the brigade required to live in close proximity to a fire station; or, in either case, if the house is let expressly on a temporary basis pending use by the force or brigade;[10]

8. A tenancy of a house which forms part of, or is within the curtilage of, a building which mainly (a) is held for non-housing

1 Ibid and s 45. But see p 52 below.
2 Ibid. For these 'management co-operatives' see p 42 above. But see also p 52 below.
3 Ibid. Category added by 1986 Act.
4 Ibid. Category added by 1986 Act.
5 1987 Act, s 44(1)(c) and (2).
6 These are now specified in amended form in Sch 2 to the 1987 Act.
7 See p 105.
8 See p 102 below.
9 See Chap 10.
10 These exceptions were added when police and fire authorities were added to the list of landlords of secure tenancies by the 1986 Act.

purposes or (b) consists of accommodation other than housing accommodation.[1]

Having regard to these criteria taken as a whole, it is clear that, with only a few exceptions, the tenants of local authorities, the new towns and Scottish Homes are secure tenants. Equally, with a few exceptions, the tenants of housing associations (other than tenants of co-operative housing associations) also became secure tenants in 1980.[2] They were never, however, in quite the same position as other secure tenants. They retained, for instance, access to the 'fair rents' provisions of the Rent Acts from which public sector tenants were excluded.[3] Initially, the secure tenants of housing associations were not given the right to buy. Following changes made by the Housing (Scotland) Act 1986 (now consolidated in the 1987 Act), many housing association tenants did have the right to buy.[4] Their position was brought closer to that of secure tenants in the public sector.

More recently, however, in the second radical change of the 1980s, the 1988 Act has reversed that trend. The line between the public and private sector has been made more explicit—'public body' and 'public sector landlord' have become statutory terms of art[5]—and housing association tenants now find themselves more firmly back in the private sector—a sector also substantially remodelled by the 1988 Act.

The key terms of the 1988 Act produced the following changes:

1. With effect from 2 January 1989, the only new secure tenancies (subject to the limited exceptions below) which may be created are those where the landlord is a body in the public sector—local authorities (including police and fire authorities), new towns and Scottish Homes.[6] An exception was made for tenancies arising from contracts made prior to 2 January 1989.[7] Of more continuing significance was an exception for a tenancy granted to a person who, immediately before the tenancy was entered into, was a secure tenant of the *same landlord*.[8] Thus a housing association tenant who became

---

1 This exception was added by the 1986 Act following difficulties related to those mentioned under exception 1 above. See also p 107 below.
2 See now 1987 Act, ss 44(1) and 45(1).
3 Now Rent (Scotland) Act 1984, Pt VI.
4 1987 Act, s 61(1), (2), (4). See p 102 below.
5 1988 Act, ss 45(4) and 56(3).
6 Ibid, s 43(3) and SI 1988/2038.
7 Ibid, s 43(3)(b).
8 Ibid, s 43(3)(c).

a secure tenant in the period up to 2 January 1989 and who moves into a different house owned by the same landlord remains a secure tenant. Similarly, a tenant remains a secure tenant if an order for possession of his original house is made against him on a 'management' ground; the new tenancy is of premises which are 'other suitable accommodation' for these purposes; and the court directs that there should be a new secure tenancy.[1]

2. As implied in (1), despite a general restriction on *new* secure tenancies where the landlord is not in the public sector, *existing* secure tenancies continue to have that status. Secure tenants of housing associations also continue to enjoy the benefits of the 'fair rent' provisions of the Rent (Scotland) Act 1984.

3. In reinforcement of (1) and (2), it was provided that any tenancies of a landlord which is a 'public body' (the public landlords mentioned in (1) plus the Crown or Government department) which cease to be tenancies of such a landlord and any tenancies which cease to be housing association tenancies (for 'fair rent' purposes) cannot thereafter be secure tenancies. Nor can they be tenancies, whether of a housing association or of a private sector landlord, subject to the Rent (Scotland) Act 1984.[2] In common with most other tenancies entered into after 2 January 1989 (ie apart from tenancies of the Crown, a Government department, a public sector landlord, or a *co-operative* housing association) the only option is an assured tenancy under Part II of the 1988 Act.[3]

5. ASSURED TENANCIES

Alongside the proposals for Scottish Homes and other changes in the public sector, the Government also used the White Paper, *Housing: The Government's Proposals for Scotland*[4] to launch changes in the private rented sector of the housing market. Landlords were unwilling, the Government argued, to let their houses because of the guarantees for tenants of security and 'fair rents' under the regulated tenancies of

---

1 Ibid, s 43(3)(d) and see p 76.
2 Ibid, s 45.
3 Ibid, s 12 and Sch 4.
4 Cm 242 (1987) Chap 4.

the Rent (Scotland) Act 1984.[1] Those people for whom renting was a sensible option were being denied the chance because of the shortage of houses available.[2]

The key change proposed was the 'assured tenancy' which would be developed in two forms. The assured tenancy itself would be the standard form of tenancy introduced to replace the protected tenancy. There would be security of tenure for tenants but rents would be 'freely negotiated between landlord and tenant.'[3] The short assured tenancy, on the other hand, would offer no security beyond the period of the tenancy itself (a minimum of six months) but would have a system of statutory registration of rents, at market levels.[4]

These proposals reached the statute book as Part II of the Housing (Scotland) Act 1988. As already described, the phasing out of protected tenancies was ensured. With limited exceptions, no new protected tenancy could be created after 2 January 1989.[5] Most new tenancies in the private sector are now assured tenancies and it may be that some properties will be brought into the housing market by landlords induced by the prospect of the 'freely negotiated' rents. Further encouragement was given by the Government in the form of its Business Expansion Scheme which offered substantial tax incentives to those who invested in companies developing housing for renting on assured tenancies.[6] This did not necessarily need to involve new-build housing and there was a close relationship between the introduction of assured tenancies, the encouragement through tax incentives of investment in private landlords, and the provisions (contained in the 1988 Act and the Housing Act 1988) for the 'choice of a new landlord' by public sector tenants and for 'voluntary disposals' of houses by local authorities.[7] There was an assumption that the assured tenancies would be financially attractive to landlords whilst the tenants who were unable to afford the rents resulting from 'free negotiation' could be supported by increased reliance on housing benefit.[8]

As already explained, another important change made by the 1988 Act was the shift of housing association tenancies (treated by the White

1 Ibid, para 4.1
2 Ibid, para 4.2.
3 Ibid, para 4.9.
4 Ibid, para 4.10.
5 1988 Act, s 42.
6 See Chap III of Pt VII of the Taxes Act 1988 as applied to private rented housing by ss 50–53 of and Sch 4 to the Finance Act 1988. The Scheme was terminated with effect from 31 December 1993.
7 See Chap 9 below.
8 Cm 242, para 4.12.

Paper as a part of the 'independent rented sector') away from the public sector and the general replacement of secure tenancies with 'fair rents' by assured tenancies with market rents. The numbers of housing association tenants are expanding to include many of those moving from Scottish Homes, new town, and local authority tenancies.[1]

The essential requirements of an assured tenancy are that the tenant (or at least one joint tenant) must be an individual; and the house must be occupied by the tenant (or again, by at least one joint tenant) as his or her principal home.[2] The letting may include land other than the house.[3] The house itself must be let as a separate dwelling, although a tenant who shares some accommodation with a person other than the landlord may hold the accommodation which he or she occupies exclusively on an assured tenancy.[4] Certain tenancies are excluded from being assured tenancies. These include tenancies in the public sector and *continuing* protected tenancies, housing association and secure tenancies[5] but also tenancies at a low rent (under £6 per week)[6] and shops, tenancies of licensed premises, agricultural holdings, tenancies of resident landlords, student lettings and holiday lettings.[7] Another exception is any tenancy granted expressly on a temporary basis in fulfilment of a duty imposed on a local authority by the homeless persons provisions in Part II of the 1987 Act.[8]

---

1 See Chap 9 below.
2 1988 Act, s 12.
3 Ibid, s 13.
4 Ibid, s 14.
5 Ibid, Sch 4.
6 Ibid, Sch 4, para 2 and SI 1988/2069.
7 Ibid, Sch 4, paras 3–9 and, in the case of students, SI 1988/2068, as amended by SI 1993/995.
8 Ibid, Sch 4, para 11A (inserted by the Housing Act 1988). See Chap 10 below.

CHAPTER 6

Tenancies in the private sector

1. INTRODUCTION

It was explained in the last chapter that it is not always appropriate to draw firm lines between so-called private sector and public sector tenancies. In particular, the treatment of housing association tenancies has in recent years blurred the distinction. On the other hand, many of the special rules which attach, almost exclusively, to public sector secure tenancies deserve separate treatment and this appears in Chapters 7–9. In this chapter, the focus is on the two important statutory regimes which operate principally in the private sector—those of the regulated tenancy and the assured tenancy (including the short-assured tenancy).

It may be objected that this approach oversimplifies a very much more complicated picture to the extent of producing distortion. Certainly it ignores the rules which have produced a number of subsidiary housing regimes including the hybrid category of the 'Part VII contract'. So called because the relevant rules were first contained in Part VII of the Rent (Scotland) Act 1971 and then in Part VII of the 1984 Act, these contracts provided limited protection for people occupying some categories of furnished premises and premises with resident landlords.[1] Since no new Part VII contracts have been created after 2 January 1989 (and earlier contracts lost their special status if their terms were changed after that date),[2] there cannot now be many still in existence. One of the consequences of providing less tenant security in the principal form of current statutory tenancy—the assured tenancy—is that there are fewer landlord and tenant disputes at its boundaries and less room for satellite hybrid regimes. The most important general rules which do continue to offer some tenant protection outwith the main categories of tenure are (a) the assurance that a person in occupation of a dwelling (whether under a formal tenancy

---

1 See 13 *Stair Memorial Encyclopaedia* paras 593 and 624–629.
2 1988 Act, s 44.

or not) cannot be evicted by the landlord without court proceedings[1] and (b) in reinforcement of that assurance, that it is a criminal offence unlawfully to evict or to harass a residential occupier.[2]

2. REGULATED TENANCIES

The tenancies to which the Rent (Scotland) Act 1984 applies have been described.[3] With only small modifications, the rules which govern them date back to the Rent Act 1965 whose principal purposes were (1) to confer security of tenure (2) to permit succession to tenancies and (3) to provide a system of 'fair rents'.

(a) Security of tenure

What has to be guaranteed to tenants who are to be afforded security of tenure of the house in which they live is that, whatever the 'agreed' terms of the tenancy, they cannot be ejected simply on the whim of the landlord. The way in which this is achieved under regulated tenancies is by the combined operation of two legal mechanisms. It is first provided that, if the landlord ends the (contractual) protected tenancy, then, as long as the tenant retains possession of the house, a new (statutory) tenancy is created.[4] Secondly, a court may make an order for possession of a house subject to either form of tenancy in only a limited number of circumstances specified in the Act. In ways later loosely paralleled by assured tenancies and also by secure (public sector) tenancies, the grounds on which a possession order may be made are divided into two groups. On the one hand, there are grounds which are 'discretionary' in the sense that the court must be persuaded of the substance of the landlord's case and also consider that it is reasonable to make an order. On the other hand there are 'mandatory' grounds which, if established by the landlord, leave the court no choice. It must make the order.

The discretionary power of the court to make an order arises in two different types of circumstance. The first is where the landlord seeks an order for possession and the court is satisfied that 'suitable alternative accommodation' is available or will become available for the

---

1 1984 Act, s 23.
2 1984 Act, s 22 and see 1988 Act, ss 36 and 37.
3 See p 47 above.
4 1984 Act, s 3.

tenant.[1] The Act provides that a certificate from the local housing authority that it will provide such 'suitable alternative accommodation' on a specified date is to be treated as conclusive evidence of its availability. Otherwise the proposed accommodation is to be deemed suitable if it consists of premises to be let as a separate dwelling subject to a protected tenancy (or, in the opinion of the court, on terms affording reasonably equivalent security of tenure). It must also be 'reasonably suitable to the needs of the tenant and his family as regards proximity to place of work' and either similar, as regards rental and extent, to accommodation provided by a housing authority in the neighbourhood to meet similar needs or reasonably suitable to the actual means and needs of the tenant and his or her family. If furniture was provided under the regulated tenancy, this should also be offered in the alternative accommodation.[2]

The other type of circumstance in which the court's discretionary power to order possession arises is where any of a list of 10 cases specified in Part I of Schedule 2 to the 1984 Act arises. In brief these are:

1. Rent lawfully due but unpaid or other tenancy obligation broken;
2. Tenant or other resident or sub-tenant guilty of nuisance or annoyance to neighbours or using the house for immoral or illegal purposes;
3. Condition of house deteriorated by neglect or default of the tenant or resident or sub-tenant;
4. Condition of furniture similarly deteriorated;
5. Landlord's need to sell or let the house would be seriously prejudiced following notice to quit;
6. Assignment of subletting of house without consent;
7. House reasonably required for person in employment of landlord;
8. House reasonably required for occupation by landlord or member of immediate family;
9. Tenant charging excessive rent for part of the house sublet; and
10. House so overcrowded as to be dangerous or injurious to health.

The other situation is where the court has no alternative but to order possession if certain facts are established. The landlord does not also

---

1 Ibid, s 11(1)(a).
2 Ibid, Sch 2, Pt IV.

have to demonstrate the 'reasonableness' of the order; the making of the order is mandatory. Here it is one of the cases (nos 11–21) in Part II of Schedule 2 which has to be shown to apply. Listed again in abbreviated form, these are:

11. A number of situations where the landlord as a former owner-occupier has specifically reserved the right to recover possession for him or herself or certain family members;
12. Where the house was acquired for eventual occupation by the landlord on retirement;
13–15. Various categories of holiday and other short lets;
16–20. House required for occupation by minister, lay missionary, agricultural worker, or person with special needs; and
21. House required by owner who is a former member of the armed services.

To the extent that the Rent Acts have, in their complicated history, 'worked', this has been achieved by the device, just discussed, of limiting the grounds on which the landlord can repossess the house, whatever the terms of the original tenancy. These basic rules are supported by supplementary provisions including, most importantly, the criminal offences of unlawful eviction and harassment of the occupier of residential premises[1] and civil liability in damages in the same situations.[2]

(b) Succession to a tenancy

Another important aspect of security of tenure is, however, the right in some circumstances for a spouse or a member of the family to succeed to the tenancy on the death of the tenant. Formerly the rules were wider in scope but, since amendments made by the 1988 Act,[3] it is provided that, when the original tenant under a regulated tenancy (protected or statutory) dies, his or her spouse (who may be a person who lived with the tenant as husband and wife) becomes a statutory tenant provided that the house was his or her only or principal home and the spouse retains possession of it.[4] Failing such a qualifying spouse, then a member of the original tenant's family is entitled to

---

1 Ibid, s 22.
2 1988 Act, ss 36–37.
3 1984 Act, s 3A and Schs 1A and 1B inserted by s 46 of and Sch 6 to the 1988 Act.
4 Subject to the need, in some instances, for the resolution of competing claims from 'spouses': 1984 Act, Sch 1A, para 2(3).

succeed but only to a statutory *assured* tenancy (see below) and then only on condition that the person resided in the house with the original tenant for the period of two years immediately before the death. There is a similar possibility of further succession by a person who is a member of the family of both the original tenant and of the spouse who earlier succeeded when that spouse died—again subject to the condition of two years immediate past residence in the house.

If there had already been a succession to a statutory tenancy, whether by a spouse or a member of the original tenant's family, prior to 2 January 1989 (the date of commencement of the 1988 Act changes), then, subject to the same conditions of residence, a member of the family (again of both the original and first successor tenants) may succeed to a statutory assured tenancy.[1]

(c) Fair rents

As already explained, the second essential element of the system of regulated tenancies has been the provision for restricting the rents landlords may charge. The mechanism employed is that of the determination of a 'fair rent' which, once registered in respect of a particular house, may not be exceeded.

Administratively, the registration of rents is in the hands of rent officers appointed by the Secretary of State and operating in registration areas based on local authority areas.[2] Rent officers maintain a register for their area[3] and applications to the rent officer for the registration of a rent may be made either by the landlord or by the tenant of a regulated tenancy (or it may be made jointly) in a prescribed form.[4] In determining a fair rent, the rent officer is bound to take into account information supplied and representations made by both sides and to notify them of the decision.[5] Either party may then object to the decision (within 28 days) in which case the rent officer must refer the issue to a rent assessment committee. These committees are drawn from a panel appointed by the Secretary of State and

---

1 For the position in relation to tenancies which *started* as assured tenancies, see p 63 below.
2 1984 Act, s 43.
3 Ibid, s 45.
4 Ibid, s 46. For the form, see the Rent Regulation (Forms and Information etc) (Scotland) Regulations 1991, SI 1991/1521.
5 1984 Act, Sch 5, Pt I.

consist of a chairman and one or two other members, save that the president of the panel may direct that in certain cases the chairman may, with the consent of the parties, act alone.[1] Once a fair rent has been registered, whether after consideration by a rent assessment committee or not, there may not be an application for a different rent for the house, unless either (a) the application is made jointly by landlord and tenant or (b) there has been 'such a change in the condition of the dwelling-house (including the making of any improvement therein)', or of the other factors relevant to the fixing of a fair rent as to make the registered rent no longer fair.[2]

Although the considerations relevant to the determination of a fair rent have been subject to much interpretation in the courts, the central statutory rules are fairly straightforward.[3] It is the duty of the rent officer (or rent assessment committee)

'to have regard to all the circumstances (other than personal circumstances), and in particular to apply their knowledge and experience of current rents of comparable property in the area, as well as having regard to the age, character and locality of the dwelling-house in question and to its state of repair and, if any furniture is provided for use under the tenancy, to the quantity, quality and condition of the furniture.'

It is to be assumed that demand for similar rented accommodation does not substantially exceed supply. Conditions of disrepair, defects, deterioration of furniture or (on the other hand) improvements attributable to the tenant are to be disregarded. Amounts payable by the tenant to the landlord for the use of furniture or for services, are to be included in a registered rent but noted separately.[4] Although a fair rent determined according to these procedures and principles takes effect, *prima facie*, at the date of registration, separate provision is made to ensure that, in some cases, any rent increase must be implemented in stages, rather than with immediate effect.[5] An appeal lies against a decision of a rent assessment committee by way of a case stated for the opinion of the Court of Session.[6]

1 Ibid, Sch 4.
2 Ibid, s 46(3).
3 Ibid, s 48.
4 Ibid, s 4.
5 Ibid, s 33 and see the Limit on Rent Increases (Scotland) Order 1989, SI 1989/2469 which limits increases of rent (not including 'service' payments) to £104 or ¼ of the previous rent or ½ of the difference between the old and new rents, whichever is the greatest.
6 Tribunals and Inquiries Act 1992, s 11(7).

3. ASSURED TENANCIES

(a) Security of tenure

Security of tenure in an assured tenancy is provided, as with protected tenancies, in two principal ways. One is the device of the 'statutory assured tenancy' which comes into effect immediately if the original contractual tenancy is terminated by a notice to quit.[1] Such a statutory assured tenancy continues on the same terms as the original tenancy, subject to modification of the terms and adjustment of rent, if appropriate, by the rent assessment committee upon application by either the landlord or tenant.[2] The other source of security under an assured tenancy is that the tenant cannot be evicted from the house save as a result of an order for possession made by a sheriff on limited grounds and in accordance with prescribed procedures.[3] The circumstances in which a sheriff may order possession are complex but may be summarised as follows: (a) the 17 grounds are listed in Parts I (grounds 1–8) and II (grounds 9–17) of Schedule 5 to the 1988 Act; (b) if any of grounds 1–8 are established the sheriff *must* make an order for possession, but, in the case of a *contractual* assured tenancy, only on ground 2 or 8 and then only if it is a term of the tenancy;[4] (c) the eight grounds in Part I relate to: (1) intended occupation by the landlord; (2) default on a heritable security (mortgage); (3) short out of season lets; (4) short lets between student lettings; (5) house required for minister of religion or missionary; (6) house to be demolished or reconstructed; (7) tenancy devolved under a will or on intestacy; (8) at least three months rent in arrears;[5] (d) if any of grounds 9–17 are established the sheriff *may* order possession (if a contractual tenancy, only on grounds 11–16) but not unless he considers it reasonable to do so;[6] (e) the nine grounds in Part II relate to: (9) availability of suitable alternative accommodation;[7] (10) expiry of tenant's notice to quit; (11) persistent delay in paying

---

1 For information to be contained in such a notice to quit, see SI 1988/2067.
2 1988 Act, ss 16–17. For the forms required, see AT1(L), AT1(T), AT3(L) and AT3(T) prescribed in SI 1988/2109.
3 Ibid, ss 16(2), 18 and 19. A notice from the landlord of intention to raise proceedings for possession is required. See form AT6 prescribed in SI 1988/2109.
4 Ibid, s 18(3), (6). In the case of grounds 1–5, it is normally (ie subject to variation by the sheriff) a statutory precondition that the landlord gave notice before the beginning of the tenancy that possession might be recovered on the ground in question.
5 Ibid, Sch 5, Pt I.
6 Ibid, s 18(4), (6).
7 See also Sch 5, Pt III.

rent; (12) some rent due and unpaid; (13) an obligation of the tenancy broken or not performed; (14) deterioration of house by neglect or default of tenant or lodger; (15) tenant or lodger guilty of nuisance or annoyance or convicted of using the house for immoral or illegal purposes; (16) deterioration of any furniture provided owing to ill-treatment by tenant or lodger; (17) house let in pursuance of employment which has ceased.[1] The sheriff may adjourn proceedings for possession except where he is satisfied that the landlord is entitled to possession on grounds 1–8.[2]

(b) Succession of spouse to tenancy

The spouse of a tenant (including a person living with the tenant as husband or wife) is entitled to a statutory assured tenancy following the death of the tenant provided that (a) the tenant was sole tenant of the house; (b) the spouse was living in the house as his or her only or principal home and (c) the tenant was not already a successor to the tenancy.[3]

(c) Rents

As already explained, the underlying principle of assured tenancies is that there is no rent control and that rents should be 'freely negotiated.' There is, therefore, no general statutory restriction on rents at the commencement of a tenancy nor is the tenant able to initiate proceedings which might lead to a reduction in rent. There is no role for the rent officer. On the other hand, the statutory measures for security of tenure require further statutory provision both to protect the tenant from excessive rent *increases* but also to enable the landlord to apply for a new rent to become payable under the tenancy. Therefore, once any contractual tenancy has been terminated and a statutory assured tenancy created, there is provision for the landlord to serve a notice on the tenant proposing a new rent. If the tenant does not agree to the new rent, he or she may refer the notice to the rent assessment committee.[4] It is then for the committee to determine the

---

1 Ibid, Sch 5, Pt II.
2 Ibid, s 20.
3 Ibid, s 31.
4 Ibid, s 24. The required forms AT2 and AT4 are prescribed by SI 1988/2109. The notice requiring an increase in rent in consequence of the introduction of the council tax is contained in SI 1993/648. See also the Rent Assessment Committee (Assured Tenancy) (Scotland) Regulations 1989 (SI 1989/81, as amended by SI 1993/659).

rent at which it considers that 'the house might reasonably be expected to be let in the open market by a willing landlord under an assured tenancy.'[1] That rent then takes effect.[2] A further increase of rent cannot be made until a year has expired.[3]

(d) Other terms of assured tenancies

The 1988 Act contains a number of other provisions relating to assured tenancies: 1. Where the tenancy is silent on the matter, there is a term implied into every assured tenancy which forbids the tenant to assign, sublet or otherwise part with possession of the house.[4] 2. The landlord must provide the tenant with a written tenancy document stating the terms of the tenancy and, where rent is payable weekly, he must provide a rent book.[5] 3. An implied term of every assured tenancy is that the tenant must allow the landlord reasonable access to the house and reasonable facilities for executing repairs.[6] 4. By incorporation of equivalent terms in the Rent (Scotland) Act 1984, it is an offence for the landlord to require premiums and payment of rent in advance of the rental period.[7]

(e) Short assured tenancies

The short assured tenancy (loosely modelled on the short tenancy under the Rent (Scotland) Act 1984) is the form of tenancy which, provided he serves the prescribed form of notice prior to the creation of the tenancy, permits the landlord to end the tenancy by notice without the possibility of further security (hence the 'shortness' of the tenancy).[8] Thus, in addition to the general grounds for possession of assured tenancies, notice by the landlord stating that he requires possession under a short assured tenancy obliges the sheriff to make an order—provided that the original term of the tenancy (which cannot be less than six months) has expired, tacit relocation is not operating

---

1 Ibid, s 25(1). Information on assured tenancy rents is required to be kept by the rent assessment panel: 1988 Act, s 49 and SI 1989/685 (as amended by SI 1993/645).
2 Ibid, s 25(6).
3 Ibid, s 24(4).
4 Ibid, s 23.
5 Ibid, s 30. For the form of notice to be contained in every rent book, see SI 1988/2085, as amended by SI 1993/649.
6 Ibid, s 26.
7 Ibid, s 27.
8 Ibid, s 32.

to continue the tenancy and no further contractual tenancy is in existence.[1] In contrast with the position under an ordinary assured tenancy, the tenant may apply to a rent assessment committee for a determination of the rent 'which, in the committee's opinion, the landlord might reasonably be expected to obtain under the short assured tenancy.' The committee must not make such a determination unless it considers (a) 'that there is a sufficient number of similar houses in the locality let on assured tenancies' and (b) 'that the rent payable under the short assured tenancy in question is *significantly higher* than the rent which the landlord might reasonably be expected to obtain under the tenancy' having regard to other rents in the locality.[2]

1 Ibid, s 33.
2 Ibid, s 34.

CHAPTER 7

Tenancies in the public sector

1. INTRODUCTION

In Chapter 5 we took account of the introduction in 1980 of secure tenancies in the public sector and then of the Housing (Scotland) Act 1988 whose effect was to transfer new housing association tenancies into the private sector. In this chapter, we look at some of the principal characteristics of public sector tenancies once created. This means, in particular, the rules governing security of tenure itself and succession to tenancies. There are then tenants' rights to a written lease; to sublet and assign; and in relation to repairs, alterations and improvements. There is then a section on rents and housing benefit. The chapter ends with a note on tenants' access to information.

First, however, there is a section on the allocation of tenancies which, although it contains some reference to housing associations, is appropriately linked to the other public sector tenancy rules. The chapter deals, in effect, with the legal aspects of many of the management functions of the public landlords. Although such functions are routinely delegated, formally or informally, within public authorities, they do normally remain the legal responsibility of the public authority concerned. However, one initiative promoted in the 1991 *Tenant's Charter* was that of the 'right to manage'—the right of local authority tenants themselves to take over responsibility for managing their own housing—and this was taken forward in the 1993 Act.

A new section 22A of the 1987 Act[1] creates a new form of co-operative—the Scottish Office has adopted the title of 'Tenant Management Organisation' (TMO)—which may agree, with the approval of the Secretary of State, to take over management functions of a local authority. Before a local authority enters into such an agreement, it must be satisfied not only that the establishment of the TMO has been approved by the Secretary of State and that it will be competent and

---

1 Inserted by s 152 of the 1993 Act. Advice by circular on the way in which s 22A should be implemented is to be given by the Scottish Office Environment Department in Spring 1994.

efficient but also that it is representative of the tenants of the houses to which the agreement relates. If, however, the authority refuses to make the agreement on the grounds that any of these prerequisites are missing, an appeal lies to the Secretary of State. His consent is also required to the terms of the agreement itself. Thus, under a scheme regulated in all important respects by the Secretary of State rather than the particular local authority, the section provides the means for groups of tenants to take over the management of (but not the other landlord responsibilities for) their own houses.

Quite separately, the Government has declared its commitment to the extension to local authority housing management of the compulsory competitive tendering regime in the Local Government Act 1988.[1] This will compel local authorities to open their management functions to competition from private contractors in stages beginning in April 1998 ie after the impending local government reorganisation. Although full implementation is, therefore, still a few years away, some preparatory steps are already being taken. Authorities are obliged to publish housing management standards and will shortly produce housing management plans.[2]

2. THE ALLOCATION OF HOUSING

One of the most sustained areas of concern about housing in the public sector—in particular, council housing—prior to the passing of the Tenant's Rights, Etc (Scotland) Act 1980 was the process of allocation by landlords of the tenancies of their houses. They were rationing a much valued commodity but until the passing of the 1980 Act, which made only a partial inroad into the area, the allocation of council houses and the related processes of transfer and exchange were subject to very little statutory control. The Housing (Scotland) Act 1966 conferred a wide discretion upon housing authorities in their allocation of tenancies and it imposed very few substantive or procedural constraints.[3] Since the removal, after the Second World War, of the requirement to provide housing for the 'working classes',[4] the only statutory guidance as to choice of tenants was contained in the 1966

---

1 Scottish Office News Release, Environmental Department Consultation Paper, 7 February 1994.
2 A further 'paving' change was made when s 157(1) of the 1993 Act removed the requirement in s 17(1) of the 1987 Act that management powers should not only be vested in but also 'exercised by' authorities themselves.
3 See s 151(2).
4 Housing (Scotland) Act 1949.

Act itself (requiring preference to be given to persons occupying houses not meeting the tolerable standard or overcrowded houses or who had large families or who were living under unsatisfactory housing conditions[1]); in the Land Compensation (Scotland) Act 1973 and in the Housing (Scotland) Act 1974 (both of which imposed a duty to rehouse persons displaced by an authority's own demolition and improvement schemes[2]); and in the Housing (Homeless Persons) Act 1977 (which required preference to be given to homeless persons[3]). Otherwise, authorities had a free hand as to whom they could select to be their tenants.

They were equally free as to the machinery by which tenants were to be selected and houses allocated. There was no single prescribed statutory procedure to be followed. Nor were there rules requiring the publication of the procedure chosen by an authority. That is not to say that authorities operated without schemes of allocation. Each authority evolved and operated its own rules.

This system did not, however, work without complaint and one indication of this came from the local ombudsman. Housing issues were, from the outset in 1975, the ombudsman's main source of business and many of the individual complaints he received were about allocations and non-allocations. In his second annual report, the ombudsman called the allocation of council houses 'a complex and difficult matter for which each district council has its own rules and regulations.'[4] The content of these rules, however, the local ombudsman was compelled to regard as a matter of policy for housing authorities and not in itself reviewable by him. Only the application of rules in circumstances amounting to maladministration (such as unfair discrimination) is reviewable—which means that the ombudsman's influence cannot directly affect the content of allocation rules (where not statutorily prescribed a matter of policy rather than administration) however deficient they may be. The ombudsman has, however, commented on procedures which require review.

Partly as a result of the defects revealed by the ombudsman and partly in consequence of recommendations made by successive official investigations, some changes were made by the 1980 Act. The 1977 Green Paper, *Scottish Housing*, had given support to the policy that authorities should, in their allocation procedures, be given maximum freedom to respond to local circumstances. At the same time, however, it had stressed that allocation procedures 'should not only be fair

1 1966 Act, s 151(1). See now 1987 Act, s 20(1)(a).
2 Section 36 in both Acts. See now 1987 Act, s 98.
3 Section 6(2). See now 1987 Act, s 20(1)(b). See also Chap 10 below. .
4 Report for 1976–77, p 9.

but should be seen to be fair.'[1] Recalling advice given to local authorities in 1968 on the basis of a report of a sub-committee of the then Scottish Housing Advisory Committee,[2] the Green Paper said that there was 'still considerable scope for improvement in this field.'

A further sub-committee of the advisory committee was subsequently convened and this reported in 1980. Its remit was

'to consider the policies of housing authorities in relation to allocations and requests for transfer; to suggest how these policies can best be adapted to meet housing needs; and to recommend any changes of organisation or procedure which are desirable.'

When it reported,[3] the sub-committee began by taking account of the changing context of public sector housing in Scotland and its impact upon allocation policies. The fact that needs for very urgent rehousing had declined did not lessen the importance of effective allocation of houses. In particular allocation and transfer policies should be fair; meet the applicants' housing needs; maintain balanced communities; be flexible; promote mobility; and make the best use of the housing stock. From the adoption of these aims, the sub-committee went on to criticise some existing local authority practices on eligibility for admission to waiting lists (eg the refusal by some authorities to admit applicants under a certain age or over a certain level of income); their methods of allocation (including, in some cases, the involvement of councillors to assess the 'merit' of applicants); and their determination of priority groups among applicants.

The sub-committee's principal recommendations were that all who wished to join a council's waiting list should be able to do so; and that councils should adopt allocation procedures combining a 'points' system (whereby applicants acquire priority as a result of eg medical considerations, overcrowding or lack of amenities, and old age) and a 'groups' system (which further divides applicants into identifiable priority categories such as homeless people and persons from areas of redevelopment) enabling houses to be allocated on the basis of need assessed by individual circumstances and 'group' affiliation.

The sub-committee also made recommendations designed to produce greater mobility through transfer and exchange; a resolution of the problem of 'difficult-to-let housing'; and greater tenant involvement in allocation policies. It was able to welcome a number of the proposed changes contained in the Bill which, at the time of its report,

1 Cmnd 6852, para 9.18.
2 *Allocating Council Houses*, HMSO (1967). The Advisory Committee was abolished in 1980.
3 *Allocation and Transfer of Council Houses*, HMSO (1980).

was on its way to becoming the Tenants' Rights, Etc (Scotland) Act 1980 which, as amended, was consolidated in the 1987 Act. The rules were further amended by the 1993 Act.[1] There are three relevant sections—19, 20 and 21. Section 21 extends to most public sector landlords and to housing associations but relates only to the publication of house allocation rules. Sections 19 and 20, which apply only to local authorities (district and islands councils), impose some restrictions on the content of their allocation rules.

Thus, section 21 of the 1987 Act requires all district and islands councils to make and publish rules governing (a) admission of applicants to a housing list; (b) priority of allocation of houses; (c) transfer of tenants from houses belonging to the body concerned to houses belonging to other bodies; and (d) exchanges of houses. Alterations to rules must be published within six months.[2] The same obligation is imposed on all registered housing associations.[3] Scottish Homes and the new town development corporations are not expressly required to make allocation rules of the four listed types but they are required to publish any such rules that they do make.

For the rules of local authorities, Scottish Homes and development corporations, the publication required involves making the rules available for perusal at reasonable times, in the case of a council or development corporation, at its principal offices and housing department offices and, in the case of Scottish Homes, at its principal and other offices. In all cases the rules have also to be available for sale at a reasonable price and available free in summary form to members of the public. Housing associations[4] must send a copy of their rules to both Scottish Homes and every islands or district council within whose area the particular association lets houses under secure tenancies. The councils are then obliged to make the rules available for perusal at their principal offices.

Another rule in the direction of rather greater openness in the allocation process is a separate requirement in section 21 to the effect that all the housing authorities already mentioned (including housing associations) must make available on request to any of their applicants

1 Sections 154–155 which made important amendments to ss 20–21 of the 1987 Act which came into effect on 27 September 1993.
2 This requirement on local authorities not only to publish any rules they have but also to make rules in the listed areas was introduced with effect from 27 September 1993 by the 1993 Act.
3 Although it should be noted that a failure to amend s 21(2) (which contains this requirement) at the same time as s 21(1) was altered by the 1993 Act makes the law less than clear.
4 Or, in the case of an English registered association, the Housing Corporation.

for housing any record kept by them of information furnished to them by the applicant. The total effect of these provisions should be to enable interested individuals to have access to the criteria according to which applications for housing (whether at the stage of admission to a waiting list or the allocation of a house) are determined and to ensure that basic relevant facts are correct and available to be matched against the allocation criteria.[1]

It will be noticed that section 21 does not lay down the detailed content of allocation rules. Except for Scottish Homes and the development corporations, it does require rules of some sort in the four areas and then in all cases requires publication. We should turn now to the actual rules themselves.

For the most part, these remain a matter for determination by individual landlords.[2] All that sections 19 and 20 of the 1987 Act (which apply only to local authority housing) do is to set out certain priority categories of applicant and then to outlaw certain types of allocation rule which might otherwise be adopted. This is done by reference to the two stages of the process—admission, in the first place, to an authority's waiting list and then the actual selection of applicants on the list to be granted tenancies. A special restriction on the participation of local authority members in allocation decisions has also been imposed.

So far as admission to a housing list is concerned, a local authority is forbidden to take into account certain characteristics of the applicant or his or her family. These are:

(a) The applicant's age, provided he or she has attained the age of 16. This is designed to prevent discrimination against young (especially young single applicants).

(b) The income of the applicant and his or her family.

(c) Whether, or to what value, the applicant or any of his or her family owns or has owned heritable property (most importantly, a house) or moveable property. These two rules are designed to prevent discrimination on the grounds of high income or property ownership.

(d) Any outstanding debt (or rent or otherwise) attributable to the tenancy of a house of which the applicant neither is nor was a tenant. For example, a person cannot be kept off a

---

1 See also 'Access to information' below.
2 Subject to the general rules which prevent all landlords from discrimination on grounds of sex or race. See Race Relations Act 1976, s 21 and Sex Discrimination Act 1975, s 30.

waiting list because of debts owed by his or her spouse or former spouse.

(e) Whether the applicant is living with or in the same house as his or her spouse or a cohabitee (of opposite sex).

A further form of discrimination is outlawed in the interests of tenant mobility and prevents the simple fact of residence in an authority's area from determining admission to its list—save that it remains permissible to refuse admission to a non-resident applicant who has none of the connections with the area specified in the Act. If, however, a non-resident either (i) is employed or has been offered employment in the area or wishes (to the satisfaction of the authority) to move to the area to seek employment; or (ii) is over 60 and wishes to move to be near a younger relative in the area; or (iii) has special social or medical reasons for being housed in the area, then he or she must be admitted to the list. At the stage of the allocation of houses, there are two forms of limitation imposed on the discretionary freedom of local authorities. They must first give 'reasonable preference' in their selection of tenants to the people listed on p 68 above, ie those occupying houses which either do not meet the tolerable standard or are overcrowded; those who have large families(!); those who are living in unsatisfactory housing conditions; and those to whom, as homeless persons, an authority owes a duty.

Secondly, an authority is obliged to take no account of the length of time for which an applicant has resided in its area nor of any of the characteristics listed as (a)–(c) above. Furthermore an authority must not impose a requirement of any of three types before an applicant is 'eligible for the allocation of housing'—a distinctly ambiguous statutory formula in this context. The three outlawed requirements are that an application for housing has been in force for a minimum period; or that a divorce or judicial separation be obtained; or that the applicant be no longer living with, or in the same house as, some other person.[1] Finally, an authority is required to treat an applicant from outwith its area (but with one of the connections with its own area listed above) 'no less favourably' in its application of rules on priority of allocations than it would treat one of its own tenants, with similar housing needs, who is seeking a transfer to another house.[2]

Another procedural innovation of some importance was introduced by the 1993 Act. It has already been mentioned that one long-standing

---

1 There is considerable inelegance in the drafting of s 20 which derives from its origins as amendments made during the Parliamentary passage of the Housing (Scotland) Act 1986.
2 1987 Act, s 19(3).

criticism of local authority allocation procedures has been directed towards the involvement of councillors in the process, especially where discrimination for and against particular local residents might result. This has now been addressed directly by statute.[1] A local authority member is 'excluded from a decision on the allocation of local authority housing' (or of housing to which the local authority may nominate the tenant) where either (a) the house in question is situated or (b) the applicant for the house resides in the ward for which the member concerned was elected. This provision goes well beyond the restrictions on participation in decision-making imposed on councillors in general when they have an interest (pecuniary or otherwise) in the matter for discussion.[2] It is unique in local government practice.

Clearly these statutory restrictions operate as only a very partial guide to local authorities as to what should be the content of their allocation rules although another external constraint is added by the Matrimonial Homes (Family Protection) (Scotland) Act 1981. The creation of rights of occupation for spouses and cohabitees affects the policies of authorities on joint tenancies and, at the time of breakdown, on the allocation of houses to two householders.[3] Subject to this, authorities are left very substantially free to determine both their own priorities and their own procedures. There is no formal machinery for the review of house allocation decisions although judicial review in the Court of Session is available.[4] Complaints continue to be received by the local ombudsman.[5]

3. SECURITY OF TENURE AND PROCEEDINGS FOR POSSESSION

If the single most important innovation to be made in public sector housing law by the Tenants' Rights Etc (Scotland) Act 1980 was the tenant's right to buy, then the second must have been the new security of tenure for council (and some other) tenants. Prior to that Act, the one thing that everyone knew distinguished the private from the public sector tenant was that the former enjoyed the protection of the Rent Acts whereas the latter did not. Public sector landlords did not need to

1 1993 Act, s 154 inserting a new s 20(3) of the 1987 Act.
2 1973 Act, ss 38–42.
3 See SDD Circular 21/1982. See also p 78 for the Act's relevance to possession proceedings.
4 See *Lennon v Hamilton District Council* 1990 SCLR 514. For English decisions see eg *R v Canterbury City Council, ex p Gillespie* (1986) 19 HLR 7; *R v Port Talbot Borough Council, ex p Jones* (1987) 20 HLR 265; *R v Forest Heath District Council, ex p West* (1992) 24 HLR 85.
5 See p 16 above.

establish any special grounds to secure the eviction of tenants and a notice to quit given in proper form and followed by proceedings for recovery of possession was sufficient to end a tenancy. As a result of decisions of the English Court of Appeal, however, an argument had been developing that local authorities should exercise their powers as landlord subject to the same constraints to act reasonably as applied to most of their other statutory powers involving the exercise of discretion. They should act not only in good faith but with care to take into account relevant considerations and to disregard irrelevant considerations. In the case of eviction proceedings, these considerations might include other remedies available to the authority and the obligations falling upon an authority in the event of eviction.[1]

These views received some support in at least one Scottish case but were clearly rejected in another.[2] Since the 1980 Act the resolution of this dispute has been less pressing although there is nothing to prevent its re-emergence in other circumstances. At all events, it is quite clear that prior to the 1980 Act, the powers of an authority to dispose of its tenants were very wide. The courts could not stand in the way of normal evictions and, in the absence of maladministration in the shape perhaps of deception or dishonesty, nor could the local ombudsman.

When the 1977 Green Paper on housing[3] turned to the question of security of tenure, it recalled that both the Finer Committee[4] and the Morris Committee[5] had strongly recommended that public sector tenants should be afforded security comparable with that afforded to tenants of private landlords. It noted, however, that housing authorities had themselves taken the view that 'as responsible public bodies they should not be inhibited in carrying out their management functions, particularly where difficult tenants are involved, that they in practice secure evictions on the same grounds as do private landlords, and that statutory security is unnecessary if they are to have a statutory responsibility for housing the homeless.' The Labour Government concluded cautiously that there was no justification for any appreciable difference between the public and private sectors but that the application of the principle of security of tenure to the public

---

1 See *City of Bristol District Council v Clark* [1975] 3 All ER 976 and *Cannock Chase District Council v Kelly* [1978] 1 All ER 152.
2 See *City of Edinburgh District Council v Parnell*, 1980 SLT (Sh Ct) 11 and *City of Aberdeen District Council v Christie* 1983 SLT (Sh Ct) 57 respectively.
3 *Scottish Housing*, Cmnd 6852 (1977).
4 *One-Parent Families*, Cmnd 5629 (1974).
5 *Housing and Social Work: a Joint Approach*, HMSO (1975).

sector would need to be carefully worked out in consultation with local authorities and other housing organisations.[1]

In due course that Green Paper's proposal for security of tenure came to be adopted in the Conservative Tenants' Rights, Etc (Scotland) Bill and although relatively uncontroversial during their Parliamentary passage the new rules made a major change in their creation of the new security guaranteed to tenants. This takes the form of the statutory limits imposed upon the circumstances under which a secure tenancy (whatever its own express terms) can be terminated. Unless the landlord and tenant agree in writing to terminate the tenancy; or the tenant gives to the landlord four weeks' notice of his or her own intention to terminate; or the tenant abandons the tenancy; or the tenant dies leaving no 'qualified person' able or willing to succeed, the tenancy can be terminated by the landlord only if he gives notice of proceedings for recovery of possession on one of the 16 grounds laid down in Schedule 3 to the 1987 Act.[2] An attempt to rely upon other grounds or upon another procedure will be unsuccessful.[3] The first 15 grounds for recovery of possession may be divided into two lists. One list contains what can be called 'conduct' grounds—circumstances brought about by the tenant in which the landlord cannot be expected to provide alternative accommodation and where the court may make an order for recovery of possession if it is reasonable to do so. The other list contains 'management' grounds where the landlord wishes to gain possession of the house but is obliged to secure the availability of suitable alternative accommodation for the tenant. The sixteenth ground stands separately.[4]

The 'conduct grounds' are as follows:

1. Non-payment of rent or other breach of the terms of the tenancy.
2. Conviction of the tenant for using the house for immoral or illegal purposes.
3. Deterioration of the house owing to acts of waste by, or by the neglect or default of, the tenant (or lodger or sub-tenant).
4. Deterioration of furniture provided, as in 3.
5. Tenant and spouse absent without reasonable cuase for over six months *or* ceasing to occupy the house as their principal home.

---

1 Cmnd 6852, paras 19, 21.
2 1987 Act, s 46.
3 See *Monklands District Council v Johnstone* 1987 SCLR 480.
4 The grounds are set out in full in Pt I of Sch 3 to the 1987 Act.

   6. Tenant induced landlord to grant the tenancy by a false statement made knowingly or recklessly.[1]

   7. Tenant (or any person residing or lodging with him or her or any sub-tenant) guilty of conduct in or in the vicinity of the house which is a nuisance or annoyance and it is not reasonable that the landlord be required to make other accommodation available to him (or her).[2]

The 'management grounds' are:

   8. Tenant guilty of conduct as in 7 and in the opinion of the landlord it is appropriate to require the tenant to move to other accommodation.

   9. House overcrowded rendering occupier guilty of an offence.[3]

 10. Landlord intends within a reasonable period of time to demolish or carry out substantial work on the building and for which possession is reasonably required.

 11. House designed or adapted for a person with special needs and
    (a) there is no longer a person with such special needs; and
    (b) the landlord requires the house for occupation by such a person.

 12. Similarly in relation to a house forming part of a group of houses designed or provided with or located near facilities for persons in need of special social support.

 13. Similarly where the landlord is a housing association providing housing for special categories (aged, infirm, disabled, special social circumstances).

 14. Landlord's interest in the house is that of a lessee under a lease which either
    (a) has terminated or
    (b) will terminate within six months.

 15. Where the landlord is an islands council, the house is held for educational purposes and is required for the accommodation of a person employed for those purposes, the council

---

1 This ground was inserted by the Housing (Scotland) Act 1986. There is some discussion in *Monklands District Council v Johnstone* (above) of the way it might have been used in that case, had it been on the statute book.
2 See *SSHA v Lumsden* 1984 SLT (Sh Ct) 71 in which it was held that a tenant could be held responsible for the nuisance or annoyance caused by his wife even though he himself was in prison. See also *City of Glasgow District Council v Brown* 1988 SCLR 433 and 679 discussed at p 77 below.
3 For overcrowding generally see p 193.

cannot reasonably provide an alternative house, and the educational employment of the present tenant is at an end.

The 'suitable accommodation' which a landlord relying on 'management' grounds 8–15 (and ground 16 below) is obliged to provide is defined as premises to be let as a separate dwelling under a secure tenancy (or protected or assured tenancy) and 'reasonably suitable to the needs of the tenant and his family.' Such suitability is to be determined having regard to such factors as proximity to place of work; extent of accommodation required; comparability of character, furniture and terms of tenancy in relation to the existing tenancy; and any special needs of the tenant or his or her family.[1] In many cases, the question of what is suitable accommodation (and how it is to be made available) may be unproblematic. Particular problems did arise, however, in *Charing Cross and Kelvingrove Housing Association v Kraska*[2] which were exacerbated by its being also an action for recovery of possession based on ground 10 (demolition or substantial works).[3] In that case, however, it was held that to be 'suitable' the accommodation had to be actually *intended to be let* as a separate dwelling under a secure tenancy and not merely likely to become so by operation of law. The case also confirmed that the procedure[4] for a written offer (by the landlord to the tenant) of accommodation claimed to be suitable is permissive only. If used, it tends to shift the burden of proving lack of suitability on to the tenant.

The case of *City of Glasgow District Council v Brown*[5] raised the question of alternative accommodation (or lack of it) under ground 7—misconduct which is a nuisance or annoyance. In circumstances where only one of two cohabiting joint tenants was guilty of the misconduct it was held by the Sheriff Principal (overruling the sheriff) that the question of the reasonableness of not providing alternative accommodation related only to that tenant. This might have left the 'innocent' tenant without even the protection of consideration of the need for alternative accommodation for her. An answer in that case was, however, found in the need for the court to find not only that the ground was established but also that the making of the order for possession would be reasonable—the 'ultimate test of reasonableness.'

1 1987 Act, s 48(3) and Pt II of Sch 3.
2 1986 SLT (Sh Ct) 42.
3 See p 82 below.
4 1987 Act, Sch 3, Pt II, para 3.
5 1988 SCLR 433 and 679.

The Sheriff Principal refused the order because he was not persuaded that it would be reasonable to make it.[1]

Although these two lists of grounds upon which a landlord may be able to evict his secure tenant may seem quite long, there can be little doubt that they represent a marked limitation upon a public sector landlord's freedoms prior to 1980. The restricted 'management' grounds in particular circumscribe closely an authority's competence to deploy its housing stock simply on the basis of its view of general housing policy.

The final ground for possession is:

> 16. Where the landlord wishes to transfer the secure tenancy to (a) the tenant's spouse (or former spouse); or (b) a person with whom the tenant has been living as husband and wife. In either case, the conditions are that the spouse, former spouse or cohabitee has to apply to the landlord for the transfer; and that either the tenant or the spouse (or former spouse) or cohabitee 'no longer wishes to live together with the other in the house.' This provision gives to the landlord the opportunity to be directly involved in the resolution of housing difficulties in a matrimonial dispute. Suitable alternative accommodation must be made available to the displaced tenant.

It should also be borne in mind that, since the passing of the Matrimonial Homes (Family Protection) (Scotland) Act 1981 and the extended occupancy rights it introduced, recovery of possession will not always be successful even if one of grounds 1–15 is established if it relates to one spouse (the tenant) only. The other spouse (or cohabitee) may defend the proceedings. Furthermore, the 1981 Act created new powers (not requiring an initiative by the landlord under ground 16 above) to transfer a tenancy from one spouse (or cohabitee) to another. The Act contains a comprehensive code conferring occupancy rights upon a spouse not previously entitled to them; giving power to a court (sheriff court or Court of Session) to declare, enforce or restrict the occupancy rights of a spouse having regard to *inter alia* the conduct of the spouses and the needs of them and their children; and the making of exclusion orders. Section 13 of the Act is important here because under that section the court may order the transfer of the tenancy (which may be a secure tenancy) of the matrimonial home from the entitled to the non-entitled spouse or from them both to one alone. The court may order the payment of compensation by the

---

1 Ibid at 681. See also p 80 below.

entitled to the non-entitled spouse but, in assessing the amount of any compensation, no account is to be taken of the loss of a right to purchase the house under Part II of the 1987 Act. The landlord is to be informed of any transfer made.

(a) What procedure has to be adopted by a landlord seeking possession of a house subject to a secure tenancy?

In addition to restricting the grounds upon which possession of a house subject to a secure tenancy may be obtained, the 1987 Act affords further protection to the tenant by prescribing clearly the procedure according to which possession may be sought by the landlord.[1]

If the landlord does wish to obtain possession in reliance upon one or more of the statutory grounds, he has first to serve upon the tenant a notice of proceedings for recovery of possession prescribed by the Secretary of State under the Act.[2] What this notice amounts to is a warning to the tenant that the landlord may be going to raise proceedings in the sheriff court to gain possession of the house. As the notes on the form explain to the tenant:

'It is not a notice to quit and it does not affect your right to continue living in the house or your obligation to pay rent. You cannot be evicted from your house unless the sheriff court grants your landlord a possession order.'

Court proceedings cannot be commenced before the date indicated in the notice—which cannot be earlier than four weeks after the date of the notice itself—but have to be started within six months of the notice. The notice has to indicate the grounds for seeking possession by reference to a specific paragraph or paragraphs in Part I of Schedule 3 to the Act.[3]

The prescribed notes on the notice itself provide a full account of the procedure which is involved if the landlord does choose to follow up the notice by raising proceedings by summary cause in the sheriff court. If the proceedings are raised on any of the conduct grounds (paras 1–7 of Part I of Schedule 3) such as non-payment of rent, or on ground 16, then the court has, in the first place, the power to adjourn the proceedings and thus postpone a decision on the case.[4] If the sheriff does adjourn the proceedings in this way, he is also empowered to

---

1 1987 Act, ss 47–48.
2 SI 1980/1389.
3 For discussion of the meaning of 'proceedings' and the date of their commencement for this purpose see *City of Edinburgh District Council v Davis* 1987 SLT (Sh Ct) 33.
4 1987 Act, s 48(1).

impose conditions upon the tenant regarding, for instance, the payment of outstanding rent. The sheriff can require payment of rent by instalments and, if tenants comply with the terms of the condition, they can expect not to have a final order of possession made against them. Although it may have been imagined that this power to adjourn proceedings and thus to defer, perhaps indefinitely, the need to order an eviction would be quite significant, a Scottish Office research report showed that in its early years the power was being used very selectively. Only in the sheriff courts in Edinburgh and Glasgow was there routine use of adjournments under the Act. In many courts, the power was not used at all.[1]

Subject to the possibility of adjournment of proceedings, the court is obliged to make an order for recovery of possession:

(a) if it appears that the landlord does indeed have a 'conduct' ground for possession and that it is reasonable to make the order.

Although the need to apply this test of 'reasonableness' was incorporated in the original version of these provisions[2] and its existence did not go altogether unnoticed—it was in one case referred to as the 'ultimate test of reasonableness'[3]—it was not until relatively recently that the obligation imposed on pursuer public authorities to establish reasonableness achieved any prominence. It is now accepted that the onus is on the pursuer formally to claim ('aver') and then prove that the granting of an order of possession would be reasonable[4] and that a failure to do so ought normally to result in a refusal by the court, even if the case is not defended, to grant the order. However, it appears that

1 See Adler, Himsworth and Kerr *Public Housing, Rent Arrears and the Sheriff Court*, Scottish Office, CRU, 1985. See also Adler and Himsworth 'Tenants in Arrears: A New Role for the Sheriff Court' (ed McCrone) *Scottish Government Yearbook 1985* and, also on recovery procedures, *Fighting Evictions: A Practical Guide for Public Sector Tenants in Scotland*, Shelter/CRO.
2 There is a parallel provision in the Rent (Scotland) Act 1984, s 11(1) (regulated tenancies) and also in the Housing (Scotland) Act 1988, s 18(4) (assured tenancies).
3 The phrase used by the Sheriff Principal in *City of Glasgow District Council v Brown* (see p 77 above). In *Nairn v City of Edinburgh District Council* 27 January 1983, unreported, 1983 SCOLAG 44, interim interdict was issued in the Court of Session to prevent the eviction of a tenant whose case was not adequately presented in the recovery proceedings because of a strike by social workers. See also *City of Edinburgh District Council v Davis* 1987 SLT (Sh Ct) 33 and as reported at 1984 SCOLAG 86.
4 See *Midlothian District Council v Drummond* 1991 SLT (Sh Ct) 67; *Gordon District Council v Acutt* 1991 SLT (Sh Ct) 78; *Midlothian District Council v Brown* 1991 SLT (Sh Ct) 80; *Renfrew District Council v Inglis* 1991 SLT (Sh Ct) 83. All were discussed in *City of Glasgow District Council v Erhaiganoma* (Inner House) 24 March 1993, unreported, 1993 SCOLAG 89.

in some circumstances at least the narration of facts from which an inference may *prima facie* be drawn that the making of an order would be reasonable will suffice,[1] ie leaving it for the tenant to show otherwise, and it is also clear that a failure to aver reasonableness should not, in most circumstances, be fatal for the pursuer's case. Unless the tenant's interests would be prejudiced, the action should be adjourned. Similarly, if the landlord *does* aver reasonableness and the tenant produces contrary arguments at the hearing the pursuer is not compelled instantly to rebut these arguments, on pain of loss of the case. Again adjournment is the preferred option rather than outright dismissal of the action, although landlords have, for their part, been warned that they should not abuse the recovery procedure by using it 'not to regain possession of let properties but simply in order to acquire a "sword of Damocles" with which to try to enforce payment of rent arrears.' An additional warning to pursuer landlords was later given by Sheriff Principal Nicholson in *City of Edinburgh District Council v Robbin*[2] where it was joined by his condemnation of the apparently general practice of the District Council to accompany its pursuit of an order for recovery of possession with an initial application for an order of consignation in all those cases where the defender entered a defence that essential repairs or maintenance had not been carried out by the landlord. Such an order would require the defender to pay into court in advance the amount of the unpaid rent. This was, in the Sheriff Principal's view, incompetent in circumstances where no action for payment was formally involved and might 'put quite improper pressure on at least some defenders'.

What amounts to reasonableness will clearly vary from case to case but in spite of arguments that, in considering reasonableness, the court should confine itself to the personal circumstances of the tenant and ignore the facts which constitute the actual grounds for possession, it has been held that *all* such facts may be treated as relevant.[3] In a case based on arrears of rent, the amount of the arrears and the length of time for which they have been outstanding are as relevant as the tenant's personal and financial circumstances at the time of the action.[4]

---

1 *Erhaiganoma* above.
2 1994 SCLR 43. See p 90 below.
3 *Erhaiganoma* above.
4 It has been held that, as to personal circumstances, the landlord does not have to 'produce something in the nature of a social inquiry report' although exceptional circumstances might call for more information than is immediately available to the landlord. See *Midlothian District Council v Drummond* 1991 SLT (Sh Ct) 67 at 68.

(b) where the landlord invokes a 'management' ground for possession and it appears to the court that other suitable accommodation will be available to the tenant;

(c) where the landlord invokes ground 16 (transfer in response to matrimonial dispute) and it appears to the court both that it is reasonable to make the order and that other suitable accommodation will be available.[1]

If proceedings are being taken by the landlord on the 'management' ground (no 10) that substantial works are to be carried out on the house following which the tenant will return, the court, in addition to giving the landlord the right to recover possession, must also make an order entitling the tenant to return to the house on completion of the works. (In other circumstances ie the 'demolition situation' including that in which the original house will cease to exist in a process of conversion, there will be no question of a return to that house and tenancy.)[2] In this case alone, the court's order does not, in addition to giving the landlord the right to possession, terminate the tenancy. In all other cases the tenancy is terminated from a date appointed by the court and, as the notes on the prescribed form indicate to the tenant, this means that where 'conduct' grounds are relied on:

'your landlord will have to evict you once the date given in the order is passed, unless it (the landlord) decides to grant you a new tenancy of your house. If it evicts you it will not be under any obligation to rehouse you. Any action which might be taken by a local authority under its powers and duties in relation to some categories of homeless people is a separate matter and you should not assume that you will be entitled to rehousing.'[3]

That concludes considering of the normal statutory procedure according to which a landlord can recover possession of a house subject to a secure tenancy. One special circumstance is not covered by these rules and we should now refer to it briefly. It concerns the situation where a house is 'abandoned' by the tenant.

When the landlord of a house subject to a secure tenancy reasonably believes both that the house itself is unoccupied and that the tenant does not intend to occupy it as his or her home (ie the house has been

1 1987 Act, s 48(2).
2 See eg *Charing Cross and Kelvingrove Housing Association v Kraska* 1986 SLT (Sh Ct) 42 for a useful discussion of the distinction to be drawn between the 'demolition situation' (including where the house ceases to exist through conversion) and the 'decanting situation.'
3 See 1987 Act, s 48(4). This interpretation appears to be technically correct in its assumption that the order for recovery automatically terminates the tenancy on a named date. It does not appear to accord with common practice under which actual termination of a tenancy seems rarely to result.

'abandoned') then the landlord becomes entitled to take two separate courses of action.[1] In the first place, the landlord can enter the house, by force if necessary, for the purpose of securing the house and its contents against vandalism. Secondly, the landlord is empowered to take possession of the house. This, of course, is a very drastic step and it is not surprising that the Act affords some protection to the tenant against possible abuse by the landlord. Such protection takes the forms of (a) a special procedure which the landlord is bound to observe before exercising his right and (b) a right of appeal to the sheriff for an aggrieved tenant.

The procedure required of the landlord entails the service of a notice[2] on the tenant stating that he has reason to believe that the house is unoccupied and that the tenant does not intend to occupy it; requiring the tenant to inform the landlord in writing within four weeks if he or she does intend to occupy the house as his or her home; and informing the tenant that, if it appears to the landlord at the end of the four weeks that the tenant does not intend to occupy the house, the tenancy will be terminated forthwith. If, four weeks after the service of that notice, the landlord is satisfied, following inquiries, that the house has been abandoned, he may serve a second notice to end the tenancy immediately and without the need for further proceedings.[3]

Where, however, the tenant is aggrieved by the termination of the tenancy in this way he or she may raise proceedings in the sheriff court within six months of the termination.[4] If, in those proceedings, it appears to the sheriff that either the landlord failed to comply with the statutory procedure or did not have reasonable grounds for finding that the house was abandoned or that he was in error in finding that the tenant did not intend to occupy the house as his or her home and the tenant had reasonable cause, by reason of illness or otherwise, for failure to notify the landlord of his or her intention, then the sheriff must make an appropriate order. In a case where the house has not been re-let to a new tenant; then the order is that the old secure tenancy continues. If the house has been re-let, the order is to direct the landlord to make other suitable accommodation available to the tenant.

---

1 1987 Act, ss 49–50 and see *City of Edinburgh District Council v Davis* as reported at 1984 SCOLAG 86.
2 In this situation and in others governed by Pt III of the 1987 Act service of a notice on a person does not necessarily require delivery in person but may include leaving the notice at his proper address or sending it to him at that address by recorded delivery (s 84).
3 1987 Act, s 50. For the procedure governing the disposal of a tenant's property found in an abandoned house see SI 1982/981.
4 1987 Act, s 51.

(b) In what circumstances may a secure tenancy pass by succession from one tenant to another?

The benefits under a public sector secure tenancy are capable of being handed on to another 'qualified person' when the original tenant dies.[1] Section 52 of the 1987 Act makes provision for succession to secure tenancies quite separately from the provision later made for the assignation of a lease during the tenant's lifetime.

The central rule is that on the death of a tenant, the tenancy passes automatically to a 'qualified person' as defined in the Act unless either (a) there is no such 'qualified person' or (b) the 'qualified person' declines the tenancy by giving the landlord written notice within four weeks of the death following which he or she must vacate within three months or (c) the tenancy has already (subject to what is said below) passed on succession from one tenant to another, ie only one succession is permitted. The failure of a 'qualified person' to succeed for any of these reasons terminates the secure tenancy.[2]

Section 52 sets out who is a 'qualified person' to succeed as follows:

    (a) the tenant's spouse (or person living with the tenant as husband and wife) where the house was his or her only or principal home at the tenant's death;

    (b) in the case of a joint tenancy, a surviving tenant where the house was his or her only or principal home as above;

    (c) in the absence of anyone in categories (a) and (b), a member of the tenant's family[3] provided that he or she is over sixteen and provided that the house was his or her only or principal home throughout the period of twelve months up to the tenant's death.

In the event of there being more than one 'qualified person' under these provisions the secure tenancy passes to the person (or two or more as joint tenants) decided either by agreement between them all or, failing such agreement within four weeks, by the landlord.[4]

---

1 The rule that 'succession' to a tenancy can occur only on the death of a tenant was confirmed in *Robb v Kyle and Carrick District Council* 1989 SLT (Lands Tr) 78.
2 1987 Act, s 46(1).
3 As defined in the 1987 Act, s 83. See p 109 below.
4 For failure to become a 'qualified person' in attempted reliance on these (and other) grounds see *Hamilton District Council v Lennon* 1990 SCLR 297.

As mentioned above, a tenancy can normally pass on succession to a 'qualified person' only once. Two qualifications to this rule should, however, be noted. The first is that the limitation does not operate to terminate the tenancy of a formerly joint tenant where he or she continues to use the house as his or her only or principal home. An unlimited number of successions is theoretically possible in the case of such joint tenancies. The other qualification is that where a secure tenancy would pass on succession to a 'qualified person' but for the fact that it has passed on succession once already, then the 'qualified person' (or if there are more than one, the one chosen as above) is entitled to continue to occupy the house as a tenant (but not a secure tenant) for a period of six months. This entitlement is assured by the Act without prejudice, of course, to the possibility that the landlord may grant a completely new secure tenancy.

4. THE RIGHT TO A WRITTEN LEASE

The principal importance of the creation of a secure tenancy is, of course, the security of tenure itself. What the Act also does, however, is to confer some additional 'tenants' rights' upon secure tenants. Most prominently, the majority of secure tenants are given the right to purchase their own home, but there are other consequential benefits in Part III of the 1987 Act. These are applied only to secure tenants but with one small extension. A tenant who is excluded from being a secure tenant solely because either he or she occupies the premises by virtue of a contract of employment requiring him or her to do so for the better performance of their duties or because the house is within the curtilage of another building, enjoys nevertheless the right to a written lease, the right to sub-let, and the right to undertake works of repair.[1]

Until the passing of the Tenants' Rights, Etc (Scotland) Act 1980, there was not only considerable flexibility in the terms and conditions of tenancies entered into by housing authorities but even the existence of a written lease was not statutorily required. Now a written lease is obligatory for all secure tenancies. The landlord of every secure tenant must draw up and secure the execution of the necessary document before the commencement of the tenancy and a free copy must be supplied to the tenant.[2] (The absence of a written lease cannot,

1 1987 Act, s 44(5).
2 Ibid, s 53.

however, be used by a landlord as grounds for denying the existence of a secure tenancy or the tenant's right to purchase.[1])

The 1987 Act also makes provision for the circumstances and the manner in which the terms of a secure tenancy may be varied.[2] These are limited to the following three situations:

(a) By agreement (in writing drawn up by the landlord) between the landlord and the tenant;

(b) In relation to an increase in rent (or other charge payable) only when the landlord gives not less than four weeks' notice of an increase to take effect from the beginning of a rental period;

(c) By order of the sheriff where either (i) the tenant refuses to agree to a change proposed by the landlord or (ii) the landlord refuses to agree to a variation sought by the tenant in any term of the tenancy which restricts his or her use or enjoyment of the house. In the latter case the tenant's wish for a variation must be based upon changes in material circumstances including changes in the character of the house or the neighbourhood making a term unreasonable or inappropriate; or upon showing that a term is unduly burdensome compared with any benefit which would result from its performance; or that the existence of the term impedes some reasonable use of the house. In proceedings brought upon the application of either the landlord or the tenant, the sheriff may make such order varying the tenancy as he thinks reasonable in the circumstances having particular regard to the safety of any person and to any likelihood of damage to the house. Before making an order in favour of a tenant, the sheriff may require service of a copy of the application on any person (owner or tenant of any land) who appears to the sheriff either to benefit from the term to be varied or to be adversely affected by the proposed variation.

5. SUB-LETTING AND ASSIGNMENT BY TENANTS (INCLUDING EXCHANGE)

At common law a tenant has no general implied power to give up his or her premises either by assignation to a new tenant or by sub-letting to

---

1 See *MacDonald v Strathclyde Regional Council* 1990 SLT (Lands Tr) 10.
2 1987 Act, s 54.

a sub-tenant. This position has, however, been the subject of statutory modification in relation to secure tenancies.[1]

It is provided that it shall be a term of all secure tenancies that the tenant shall not assign or sub-let the house (or any part of it) or take in a lodger except with the landlord's written consent.[2] That consent is not, however, to be unreasonably withheld and the only circumstances in which the landlord is bound to refuse his consent are where it appears that payments other than reasonable rent or certain reasonable deposits are being received by the tenant in consideration of the transaction. The procedure according to which a tenant requests the landlord's consent to an assignation or sub-letting and the landlord intimates his consent or refusal is set out in Schedule 4 to the 1987 Act. In the case of a refusal of consent (the landlord is deemed to have consented by his failure to respond within one month to a tenant's request) the tenant may apply to the sheriff who is bound to order the landlord to consent unless he is satisfied that refusal is reasonable. In making this decision the sheriff must have regard in particular to the likelihood of overcrowding being the result of the grant of consent and to any proposal by the landlord to carry out works likely to affect the accommodation. It is interesting to note that, even in the case of an assignation (where the tenancy passes in its entirety from one tenant to another), the Act makes no specific allowance for refusal of consent by the landlord on the grounds that he would prefer to substitute a tenant with high priority on the waiting-list in place of the existing tenant's own choice of assignee. This is an important matter since a new tenant by assignation becomes a secure tenant under the Act (although a sub-tenant or lodger does not become a protected or assured tenant[3]).

One result of the right to assign has been the introduction of schemes to assist tenant exchanges. There are local arrangements but also schemes in which secure tenants from the whole of the United Kingdom can participate if they wish to move to another area. Tenants provide particulars of their own house and the location and type of house they require.[4] The Secretary of State has the power to make grants or loans towards the cost of arrangements for facilitating transfers and exchanges.[5]

---

1 Extended by 1987 Act, s 44(5). See p 85 above.
2 1987 Act, s 55.
3 Ibid, s 55(4).
4 See the Home Swap Scheme and the National Mobility Scheme organised by HOMES—the Housing Organisations Mobility and Exchange Service.
5 1989 Act, s 168 (which repealed and replaced s 80 of the 1987 Act).

6. REPAIRS, ALTERATIONS AND IMPROVEMENTS

Two principal matters of concern arise under this head. Seen from the tenant's point of view the first is the extent to which the landlord can be held responsible for repairs to the house and the way in which that responsibility can be enforced. The second is the extent to which a tenant is free to undertake his or her own works of alteration, improvement and repair.

Looking first to the landlord's own responsibility to repair, this may arise from three different sources. In the first place, there are some rather imprecise common law rules which, even in the absence of any other obligation, require the landlord to maintain the structure of the house in wind and watertight condition and keep it 'in proper tenantable condition.'[1] These limited obligations are supplemented by rules from the second source which is statute.

By virtue of Schedule 10 to the 1987 Act,[2] implied repairing obligations are imposed upon certain landlords, including landlords in the public sector. Thus, in the first place, there is an implied condition in every contract for letting a house for human habitation (at a rent less than £300 per week[3]) that the house is, at the commencement of the tenancy 'in all respects reasonably fit for human habitation' and that the landlord will keep it so during the tenancy. In determining whether a house is fit for human habitation, regard must be had to the extent to which it falls short of the provisions of building regulations by reason of disrepair or sanitary defects. The term 'sanitary defects' is to include lack of air space or of ventilation, darkness, dampness, absence of adequate water supply or sanitary arrangements or other conveniences, and inadequate paving or drainage.[4]

Secondly, and of greater general significance, there is implied into the lease of all houses (leased for a period of under seven years—which includes virtually all tenancies in the public sector) a duty upon the landlord to keep in repair the structure and exterior of the house (including drains, gutters and external pipes);[5] and also to keep in repair and proper working order installations for the supply of water, gas, and electricity,

---

1 *Rankine on Leases* (3rd edn) p 241.
2 Schedule 10, which was amended in important ways by Sch 8 to the Housing (Scotland) Act 1988, is given effect by s 113.
3 See SI 1988/2155.
4 Schedule 10, para 1, as amended. Para 2 makes provision for the application of the terms of para 1 to houses occupied by agricultural workers otherwise than as tenants.
5 In *Hastie v City of Edinburgh District Council* 1981 SLT (Sh Ct) 61 and 92, this was held to include an external window. It had been broken by vandals and the landlord was held to be responsible for the repair.

for sanitation, and for space or water heating.[1] Installations to be repaired by the landlord include basins, sinks, baths and sanitary conveniences but not fixtures, fittings and appliances for making use of the water, gas or electricity supply. The landlord's duty is further limited to exclude, amongst other things, the repair or maintenance of anything the tenant is entitled to remove from the house and, in determining the standard of repair required, regard is to be had to the age, character and prospective life of the house and the locality in which it is situated. A recent extension of the scope of Schedule 10 has brought within the 'implied repairs provision' houses which form part only of a building in such a way as to require the repair of relevant parts of the building and installations in it which serve the house in question. There are some qualifications attached to this extension which relate, in particular, to legal limitations on the landlord's ability to comply. It does not apply to leases (or contracts to make leases) entered into before 1 April 1989.[2] Another source of a statutory standard of maintenance is section 85 of the 1987 Act which requires local authorities to secure that houses in their districts are brought up to the 'tolerable standard.' This standard which is discussed in Chapter 11 may be the basis of an obligation of a landlord authority to its tenants.

The other source of a landlord's obligations is the tenancy agreement itself. This can modify and extend the common law and implied statutory obligations but cannot reduce those secured under Schedule 10.[3] Because the tenancy agreement is likely to contain the most comprehensive catalogue of the rights and duties of both parties, it will be the starting point for working out a landlord's obligations in a specific case. Tenancy agreements vary, however, and it is impossible to provide a universally applicable list of a landlord's (or tenant's) duties. What we can do is to look at a few illustrations of disputes which have reached the courts since these show not only what a landlord's obligations may be but also how they have been enforced. The means of enforcement have more general application and will be taken in turn.

(1) In the first place, it may simply be appropriate for a tenant to apply to the sheriff court for an order (a declarator) stating the

---

1 1987 Act, Sch 10, para 3.
2 Ibid, para 3(1A)–(1C) and 3(3A) inserted by Sch 8 to the Housing (Scotland) Act 1988.
3 But the agreement, even if loosely based upon Sch 10, can extend the tenant's rights. See *Lawrie v City of Edinburgh District Council* 1982 SLT (Sh Ct) 83. Like *Hastie*, this case concerned responsibility for damage caused by vandals.

landlord's obligations based either upon common law, statute[1] or the tenancy agreement.

(2) Unless specifically excluded in the lease, the tenant will normally be entitled to withhold rent on the basis that the landlord is in default. This may lead to the landlord's undertaking the repair which may then make the rent withheld due and payable.[2] It may instead lead to the landlord's taking his own legal action either simply for debt or for recovery of possession. It is possible for the two actions to be conjoined and taken together.[3] In such an action, the defence of a tenant that repairs have not been carried out may be met by an application by the landlord for an order of consignation requiring the tenant to pay into court in advance the amount of the unpaid rent, a practice recently criticised in circumstances where the landlord's action is one for recovery of possession only and where the order of consignation may be oppressive in its effect on the tenant.[4]

(3) Another possibility is for the tenant to raise an action for damages for injury caused by the failure to repair. Such actions have, for instance, been based upon the landlord's failure to keep the house in habitable condition in that he has failed to secure against rising damp and to prevent damp through condensation.[5] In another case the widow and son of a tenant were awarded damages (for loss of society) after it was established that the tenant's death by broncho-pneumonia was the result of dampness caused by broken water pipes which had made the house not reasonably fit for human habitation.[6] There is also the related possibility of an action against the landlord for damages based not on his failure as landlord but as the owner of adjacent property as in the case where injury was caused through persistent flooding from a flat above.[7]

(4) Another basis for an action is breach of the landlord's duties under section 3(1) of the Occupiers' Liability (Scotland) Act 1960.

1 Including perhaps s 85 of the 1987 Act. See *Davis v City of Edinburgh District Council* (Sh Ct) 1984 SCOLAG 86.
2 For practical guidance on this and other matters of enforcement, see Brown and McIntosh, *Dampness and the Law*, Shelter (Scotland), 1988.
3 See *Davis*, above.
4 *City of Edinburgh District Council v Robbin* 1994 SCLR 43. See p 81 above.
5 See *Gunn v NCB* 1982 SLT 526 and *Davis*, above, respectively.
6 *Morrison v Stirling District Council* 13 February 1991, Outer House, unreported. See 1991 SCOLAG 76. This case also appears as the last of some 27 (otherwise entirely sheriff court decisions) contained in volume 1 'Disrepair' of *Scottish Housing Law Reports* published by Shelter (Scotland) in 1991.
7 Again see *Davis*.

This requires a landlord to show care to an occupier in respect of dangers arising from a failure to maintain or repair. Actions under this section have been successfully based upon injury caused by a broken toilet bowl which required to be repaired if the house was to be kept in a habitable condition; and upon damage caused by flooding after a failure to lag waterpipes in the roof.[1]

(5) A separate remedy may be available under section 146 of the Public Health (Scotland) Act 1897. This provision can be used to require local authorities to take action against nuisances such as those which might create a risk to health and, although not principally intended for this purpose, it can be used to order the authority itself to remove nuisances affecting its own tenants. The section has been used to require the removal of dampness.[2]

(6) Finally, the local ombudsman should be mentioned. Although he has no direct power to order remedial work, a failure to repair may, in appropriate circumstances, amount to maladministration and the ombudsman could recommend action.

Thus, in these various ways a tenant may require his or her landlord to carry out certain works of repair. Another concern, however, may be with the tenant's freedom to carry out his or her own works of alteration and improvement and repair. Until the passing of the 1980 Act the position was not regulated by statute and varied from one authority to another according to the terms of tenancy agreements adopted. Frequently the tenant's freedom to make even modest improvements to his or her own home was, in the view of many people affected, quite unnecessarily curtailed.

The change made by the 1980 Act, the terms of which are now contained in section 57 of the 1987 Act, is again cast in initially negative mode. The section declares that it shall be a term of every secure tenancy that the tenant shall not carry out work (other than simply interior decoration) without the landlord's written consent. 'Work' is defined to mean the alteration, improvement or enlargement of the house or of any of its fittings or fixtures; the addition of new fittings or fixtures; and the erection of a garage, shed or 'other structure.' It does not, however, include the mere repair or maintenance of any of these items which, along with internal decoration, can, therefore, be undertaken without the need for consent.

---

1 See *Hughes' Tutrix v City of Glasgow District Council* 1982 SLT (Sh Ct) 70 and *Cameron v City of Glasgow District Council* (Sh Ct) 1984 SCOLAG 9, respectively. In *Cameron* it was also held that the authority was in breach of the water byelaws.
2 See *McGourlick v Renfrew District Council* (Sh Ct) 1982 SCOLAG 158. See also 1985 SCOLAG 109. (For subsequent attempts to dislodge the sheriff's decision in *McGourlick* see 1987 SLT 538 and 1988 SLT 127.)

The landlord's written consent to any of the forms of 'work' is, however, required but, as in the case of consent to sub-letting, that consent is not to be unreasonably withheld and, once again, a specific procedure must be adopted where consent is refused or where consent with conditions unacceptable to the tenant is granted.[1] The landlord is bound to respond to an application from the tenant to undertake works within one month of its receipt. A failure to respond within the time limit implies consent.

Appeal is to the sheriff who must order the landlord to consent or to withdraw a condition unless the sheriff finds the refusal or the condition to be reasonable. In making his assessment of such reasonableness, the sheriff is required to have regard in particular to the safety of occupiers of the house or of other premises; any likely resultant expenditure for the landlord; any likely reduction in value of the house or building or in their suitability for letting or for sale; and any likely effect of the work on the extent of accommodation provided by the house.

Apart, therefore, from restrictions which may reasonably be imposed by the landlord, a public sector tenant's freedom to improve his or her house has been quite substantially guaranteed.

Two other related matters should be noted. One is that specific authority is given by the 1987 Act for the landlord, if he wishes, to reimburse the tenant for any works of improvement carried out with the landlord's consent which have materially added to the price which the house might fetch if sold on the open market. The amount of such a payment cannot exceed the cost of the actual works themselves (and reduced by the amount of any improvement grant paid or payable).[2] This provision for voluntary payments of compensation to be made by landlords to tenants was supplemented with effect from 1994 with a mandatory scheme proposed in the 1991 *Tenant's Charter*.[3] A 'qualifying person' (who is a tenant of a local authority, development corporation or Scottish Homes when a tenancy comes to an end and who carried out 'qualifying work')[4] is entitled to be paid a prescribed amount of compensation. Rules defining 'qualifying work' and the prescribed amounts of compensation have been issued in regulations made by the Secretary of State.[5] The other important point is that the Act also specifically forbids taking into account, when assessing rent,

---

1 1987 Act, Sch 5.
2 Ibid, s 58. For improvement grants see Chap 12 below.
3 Section 48A of the 1987 Act inserted by s 147 of the 1993 Act.
4 Or is a joint tenant of a tenancy in which such work was done, or a successor to a tenant who carried out the work.
5 SI 1994/632.

any improvement in the value or amenities of the house resulting from work carried out by the tenant.[1]

Recently, these rules on repair and improvement have been joined by a further innovation. As early as 1984, framework legislation was enacted which was designed to expand the rights of secure tenants by permitting them to carry out repairs—not, of course, the repairs which they were already legally bound to undertake but some of the repairs for which landlords were responsible—and to do so at their landlords' expense. Re-enacted as section 60 of the 1987 Act, the statutory provisions were skeletal and required supplementation by regulations to be made by the Secretary of State. These were, however, never made but Government recommitment to the introduction of a right to repair came in the 1991 *Tenant's Charter* and then in the substitution of a new section 60.[2] This too relies upon supplementation by regulations and these have since been made as the Secure Tenants (Right to Repair) (Scotland) Regulations 1994.[3] What the regulations do is to identify 'qualifying repairs' as the works (costing no more than £250) necessary to repair any of a list of some specified defects such as 'loss of water supply', 'partial loss of water supply', 'loss of electric power' and 'blocked sink, bath or basin' and then, when a tenant applies to the landlord to have such a repair carried out, to require the landlord to order its 'usual contractor' (the direct services organisation or the person to whom the landlord has generally contracted its repairs) to undertake the works. Also specified in the regulations is a 'maximum time' expressed in days from the first working day after receipt of the tenant's request (or, if the landlord first inspects the house, from the date of the inspection) within which the repair is to be completed (eg loss of water supply 1 day, partial loss of water supply 3 days). If the repair has not started by the last day of the maximum time, the tenant may instruct the repair to be done by a different contractor drawn from a list which must be maintained by the landlord. If the works have not then been completed within the maximum time, the tenant may claim compensation from the landlord. The amount payable is a basic figure of £10 plus £2 per working day after the maximum time (calculated this time by reference to the *second* contractor's appointment) up to the date on which the repair is

---

1 Ibid, s 59. The value of the tenant's improvements cannot be taken into account when calculating the price of his or her house if he or she exercises the right to purchase. See p 112 below.
2 1993 Act, s 146.
3 SI 1994/1046 effective from 1 October 1994.

completed (up to a maximum of £750). There is provision for the suspension of the running of time where exceptional circumstances intervene.

7. COUNCIL HOUSE RENTS AND RENT REBATES

(a) Rents

Although one of the principal effects of the Tenants' Rights, Etc (Scotland) Act 1980 was to introduce for council (and many other public sector) tenants a form of security of tenure parallel to that offered in the private sector by the Rent Acts, there has been no radical change in the system of establishing levels of council house rents. Local authorities enjoy the *prima facie* freedom to decide the level of rents on their housing stock. Under Part XI of the 1987 Act an authority may charge such reasonable rents as it may determine although there is a requirement to review rent levels from time to time and make such changes as circumstances require.[1] In its determination of rents an authority may take no account of the personal circumstances of tenants.[2]

It should not, however, be assumed that Part XI of the 1987 Act reveals the whole story. Quite apart from any political considerations and factors relating to housing management policy which an authority may be expected to take into account when determining rent levels, two important legal constraints are brought to bear. One has operated for many years; the other has developed more recently.

The first depends upon default proceedings which have been initiated by the Secretary of State against authorities whom he believed to be fixing rents at too low a level. In a number of cases brought by the Secretary of State against housing authorities between 1958 and 1971 it was made clear that under the Housing (Scotland) Acts of 1950 and 1966, which afforded a similar freedom to authorities as is now conferred by the 1987 Act, an unreasonably low level of rents would not be permitted. Importing a test employed in decisions of English courts of the time, 'unreasonableness' in this case was taken to mean failure to maintain an equitable balance between rentpayer and

---

1 1987 Act, s 210(1)–(2). Since consolidation, an original duty to make 'changes' appears to have become one to make 'charges'. Under s 211, the authority may make additional service charges for facilities such as garages.
2 Ibid, s 210(3).

ratepayer.[1] Such instances of the charging of unreasonably low rents may now be made the subject of the audit procedures in the Local Government (Scotland) Act 1973 under which the Controller of Audit may make a special report to the Commission for Local Authority Accounts where he is of the opinion *inter alia* 'that any loss has been incurred or deficiency caused by the negligence or misconduct of any person or by the failure of the authority to carry out any duty imposed on them by any enactment.' Such a special report, if the facts are confirmed following inquiry, could lead to the surcharge of those responsible.[2] In a case involving Dumbarton District Council the Commission held that the Council's rents in 1976 were unreasonably low and failed to maintain an equitable balance between rentpayer and ratepayer.[3] Thus, although this is a matter not authoritatively tested in a Scottish court, it must be assumed that the freedom conferred upon local councils by the 1987 Act has to be read subject not only to the statutory qualifications imposed by the Act itself but also to this general duty when fixing rents to behave equitably as between those who pay rents (and rates and, latterly, council tax) and those who pay rates and/or council tax alone.

The other, more recently developed, form of control over the freedom of manoeuvre enjoyed by housing authorities when determining rents arises from the intervention by central government which has developed since 1980. In their efforts to hold down rate levels, Conservative Secretaries of State have sought to curb rate fund (now general fund) contributions to housing revenue accounts and this inevitably implies corresponding increases in rent levels to keep the accounts in balance.[4]

Apart from these constraints which tend to affect only overall levels of rent, the determination of rents of individual houses is a matter for the housing authority. Authorities are free to determine individual 'reasonable' rents and, as noted above,[5] the tenancy agreements can be varied, upon notice from the landlord, to accommodate rent increases.

Whilst rents are fixed on a weekly basis, they are nowadays most commonly collected either fortnightly or monthly. If rent is unpaid, the landlord has the ordinary remedies of a creditor for its recovery

1 See eg *Report by A M Morrison on a Local Inquiry in the Matter of a Review of Rents of Council Houses in Coatbridge*, SDD 1971.
2 1973 Act, ss 96–106.
3 See Special Report by Controller of Audit (15 October 1976) and Recommendations of the Commission (30 June 1977).
4 See p 14 above.
5 See p 86.

and non-payment is also a ground upon which a court may grant the landlord an order of possession of the house and termination of the tenancy.[1]

(b) Rent rebates under the Housing Benefit Scheme

Although authorities are not permitted to take the personal circumstances of tenants into account when rent levels themselves are determined, they are obliged to do so as they operate within their areas the statutory scheme for the granting of housing benefit to their tenants and to others under the Social Security Contributions and Benefits Act 1992 and the Social Security Administration Act 1992. The details of the scheme are contained in the Housing Benefit (General) Regulations 1987 as amended.[2]

Although the housing benefit scheme is, for the purposes of its administration, primarily the responsibility of housing authorities (including for these purposes new town development corporations and Scottish Homes), it extends far beyond the scope of this book. Housing benefit is one of the principal pillars of social security provision and, from that point of view, the scheme is best understood as an important adjunct to the rules governing the award of social security benefits generally. This substantial area of the law cannot be accommodated here. There are several sources to which those who do want a comprehensive review of housing benefit law can turn.[3] Here we shall focus, within this section on rents, upon the principal forms of assistance with rents which tenants may claim. Although the scheme of housing benefits is complex in its detailed application, its central principles are straightforward. Tenants who are in receipt of income support are entitled to receive 100% of eligible rent, less a deduction normally made for each non-dependent person living in the applicant's home. In the case of other tenants, they receive the same amount but with a further deduction of 65% of the amount (if any) by which the applicant's net income exceeds his or her 'applicable amount'—a prescribed amount deemed to represent the applicant's needs and those of his or her family.[4] An individual's applicable

---

1 See p 75 above.
2 SI 1987/1971. For rates of benefit for 1994/95 the regulations are amended by SI 1994/542.
3 The most accessible and comprehensive study is Ward and Zebedee, *Guide to Housing Benefit* (revised each year), Institute of Housing/SHAC.
4 The figures appear in Sch 2 to SI 1987/1971 as most recently adjusted by SI 1994/542.

amount starts with a personal allowance and additional allowances are made in respect of children and young persons. A number of premiums—lone parent, pensioner, disability, severe disability, disabled child—may then be added to personal allowances in appropriate cases. No housing benefit is payable to persons with capital valued at over a prescribed amount.[1] Under a power conferred by the Housing (Scotland) Act 1988,[2] the Secretary of State may by order require rent officers to 'carry out such functions as may be specified in the order in connection with housing benefit'—a power enabling levels of benefit to be restricted in areas determined by rent officers.[3]

Procedurally, housing benefit is granted upon application to the housing authority. Normally benefit is payable from the date of first application but there is the possibility of backdating of payments for up to 12 months.[4] An applicant dissatisfied by a decision on his or her housing benefit may first make representations to the authority and may then appeal. Appeals are decided by a review board appointed by the authority. The board must consist of no fewer than three members of the authority.[5]

Authorities are paid a subsidy by central government to cover much of the cost of benefit payments and the administration of the scheme.[6]

8. ACCESS TO INFORMATION

It is sometimes of importance to tenants in the public sector to be able to gain access to information concerning them which is held by their landlord. Specific reference has already been made to this as an aspect of the allocations process[7] but more general provision for (limited) access was made in the Access to Personal Files Act 1987, implemented in relation to housing in Scotland by regulations which came into effect in August 1992.[8] What these do is to enable a tenant (or former tenant or applicant for a tenancy) to request his or her landlord

1 SI 1987/1971, reg 37.
2 Section 70.
3 See now SI 1990/396 as amended by SI 1991/533 and SI 1993/646.
4 SI 1987/1971, reg 72.
5 Ibid, reg 81. There is no further statutory appeal but judicial review is available. See eg *Macleod v Banff and Buchan District Housing Benefit Review Board* 1988 SLT 753 and *Girvan v Irvine Development Corporation* 1989 SLT 145 (noted at 1989 SCO-LAG 42).
6 Social Security Administration Act 1992, s 135.
7 See p 70 above.
8 The Access to Personal Files (Housing) (Scotland) Regulations 1992, SI 1992/1852.

for information in writing as to whether the landlord holds 'accessible personal information' about the tenant and for access to that information. Such 'accessible personal information' is, subject to prescribed exceptions,[1] information held for any purpose of any of the landlord's tenancies and which relates to a living individual (including an expression of opinion about the person). The landlord must comply with a tenant's formal request for access and there is provision for the rectification or erasure of inaccurate or misleading information.

A quite separate duty on landlords to supply information to secure tenants arises under the 'right to buy' provisions and requires the landlord, at the time of the creation of the tenancy or (if relevant) thereafter, to inform secure tenants of circumstances which may restrict the tenant's right to buy.[2]

---

1 Including where information also concerns another person and certain health information and information subject to professional legal confidentiality.
2 1987 Act, s 76. See Chap 8.

CHAPTER 8

The sale of public sector houses: the tenant's right to purchase

1. INTRODUCTION

In the period between 1945 and 1979, governments adopted opposing policies towards the sale of public housing. Conservative governments favoured sales as strongly as Labour governments sought to restrict them. The ideology of individual home ownership opposed the ideology of maintaining a large scale public housing stock to cater for Scotland's needs.

The legal framework, within which that political football was kicked, was, until 1980, based upon the Secretary of State's power to grant or withhold his consent to all sales of council houses (held by authorities on their housing revenue accounts).[1] This enabled Conservative Secretaries of State to grant general consents and to issue encouragement to housing authorities to sell to those who wished to buy. Labour ministers, on the other hand, would come into power, withdraw the general consent and indicate the limited circumstances in which individual consents to sales would be issued.

The most recent and most substantial change in political direction occurred immediately after the Conservative Government was elected in 1979. The SDD circular of 18 May 1979[2] gave a general consent for sales to sitting tenants. That circular, however, also heralded a revolutionary change in the policy and legal framework of council house sales. It forecast the introduction of a complete newcomer to the scene—not a permission for local authorities to sell but the right of tenants to buy:

'The Government wish to encourage the spread of home ownership, and the Secretary of State considers that the sale of local authority houses has an important part to play in this policy in Scotland. He believes that many local authority tenants would like to purchase the houses in which they live and that they should be encouraged to do so by conditions of sale which recognise their

---

1 Housing (Scotland) Act 1966, s 145(6) now consolidated as s 12(7) of the 1987 Act. For the significance of this provision in 'voluntary disposals' see p 147 below.
2 No 27/1979.

existing interest in the house. He intends therefore to introduce legislation during the current session of Parliament to give sitting tenants a right to buy the house which they occupy on terms specified in the legislation.'

It was this legislative proposal which was the first step on the path leading to the royal assent to the Tenants' Rights, Etc (Scotland) Act 1980 on 8 August 1980—with the public sector provisions coming into force on 3 October. That Act contained a variety of new provisions affecting public sector housing (in addition to introducing a number of changes in the private sector) but what we are primarily concerned with, in this chapter, are the 'right to purchase' sections in Part I of the Act as subsequently amended (especially by the 1986 Act) and now consolidated (and further slightly amended) in Part III of the 1987 Act. Further changes have since been made, especially by the 1993 Act.

These provisions dominate the legal picture of public sector sales. However, in addition to the rules governing the right of tenants to purchase their own houses there are others governing other public sector sales (see Chapter 9). In the case of some of these disposals which leave the tenants as tenants of private sector landlords, their right to purchase is statutorily preserved.[1]

2. THE TENANT'S RIGHT TO PURCHASE

The rules in the 1987 Act (as amended) and the related regulations which govern the tenant's right to purchase his or her house do not make very easy reading. One response to the increasing complexity of the rules (and also to a wish to encourage further house sales) was the introduction by the 1993 Act of a duty imposed on every local authority to supply each of its secure tenants at least once every year with information about the right to purchase. The information must be in such form as the landlord considers best suited to explain the right to buy in simple terms.[2]

In this summary, the rules are dealt with under six heads designed to answer the following questions:

1. Which tenants have the right to purchase?
   This necessarily also covers the question of which landlords may be obliged to sell. The right of a tenant to purchase jointly with other persons is also dealt with.

---

1 1987 Act, s 81A. See p 150 below.
2 1993 Act, s 148 inserting a new s 75A in the 1987 Act.

2. What will be the price of the house?
   This includes consideration of the discount to which the tenant may be entitled and the circumstances under which the discount may become repayable.
3. Will the tenant be entitled to a loan to assist with the house purchase?
   Relevant here too is the tenant's right in some circumstances to a 'fixed price option' where he or she cannot raise sufficient funds for the house immediately.
4. What conditions can the landlord place on the sale?
   In particular, can the landlord impose a condition requiring the tenant to sell back the house if the tenant subsequently decides to resell following purchase under the Act?
5. What is the procedure to be followed?
   The Act sets out the procedure that both the tenant and landlord must follow. It also provides for the way in which disputes must be settled eg if the landlord refuses to sell or is dilatory or fails to offer a loan under the Act.
6. Does the tenant have a remedy if the house is defective?

After discussion of these issues (in sections A–F below) the chapter concludes with a note on the rent to mortgage (or rent to loan) scheme introduced by the 1993 Act.

A. Which tenants have the right to purchase?

Two main conditions have to be satisfied before the right to purchase will arise. The tenant must be a public sector 'secure tenant' who has occupied his or her house (or another qualifying house) for two years.

1. The tenant must be a public sector 'secure tenant'[1] and must be so at the date of the application to purchase.[2] The concept of the secure tenancy has already been discussed and means, for instance, that the house must be let as a separate dwelling. A room in a hostel will not suffice.[3] The house must be the tenant's only or principal home.[4] (If a person has a tenancy of more than one house, which of them is the principal home will be a question of fact. A person cannot have two principal homes at one and the same time and thus be able to

---

1 1987 Act, s 44 and Sch 2. See p 50 above.
2 *Lamont v Glenrothes Development Corporation* 1993 SLT (Lands Tr) 2.
3 *Thomson v City of Glasgow District Council* 1986 SLT (Lands Tr) 6.
4 1987 Act, s 44(1)(a).

purchase two public sector houses.[1]) It also means that a letting expressly on a temporary basis pending development will not be a secure tenancy.[2] Nor will there be a secure tenancy if a letting is expressly on a temporary basis and to a person moving into an area to take up employment and for the purpose of enabling the person to seek accommodation in the area.[3] But in two Lands Tribunal cases these exceptions have been construed narrowly and, therefore, in favour of people claiming to be secure tenants.[4] There is no secure tenancy if the house in question is let in conjunction with business, trade or professional purposes.[5]

Not quite all 'secure tenants', however, have the right to buy, but, once that right is established, it cannot be excluded by the terms of the tenancy or other agreement between the landlord and tenant.[6] To have the right to buy,[7] one has to be the tenant of

> an islands or district council;[8] or
> a regional council;[9]
> a new town development corporation;[10] or
> Scottish Homes; or
> the Housing Corporation; or
> a registered housing association (but see below); or
> a housing co-operative;[11] or
> a police authority; or
> a fire authority.

The principal type of secure tenant who did not at first enjoy the right to buy was the housing association tenant. The 1986 Act, however, amended the 1980 Act to add housing association tenants to the list of qualifying tenants.[12] The inclusion of these tenants is subject to some very important reservations:

---

1 *Miller v Falkirk District Council* 1990 SLT (Lands Tr) 111 or *Matheson v Western Isles Islands Council* 1992 SLT (Lands Tr) 107.
2 Ibid, Sch 2, para 3.
3 Ibid, para 2.
4 *Shipman v Lothian Regional Council* 1989 SLT (Lands Tr) 82; *Campbell v Western Isles Islands Council* 1988 SLT (Lands Tr) 4.
5 See *Fleck v East Lothian District Council* 1992 SLT (Lands Tr) 80.
6 1987 Act, s 61(1).
7 Ibid, s 61(2).
8 Or a joint board or joint committee or common good of an islands or district council; or a trust under the control of a council.
9 Or a joint board or committee or trust as in note 8.
10 Or any urban development corporation which may be created.
11 Ie a 'section 22 co-operative.' See p 42 above.
12 Regional councils and police and fire authorities were added at the same time.

(i) The right to buy does not extend to tenants of co-operative housing associations since they are not secure tenants.[1]

(ii) Nor does the right to buy extend to tenants of associations which have never received grants from public funds; which have never let (nor had available for letting) more than 100 dwellings at a time; or which have charitable status.[2]

(iii) Another exclusion is of groups of (up to 14) houses of housing associations which are in the same neighbourhood and where it is normal practice for at least half to be occupied by people in need of special facilities because of mental illness, drug addiction or certain other difficulties.[3]

(iv) Finally, and most importantly, because only *secure tenants* have the right to purchase and because very few new secure tenancies can, since 2 January 1989, be created in the housing association sector, the right to purchase is confined to those tenants who became secure tenants before that date.[4]

Otherwise, a secure tenant of one of the bodies listed above has a *prima facie* right to purchase—subject to two small qualifications. In the first place, the right to purchase does not extend to sheltered housing ie groups of houses provided with facilities (including a call system and the services of a warden) specially designed or adapted for the needs of elderly or disabled persons.[5] Tenants of houses of this type, even if secure tenants and qualified on other grounds, have no right to buy at all. The question of whether, in a particular case, a house satisfies the statutory tests will turn on its actual physical characteristics. In a number of cases, the Lands Tribunal has regarded the requirements of a 'group' of houses with call system and warden as definitive and rejected claims that the tenants had no right to buy.[6]

The Act also recognises, however, a further category of houses adapted for elderly people and which falls between 'ordinary' housing and 'sheltered' housing. It is commonly called 'amenity' housing and a house in this category is defined to mean a house which has facilities substantially different from those of an ordinary house and which has

---

1 1987 Act, s 45.
2 Ibid, s 61(4)(8b)–(e).
3 Ibid, s 61(4)(f).
4 1988 Act, s 43(3).
5 1987 Act, s 61(4)(a).
6 *Crilly v Motherwell District Council* 1988 SLT (Lands Tr) 7; *Heenan v Motherwell District Council*, 6 August 1987, Lands Tr, unreported; *Martin v Motherwell District Council* 1991 SLT (Lands Tr) 4 and *Hollovan v Dumbarton District Council* 1992 SLT (Lands Tr) 73; but contrast *Moonie v City of Dundee District Council* 1992 SLT (Lands Tr) 103. See also *City of Dundee District Council v Anderson* 1994 SLT 46.

been designed or adapted for occupation by an elderly person whose special needs require accommodation of the kind provided by the house. Such a house does not have the facilities of sheltered housing and a secure tenant can apply to exercise the right to purchase it. If the tenant does so, however, the landlord is placed in a special position. Either it can offer to sell according to the normal procedure to be discussed below. If it does so, it can, if it wishes, impose a condition incorporating a right of pre-emption should the tenant ever wish to · sell. This was the outcome suggested in certain of the Lands Tribunal cases referred to above.[1] Alternatively, the landlord may wish to resist the sale altogether. In this case it is entitled, instead of offering the house for sale, to apply to the Secretary of State for authority to refuse to sell—setting out the facilities and features of the house upon which the landlord relies. If it appears to the Secretary of State that the house does indeed fit the definition in the Act then he must authorise the refusal to sell—which is then to be communicated (within a month at the most) to the tenant. If the Secretary of State does not authorise refusal, the sale must go ahead according to the normal procedure.[2]

The other qualification which may affect the right of some tenants to purchase is that the landlord must itself be the 'heritable proprietor' of the house.[3] It may be assumed that, when this requirement was originally included in the 1980 Act, it was intended to be something of a formality designed simply to cover the obvious point that only houses actually owned by the landlord can be sold by it. However, three difficulties arose all of which have been met by amending legislation. The first was that some local authorities, opposed to the implementation of the Act at all, took the view that, having received their houses by statutory transfer at the time of local government reorganisation in 1975, they were not in law the 'heritable proprietor.' Whether this was correct or not the objection was met, apparently successfully, by inserting a definition of the term to include any landlord entitled to grant a disposition of the house.[4] In cases where this does not apply, the right to purchase cannot be exercised.

A particular case of this sort led to the second difficulty and the second amendment. It involved the position of an estimated 9,000

---

1 But not eg in *Hollovan*, above.
2 1987 Act, s 69. Since amendment by 1989 Act, these restrictions apply only to houses first let on a secure tenancy before 1 January 1990. Guidance on their use was given in Env Circular 12/1992.
3 Ibid, s 61(2)(b). A technical exception occurs in the case of a housing co-operative where the district council must be the heritable proprietor.
4 Tenants' Rights, Etc (Scotland) Amendment Act 1980, s 2(1). See now 1987 Act, s 82.

tenants of the SSHA occupying houses on land leased to the SSHA by the district councils of Glasgow and Dundee. In this situation the landlord was not the 'heritable proprietor' and since the councils were not prepared voluntarily to transfer ownership, the tenants could not exercise the right to purchase. The problem was removed by giving powers to the Secretary of State to make orders (by statutory instrument) vesting the heritable proprietor's interest in the land in the landlord in circumstances where the heritable proprietor (as well as the landlord) is one of the bodies against which the right to purchase may normally be exercised.[1]

A third problem with the 'heritable proprietor' restriction arose when the Lands Tribunal held that, where the landlord was itself a lessee under a long (999 year) lease, it was not the 'heritable proprietor' and could not, therefore, be obliged to sell under the Act.[2] This position was reversed by the 1989 Act which extended the right to buy to tenants of a lessee under a registered lease.[3] Mere title restrictions (eg a right of reversion to superiors under a feu charter if a house ceases to be used for a particular purpose) do not stand in the way of a right to purchase.[4]

These (rather technical) issues apart, the identification of qualifying secure tenants and their landlords has not been the cause of great difficulty. There have, however, been some disputes about the status of tenants employed by their landlord. If a tenant (or one of joint tenants) is an employee of his or her landlord (or of any local authority or development corporation) and 'his contract of employment requires him to occupy the dwelling-house for the better performance of his duties' he or she is not a secure tenant.[5] The Lands Tribunal for Scotland hears challenges to the right to purchase and in a number of early cases held that certain district council parks department employees did not have security.[6] In three later cases it reached the contrary conclusion on different facts.[7] The tribunal does not

---

1 1987 Act, s 77. See eg SI 1981/1860 and SI 1992/900.
2 *Graham v Motherwell District Council* 1985 SLT (Lands Tr) 44.
3 1987 Act, s 84A. For the statutory obligation of landlords to inform secure tenants of any restrictions on their right to buy, see p 98.
4 *Walker v Strathclyde Regional Council* 1990 SLT (Lands Tr) 17. In the same case the Lands Tribunal expressed the view that although, in an appropriate case, it might be able to entertain an application under the Conveyancing and Feudal Reform (Scotland) Act 1970 to remove the restrictions, this would not be competent under the 1987 Act. See also *MacDonald v Strathclyde Regional Council* 1990 SLT (Lands Tr) 10.
5 1987 Act, Sch 2, para 1.
6 *Douglas v Falkirk District Council* 1982 SLT (Lands Tr) 21; *Kinghorn v City of Glasgow District Council*, 28 January 1982, Lands Tr, unreported; *Naylor v City of Glasgow District Council*, 12 January 1983, Lands Tr, unreported; *Neillie v Renfrew District Council*, 7 January 1985, Lands Tr, unreported.
7 *Forbes v City of Glasgow District Council; Hastie v City of Glasgow District Council; Gilmour v City of Glasgow District Council* 1989 SLT (Lands Tr) 74.

confine itself to the express terms of the contract of employment to establish the requirement to occupy the house. It will look to all the surrounding evidence of the employee's duties to ascertain whether there is an implied requirement.[1] In another case, the tribunal found in favour of the manager of a council swimming pool.[2] It was the tenant rather than his landlord who had taken steps to live near his work. Until that time the landlord council had expressed no wish for him to do so in the interests of the better performance of his duties. Similarly the tribunal upheld the right to purchase of an employee whose initial contracts required the occupation of a particular house but whose later contracts of employment relating to promoted posts did not.[3] The tribunal, on the other hand, found against the tenants in two notable Edinburgh cases in which the occupants of houses in the grounds of Laurieston Castle and in Princes Street Gardens were held not to be secure tenants.[4] In a later case, it was held that the application to purchase made by a retired school janitor should be refused both because he lacked security of tenure on grounds of his employment and also because, on this account, a notice to quit had been sufficient to end the tenancy altogether.[5] Lands Tribunal cases have continued to arise in which the contract of employment of the tenant has been at issue[6] and there has also been an important contribution from an Extra Division of the Court of Session. In *De Fontenay v Strathclyde Regional Council*[7] which concerned an application to purchase made by an assistant principal teacher of French at the only secondary school on Tiree it was held that the phrase 'the better performance of his duties' meant that the teacher's duties would not be so well performed if he lived elsewhere and that, in the conditions of extreme housing shortage on the island, without the teacher's occupancy of the particular house there would have been no performance

---

1 See also, on implied terms, the House of Lords' decision in the English case of *Hughes v Greenwich London Borough Council* [1993] 4 All ER 577.
2 *Stevenson v West Lothian District Council* 1985 SLT (Lands Tr) 9.
3 *Little v Borders Regional Council* 1990 SLT (Lands Tr) 2.
4 *Campbell v City of Edinburgh District Council*, 15 November 1984, Lands Tr, unreported, upheld on appeal, 1987 SLT 51; *Docherty v City of Edinburgh District Council*, 14 April 1985, Lands Tr, unreported. Note that in *Campbell* it was also held that the city council's tenure of Laurieston Castle and grounds as trustees for the nation was not itself a barrier to the sale of the house.
5 *Archibald v Lothian Regional Council* 1992 SLT (Lands Tr) 75.
6 In addition to the cases already cited, see *Logan v East Lothian District Council*, 10 April 1986; *Maxwell v Lothian Regional Council*, 8 March 1988; *Bruce v Borders Regional Council*, 25 May 1988; *McTurk v Fife Regional Council* 1990 SLT (Lands Tr) 49; and *McKay v Livingston Development Corporation* 1990 SLT (Lands Tr) 54.
7 1990 SLT 605.

of his duties at all. The Lands Tribunal's decision refusing a right to buy was upheld.[1]

These cases, focussing on the applicants' employment relationship to the property, might have been expected to subside when, by an amendment made by the 1986 Act, the 'curtilage' exception was added to the list of exceptions from qualifying secure tenancies. A house is not the subject of a secure tenancy if it forms part of, or is within the curtilage of, a building which mainly (a) is held by the landlord for purposes other than the provision of housing accommodation and (b) consists of accommodation other than housing accommodation.[2] There is a potential overlap between the 'employee' exception and the 'curtilage' exception. There is also, however, obvious ambiguity in the meaning of 'curtilage.' In practice, drawing some guidance from earlier cases offering interpretations of 'curtilage' in other contexts,[3] the Lands Tribunal has been reluctant to hold a house to be within the curtilage of another building, however closely the two have been associated in use.[4] In particular, a house is not in the curtilage of a building or buildings simply because it is in the grounds of or on the campus of a large institution.[5] On the other hand the fact that a house has a garden, and thus arguably a curtilage of its own, has not prevented the tribunal from holding it to be within the curtilage of a larger building.[6]

An early victory for a tenant with far-reaching consequences came, on a rather different issue, in the case of *Hill v Orkney Islands Council*.[7] There the Lands Tribunal held that a teacher employed by the islands council as education authority was entitled to purchase his house. The council did not in this case try to establish that the tenant was occupying his house for the better performance of his duties but relied upon what it argued was an implied exclusion of education (as

---

1 But cf *Jack v Strathclyde Regional Council* 1992 SLT (Lands Tr) 29.
2 See now 1987 Act, Sch 2, para 8.
3 *Sinclair Lockhart's Trustees v Central Land Board* 1951 SC 258; *Paul v Ayrshire CC* 1964 SLT 207; *Assessor for Lothian Region v BP Oil Grangemouth Refinery Ltd* 1985 SLT 453.
4 *Barron v Borders Regional Council* 1987 SLT (Lands Tr) 36; *Burns v Central Regional Council* 1988 SLT (Lands Tr) 46; *Richardson v Central Regional Council*, 19 February 1986, Lands Tr, unreported; *Fisher v Fife Regional Council* 1989 SLT (Lands Tr) 26; *Allison v Tayside Regional Council* 1989 SLT (Sh Ct) 65; *Pratt v Strathclyde Regional Council*, 22 November 1988, Lands Tr, unreported. See also *Little* above.
5 *Shipman v Lothian Regional Council* 1989 SLT (Lands Tr) 82 and see also *Dyer v Dorset County Council* [1988] 3 WLR 213. See too *MacDonald v Strathclyde Regional Council* 1990 SLT (Lands Tr) 10.
6 See eg *McTurk v Fife Regional Council* 1990 SLT (Lands Tr) 49.
7 1983 SLT (Lands Tr) 2.

opposed to housing) tenants from the right to buy. The tribunal rejected this argument but legislative change followed. The Tenants' Rights, Etc (Scotland) Amendment Act 1984 inserted a new section 3 into the 1980 Act[1] which empowered an islands council holding a house for its functions as education authority to refuse to sell in certain circumstances. The house must be required for the accommodation of a person who is or will be employed by the council for educational purposes (not necessarily a teacher); and the council must be 'not likely to be able reasonably to provide other suitable accommodation for that person.' Notice of refusal must be served within one month of the application to purchase.[2]

2. To have the right to buy the tenant must have occupied his or her house for a period of at least two years[3] immediately prior to the date when he or she initiates the procedure to purchase. (The Lands Tribunal has held that a person hospitalised for 15 months prior to her application to purchase and prevented only by her illness from returning home should be treated as being in occupation of her house and entitled to exercise her right to purchase.[4]) Alternatively some of the two years of occupation may have been spent in houses provided by registered housing associations and certain prescribed public authorities. The list of such authorities (which becomes relevant again below in relation to discount) is as follows[5]:

    (i) regional, district or islands councils in Scotland or equivalent authorities in England and Wales and Northern Ireland;

   (ii) a new town or urban development corporation anywhere in the UK;

  (iii) Scottish Homes, the Housing Corporation and the SSHA;

  (iv) a 'section 22' housing co-operative,[6] or equivalent in England and Wales;

   (v) the Development Board for Rural Wales;

  (vi) the Northern Ireland Housing Executive which provides 'council' housing for the Province;

 (vii) a police, fire, health or water authority anywhere in the UK;

---

1 See now s 70 of the 1987 Act. For an attempt to argue that Strathclyde was, in its island areas, an 'islands council' see *MacDonald* above.
2 Ibid, s 70(1). For notices of refusal see p 125 below.
3 Ibid, s 61(2)(c). Originally (until amended in 1984) the qualifying period was three years.
4 *Matheson v Western Isles Islands Council* 1992 SLT (Lands Tr) 107.
5 1987 Act, s 61(11).
6 See p 42 above.

(viii) the prison service in the UK;
(ix)   the regular armed forces (in this case 'house' is expanded to 'accommodation' and without any restriction that the accommodation concerned be in the UK);
(x)   the Forestry Commission;
(xi)   the Secretary of State where the house was used for the purposes of a State Hospital (Carstairs or English equivalent);
(xii)   the Commissioners of Northern Lighthouses;
(xiii) the Trinity House (lighthouses in England and Wales);
(xiv)   the Secretary of State where the house was used for coastguard purposes;
(xv)   the United Kingdom Atomic Energy Authority;
(xvi)   the Secretary of State where the house was used for MoD purposes;[1]
(xvii) such other persons as the Secretary of State may prescribe. The list has been extended to include a wide range of further landlords including ministers, government departments, the Post Office, and Scottish Natural Heritage.[2]

Thus, in order to qualify, the tenant (who must be a secure tenant at the time of application to buy) must have built up his or her period of two years' occupation whether in the present or another relevant house. Rent-free occupation of a relevant house can count and so too can occupation as the spouse of a tenant of a relevant house.[3] Thus, for instance, a woman recently widowed who is now a secure tenant, but who has not herself previously been a public sector tenant, may count any period of occupation built up by her late husband.[4] Furthermore, a period of occupation spent as the child (over 16) or spouse of a child or 'member of the family' of a relevant tenant will count.[5] Members of the family include grandchildren and nephews and nieces.[6]

Provided a tenant satisfies the two main conditions described above, he or she has the right to buy although if the tenant has a

---

1   The addition of this head to the list in 1984 removed the difficulties for civilian occupants of MoD houses which had been found in *Cook v Renfrew District Council*, 8 June 1982, Lands Tr, unreported. But cf *Woods v Angus District Council*, 11 May 1983, Lands Tr, unreported.
2   SI 1993/1625.
3   1987 Act, s 61(1)(a)(iii).
4   This provision does not, however, benefit a spouse who has divorced the tenant and ceased to live with him. There is no longer sufficient 'occupation' of the house. See *Webster v Cunninghame District Council*, 31 January 1983, Lands Tr, unreported.
5   Ibid, s 61(10)(a)(iv)–(v).
6   Ibid, s 83.

spouse, who is not a joint tenant, the tenant may not exercise his or her right to purchase, without the spouse's consent.[1] This mention of a joint tenant enables two final points to be made on entitlement to purchase. The first is that if there is a joint tenancy, for instance where both husband and wife are tenants, the right to buy is conferred upon such one or more of the joint tenants as may be agreed between them. So far as the period of occupation is concerned, a joint tenant may count the period of his own or another joint tenant's occupation.[2] This will normally mean that two joint tenants will agree to exercise their right to purchase jointly and subsequently become joint owners. By agreement, however, it may be that only one of the entitled joint tenants will actually exercise the right and become the purchaser. The second point also relates to joint purchase but this time involving the entitled tenant together with some other member or members of his family not presently a tenant or tenants. The Act confers the right to a joint purchase where the other member or members of the family (defined, once again, to include persons as distantly related as nephews, nieces and grandparents[3]) are over the age of 18 and have lived in the house (without breach of the tenancy) as their only or principal home for a continuous period of six months up to the date of application to purchase. Where these conditions are not satisfied, joint purchase with members of the tenant's family is permitted where the landlord consents.[4]

Apart from the opportunity that this provides for husband and wife to become joint purchasers and owners where only one was previously the tenant, the facility for joint purchase may make easier the obtaining of a loan.[5]

B. What will be the price of the house?

The Government's intention, when the 1980 Act was passed, was that the prospect of purchase should be attractive to relevant tenants and clearly one of the most important considerations was bound to be the amount to be paid. This explains the provision made for loans to assist purchase which are discussed below but it also explains the formula adopted for ascertaining the purchase price itself. The basic rule is very simple. The price is fixed at the market value of the house—its value as if it were available for sale on the open market with vacant

---

1 Ibid, s 61(5).
2 Ibid, s 61(1) and (10)(a)(i).
3 Ibid, s 83.
4 Ibid, s 61(6).
5 See p 114 below.

possession—at the date of the application to purchase less, in most cases, a discount.[1] The discount, which is required by the Act in order to reflect the reduced value of the house on the open market because of its occupation by a secure tenant, varies according to the length of time that the purchasing tenant has occupied his or her house—or the house of one or more of the bodies listed above. The initial discount is 32% (44% for a flat) of the market value but to this is added 1% (2% for a flat) per year of occupation[2] beyond two up to a maximum discount of 60% (70% for a flat) achieved after 30 years (15 years for flats) of relevant occupation.[3] Thus the discount after five years' occupation is 35%; after 10 years, 40%; after 15 years, 45% and so on. The Secretary of State has the power to increase, by statutory instrument, the percentage levels of discount.[4] Relevant occupation is not limited to that of the house to be purchased but may derive from houses previously occupied. There is also provision for occupation as an 'appropriate person' to include occupation as a succeeding child or spouse of a child (or as another succeeding member of the family).[5] A purchaser (or joint purchasers) may take advantage of whichever is the longest period of qualifying discount, whether of tenant or spouse or deceased person.[6] It is also of interest that a period of occupation qualifying for discount may include a period as a sub-tenant. In one case a purchasing tenant was permitted to count a period during which he was the tenant of his employer to whom the local authority had provided the house.[7]

Some further related points about price need to be mentioned. In the first place it is important to note that a local authority does not have the legal power (in the absence of the consent of the Secretary of State) to sell at a price below that correctly calculated in accordance with the rules in the Act. It has been held that a contract of sale which included such a lower price is void, even though the error is made by the local authority itself.[8] Secondly, the Act provides that the actual assessment of market value shall be carried out either by a qualified valuer nominated by the landlord (and accepted by the tenant) or by

---

1 Ibid, s 62(1)–(2).
2 Which, since 27 September 1993, need not be 'continuous': 1993 Act, s 157.
3 Ibid, s 62(3).
4 Ibid, s 62(5)–(6).
5 Ibid, ss 61(10) and 62(3). See also *Gliori v Motherwell District Council*, 2 May 1985, Lands Tr, unreported, upheld on appeal as *Motherwell District Council v Gliori* 1986 SLT 444.
6 Ibid, s 61(4) as substituted by s 157(3)(c) of the 1993 Act.
7 *Noble v Banff and Buchan District Council*, 11 January 1984, Lands Tr, unreported.
8 *McGroarty v Stirling District Council* 1987 SLT 85.

the district valuer, as the landlord thinks fit.[1] Thirdly, although the Act is in some respects rather vague about the actual calculation of market value it does provide that no account is to be taken of any increase in value resulting from a tenant's improvements qualifying for reimbursement under section 58 of the Act.[1]

Fourthly, the Act contains rules designed to reduce the amount of discount allowable in the case of new properties. It is recognised that landlords which have recently invested in new dwellings should not be required to sell them at a price reduced so much by discount that they would be left an undue burden of continuing interest charges. The form of this protection has varied since its original appearance in the 1980 Act. The current rules were enacted in the 1988 Act[2] and pro-vides that, except where the Secretary of State so determines, the price of a house shall not be brought down by the standard discount rules below a statutorily defined 'cost floor.' This 'cost floor' is to be calculated, in accordance with a determination made by the Secretary of State, by reference to the costs incurred in respect of the period starting at the beginning of the financial year five years prior to the application to purchase.[3] If the price *before* discount is below that level, there is no discount at all.[4] Before these 1988 rules were intro-duced, the minimum price was calculated by reference to amounts of outstanding debt and to a fixed cut-off date (first in 1975, then 1978).[5] Now the restriction on discount is calculated by reference to costs incurred ('historic costs') since a cut-off date five years earlier, but rolling forward. Even though the legislation might give the impres-sion of requiring a determination by the Secretary of State for a figure of 'historic costs' for each house to be sold, a general determination has been made—the Housing (Scotland) Act 1987 (Right to Buy) (Cost Floor) Determination 1988.[6] This requires that relevant costs be the cost of erection or acquisition of the house; the acquisition of the site of the house, any works of improvement to the house (except repair and maintenance)[7], and administrative costs.[8] The

---

1 1987 Act, s 62(2).
2 Section 65 inserting new subsections in s 62 of the 1987 Act.
3 See p 122 below.
4 1987 Act, s 62(6A).
5 1980 Act, s 1(7)–(8) as amended by the 1986 Act.
6 Appended to SDD Circular No 32/1988.
7 On the need to distinguish works of improvement from works of repair with the onus of proof falling on the landlord, see *Wingate v Clydebank District Council* 1990 SLT (Lands Tr) 71.
8 Determination para 4.

Determination also provides that, where the cost floor is less than £5,000, the discount limitation does not apply.[1]

There is, fifthly, another situation in which the discount, as calculated under the normal rules, may be reduced where the purchasing tenant has, in the past, had the benefit of discount in a previous purchase from a 'public sector' landlord in the United Kingdom.[2] The discount is reduced by the amount of the previous discount (or aggregate of previous discounts) *less* any amount subsequently recovered by the landlord on an early resale (see below). The scope of this rule extends not only to a discount received by the purchasing tenant personally but also to discount or discounts received in the past by *any* of the persons who might, if the person with the longest qualifying period of occupation, be the 'appropriate person' for the purpose of calculating the discount. This restriction (effective from 27 September 1993) is designed to prevent a person (or couple) benefitting twice from access to a right to purchase discount. Finally, the Act provides that under certain circumstances some or all of any discount allowed may become repayable. One principle underlying the right to purchase is that it is a right enjoyable by tenants for their own benefit and that they should become and normally continue to be the owner-occupier of the home formerly rented. We shall note soon, however, that the Act does not allow a landlord to forbid the subsequent resale of the house by the tenant. Indeed, another principle underlying the Act is that more owner-occupation should lead to a population with a higher job mobility. The Act does, however, impose a penalty upon a tenant or the tenant's successor in title reselling within a period of three years from the original purchase by requiring repayment of a proportion of the discount allowed.[3] This liability does not arise in the case of a disposal made by an executor of the deceased owner acting in that capacity[4] nor where the disposal results from an order for compulsory purchase. There is also an exception where the disposal is for no consideration (a gift) to a member of the owner's family who has lived with him or her for a period of 12 months before the disposal.[5] But the liability does arise even though it is a part only of the dwelling-house which is disposed of—to prevent the resale of all but a tiny fraction

---

1 Ibid, para 9.
2 1987 Act, s 62(3A) inserted by 1993 Act, s 157(2)(b).
3 1987 Act, ss 72–73.
4 Such a disposal terminates all liability (ie including that potentially arising on another disposal within 3 years) to repay discount: *Clydebank District Council v Keeper of the Registers of Scotland* 1994 SLT (Lands Tr) 2. But for the position of an executor of a purchaser who dies before transfer of ownership, see *Jack's Executrix v Falkirk District Council* 1992 SLT 5 at p 132 below.
5 1987 Act, s 73.

of the house or garden and avoidance of penalty by a claim not to have sold the whole house. Resale without penalty is, however, permitted where it is either the resale of a part by one party to the original sale to another or the resale of a part leaving the former tenant or his or her successor in occupation of the remainder as his or her only or principal home.[1] Liability to repay discount arises only in the case of the first disposal even though more may follow during the three-year period— except in the case of a disposal to a member of the family as above where a further disposal by that member of the family will attract the require- ment to repay.[2]

The actual proportions of discount liable to be repaid are as follows:

if the disposal is within one year 100%;
if within two years 66%;
if within three years 33%.[3]

Once a liability to repay discount to a landlord is established, the security created has priority after any standard security (plus interest and expenses) granted for the purchase or improvement of the house and, with the landlord's consent, any other standard security over the house in relation to any other loan.[4]

C. Will the tenant be entitled to a loan to assist with his or her house purchase?

In the course of the Parliamentary passage of the Tenants' Rights, Etc (Scotland) Bill in 1980, the Government repeatedly made it clear that it did not want a tenant's right to purchase the house made a mere paper right because of lack of funds. The right to a discount was to help in many cases but there is also an important right to obtain a loan to assist with house purchase or, failing that, in some cases the right to pay a small (£100) deposit and secure the right to purchase at the same fixed price within a period of two years.

Loans of amounts not exceeding the price of the house are to be offered by the district or islands council[5] to tenants who have not been able to secure a sufficient building society loan and who have duly applied for a loan under the Act.[6] The actual amount required to be

1 Ibid, s 72(2).
2 Ibid, ss 72(4) and 73(2).
3 Ibid, s 72(3).
4 Ibid, s 72(5)–(6).
5 Or, in the case of a sale by Scottish Homes or a new town corporation, by those bodies; and, in the case of a sale by a housing association registered in Scotland, by Scottish Homes.
6 1987 Act, s 216.

lent depends principally upon the tenant's resources (the 'tenant' here means the tenant or joint tenants and others by whom the house is to be jointly purchased) in accordance with regulations made by the Secretary of State.[1] Subject to certain prescribed adjustments these provide for the net annual income of the tenant to be multiplied by an 'appropriate factor' to produce the maximum amount of the loan. The appropriate factor is normally 2.5 but is reduced to 2 for applicants aged 60–64 (at the time of application to purchase) and to 1 for those aged 65 or above. Where two or more persons are applying, their incomes are combined but the appropriate factor is only 1—the regulations do, however, permit a calculation based on one income and a higher appropriate factor if this would produce a larger maximum loan. The manner in which disputes over loans and offers of loans are to be resolved is dealt with at p 132 below.

If a loan is offered and accepted then it becomes a variable interest home loan and secured by a standard security (mortgage) over the house.[2] Repayment is by equal instalments of principal and interest combined—normally over a period of 25 years. If a loan of a sufficient amount is refused to the tenant by reason of the terms of the loan regulations, then the tenant may give notice to his or her landlord of his or her wish to have a fixed price option giving an entitlement to purchase at any time within the following two years upon repayment of £100. If the option is not exercised the £100 is recoverable at the end of the two years. If the option is exercised then the £100 again becomes recoverable but will, of course, normally be left as part-payment of the purchase price.[3]

D. What conditions can the landlord place on the sale?

The simple answer to this question is that, when the landlord makes its offer to sell, the offer may contain such conditions as are reasonable.[4] This answer must, however, be qualified. In the first place the Act lays down a limited number of types of condition which must either be included or excluded for the benefit of the purchasing tenant. If the purpose of the Act is to encourage sales, this would be undermined by a complete freedom for landlords to impose very burdensome conditions. Thus any conditions attached must, firstly, have the effect of ensuring that the tenant has as full enjoyment and

1 SI 1980/1430. For the prescribed form see SI 1980/1492.
2 1987 Act, s 219(1).
3 Ibid, s 67.
4 Ibid, s 64(1).

use of the house as owner as he or she had as tenant; they must secure to the tenant any necessary additional rights for the reasonable enjoyment and use of the house (including any common rights in the building but imposing necessary duties relating to the rights secured[1]); and they must include terms entitling the tenant to receive a good and marketable title to the house. A condition imposing a new or increased charge for provision of a service must provide for that charge to be in reasonable proportion to the landlord's costs in providing the service. These are the conditions which may or must be included for the benefit of the tenant.[2]

Two types of conditions are then outlawed under the Act. The first is quite straightforward. The tenant cannot be required to pay any of the landlord's expenses incurred in connection with the sale.[3] Tenants must pay their own expenses but no further fee can be charged by the landlord. This position is reinforced by a rule explicitly relieving a tenant applying to purchase from being required to make any advance to, or lodge a deposit with, the landlord—even if such a requirement is contained in an agreement between them.[4] The second type of prohibited condition is one which would have the effect of requiring the tenant (or successors) to offer to the landlord (or anyone else) an option to purchase the house in advance of its sale to a third party.[5] This imposition of a right of pre-emption had commonly been attached to council house sales prior to the 1980 Act as a means of trying to ensure that tenants bought with a view to owner-occupation rather than to make a quick profit on an early sale. Now, the only way in which continued owner-occupation is directly encouraged is by means of the requirement to repay discount in the case of sales within three years.[6] Otherwise, the assumption is that the full benefits of ownership should normally pass to the former tenant—including the right to resell without constraint.

There are, however, two exceptions to this general rule. One has already been mentioned and relates to a house with facilities substantially different from those of an ordinary house and which has been designed or adapted for occupation by an elderly or disabled person whose special needs require accommodation of the kind provided by

---

1 And eg to ensure the continued availability of an emergency exit from adjoining premises retained by the landlord. See *MacDonald v Strathclyde Regional Council* 1990 SLT (Lands Tr) 10.
2 1987 Act, s 64(1)–(2).
3 Ibid, s 64(3).
4 Ibid, s 75.
5 Ibid, s 64(4).
6 See p 113 above.

the house. In the case of this type of house, the requirement to offer an option to purchase may be imposed. If such an option is exercised, valuation is to be by the district valuer having regard to the house's market value at the time of the purchase and to any amount due to the landlord by way of repayment of discount.[1]

The other exception is cast in a more complicated form and relates to the sale of houses in rural areas where landlords (and here this means almost exclusively local authorities) have a limited power to impose a pre-emption condition. Such a condition can have effect only for a maximum of 10 years and, for it to be applied at all, the following conditions must first have been satisfied:

(i) The local islands or district council must have applied to the Secretary of State to have him designate the area, within which the house is, as a rural area.

(ii) The Secretary of State must have so designated the area by order. Such an order may be made only when more than a third of relevant council or housing association houses in the area have been sold; and the Secretary of State is satisfied that an 'unreasonable proportion' of the houses sold consists of houses which have been resold and are neither being used as the only or principal homes of the owners nor are they subject to regulated or assured tenancies.[2]

These tests impose a heavy onus upon an authority wishing to attach a pre-emption condition when it fears a severe running down of its stock in an attractive rural area. A wide discretion is granted to the Secretary of State.

That concludes our summary of the types of condition explicitly required or forbidden by the 1987 Act but we should remember that the Act also allows a landlord to attach to his offer to sell 'such conditions as are reasonable.' What is reasonable is not further defined in the Act but the reasonableness of some conditions has been challenged in proceedings in the Lands Tribunal for Scotland and the decisions of the tribunal are, therefore, a helpful guide.[3] Thus the tribunal has held that conditions to be attached to the sale must not derogate from the express statutory protections for the tenant already discussed. Conditions cannot be imposed which might relieve the landlord from

1 1987 Act, s 64(4). See p 103 above.
2 Ibid, s 64(6)–(8). To date, no order designating a rural area has been made.
3 For a discussion of some of the earlier decisions see Himsworth 'The Lands Tribunal for Scotland and the Government of Council House Sales' (1984) 6 Urban Law and Policy 253. See also the Court of Session decision in *City of Glasgow District Council v Doyle* 1993 SLT 604.

the duty to secure a marketable title or require the tenant to accept the title as it stands.[1] Nor, for instance, could a condition stand which forbade the occupation of a house 'by separate families.' This would leave the purchasing tenant less free as owner to sublet than he was as tenant—another derogation from the statutory conditions.[2] The tribunal has, however, made it clear that the conditions attached to an offer can certainly extend beyond those enumerated in the Act.[3]

To establish the reasonableness of a condition the tribunal has said that the interests of both purchasing tenant and selling landlord must be taken into account.[4] For this purpose it will sometimes be appropriate to supplement legal argument with the calling of supporting evidence. There is no clear onus of proof on either one side or the other.[5]

One general interest of landlords which the tribunal has recognised is that of protecting the amenity of a housing scheme as a whole. They may, therefore, impose conditions which restrict the use and occupation of a house. Conditions requiring future maintenance of the house may be required although, in one case, a condition requiring compliance with the landlord's colour scheme was held to be unreasonable.[6] Conversely, the tenant cannot, as a condition of sale, require the landlord to carry out repairs prior to the sale which he or she claims to be an obligation under the lease.[7] But nor can a landlord insist on the right to undertake repairs (*prima facie* an obligation of the tenant) where it sought to do so on the basis of its 'special social responsibilities.'[8] Particular problems arose where a landlord authority sought to protect remaining participants in a district heating scheme.[9] An attempt to impose a condition requiring repayment of a central heating grant paid to tenants was struck down by the Lands Tribunal.[10]

---

1 See *Keay v Renfrew District Council* 1982 SLT (Lands Tr) 33 and *Clark v Shetland Islands Council*, 14 June 1982, Lands Tr, unreported.
2 *Mackenzie v City of Aberdeen District Council*, 10 March 1982, Lands Tr, unreported. See also *El Bakary v City of Dundee District Council*, 21 May 1986, Lands Tr, unreported.
3 See *Keay v Renfrew*, above.
4 See *Clark v Shetland*, above.
5 See eg *Pollock v Dumbarton District Council* 1983 SLT (Lands Tr) 17.
6 *Keay v Renfrew*, above.
7 *Miller v Livingston Development Corporation*, 24 March 1986, Lands Tr, unreported.
8 See *Forsyth v Scottish Homes* 1990 SLT (Lands Tr) 37. Scottish Homes wished to take on the repairs against a background of actions based on its alleged negligence raised in the Court of Session.
9 *Irvine v Midlothian District Council*, 12 May 1982, Lands Tr, unreported.
10 *Brookbanks v Motherwell District Council* 1988 SLT (Lands Tr) 72.

Conditions must not be attached if they are designed to achieve a purpose unrelated to the sale of the house. Conditions to be reasonable must 'fairly and reasonably relate to the sale.' Thus a condition, however well-intentioned, cannot be used to restrict (in perpetuity) the resale of a house to a person resident in the area or 'who, by nature of their employment or other interest in the economic well-being of the area, requires to reside therein.'[1] Similarly, conditions cannot be used by the landlord merely to duplicate or to strengthen protections provided for it elsewhere in the legislation.[2]

There are other limits to the use of conditions. Subject to a significant exception mentioned below, one important restriction is that conditions cannot be used (this time more commonly at the tenant's initiative rather than the landlord's) if they would affect the extent of the actual land or other property to be sold. In one case, for instance, it was held not to be reasonable for a tenant to try to secure the continued use of a lock-up garage in the neighbourhood (he had already failed to persuade the landlord to include it as a part of the subjects of the sale itself). Having the garage nearby was no doubt a convenience but was not necessary for the reasonable enjoyment of a house.[3] On the other hand, the tribunal has also held that a purchasing tenant should not be deprived of the full enjoyment of the property to be sold simply as a result of an informal agreement with a neighbour under which the neighbour enjoyed a right of access over the property. The property should be sold free from any servitude designed to protect the neighbour's informal rights.[4]

Another limit on conditions is that they will be considered unreasonable if they would adversely affect the rights of third parties. This is a situation which can arise particularly acutely in the case of tenemental properties where the exclusive benefit of facilities previously shared with other tenants can be sought by a purchasing tenant. It was the adverse effect upon the rights of third parties which, in an Aberdeen case, led to a purchasing tenant being refused exclusive access to a part of a common drying green.[5] On the other hand, in two more recent cases the problem of 'common' areas or areas in some respect subject to the

1 *Pollock v Dumbarton District Council* 1983 SLT (Lands Tr) 17.
2 See *Lewis v Renfrew District Council*, 7 May 1982, Lands Tr, unreported; *Clark v Shetland*, above; *Caldwell v Renfrew District Council*, 24 February 1983, Lands Tr, unreported.
3 *Fullerton v Monklands District Council* 1983 SLT (Lands Tr) 15—see also *Hannan v Falkirk District Council* 1988 SLT (Lands Tr) 18.
4 *Arnott v Midlothian District Council*, 21 June 1983, Lands Tr, unreported.
5 *Porter v City of Aberdeen District Council*, 10 March 1982, Lands Tr, unreported. See also *Boles v Falkirk District Council*, 22 July 1988, Lands Tr, unreported.

management of the landlord, the Lands Tribunal has decided that they should not, on that ground, be excluded from the sale. The land should be included in the sale if included in the lease. The sale could, however, be made subject to a condition enabling continued maintenance by the landlord.[1] Also held to be reasonable have been conditions designed to ensure that a purchasing tenant makes financial contributions towards the maintenance of common areas in an estate owned by the landlord in such a way as to share fairly the cost between owners who have bought their homes in the past, the purchasing tenant and future purchasers. It was recognised that sometimes 'reasonableness' must be judged not just in terms of fairness between the landlord and the individual tenant but also fairness between the other parties involved, past and future.[2]

Rather different questions were raised in two cases where the Lands Tribunal was forced to decide on the limits of the purchasing tenant's rights, not as against other tenants and would-be purchasers but in relation to former tenants who have already purchased their homes. The problem arises where the purchasing tenant claims that the land to be acquired should include land already sold to an adjoining tenant or should be acquired free from rights already formally granted to a neighbour in such an earlier sale. The purchasing tenant's claim rests on a right to purchase what was leased to him. The landlord's difficulty lies in being compelled to sell something already conveyed to a neighbour. In both of the cases which came before the Lands Tribunal, the tribunal made orders against the selling councils requiring them to include in their offers the whole subjects leased, whilst acknowledging that this might lead to disputes to be resolved in another forum.[3]

More recently, the decision of an Extra Division of the Court of Session in *City of Glasgow District Council v Doyle*[4] has provided important clarification of some aspects of this dilemma. The case concerned an offer to sell which contained a description of the subjects as the dwelling house together with garden ground 'as the same shall be determined by the council.' When, after the contract had apparently

---

1 *Neave v City of Dundee District Council* 1986 SLT (Lands Tr) 18 and *Robb v East of Scotland Housing Association*, 10 September 1987, Lands Tr, unreported.
2 *McLuskey v Scottish Homes* 1993 SLT (Lands Tr) 17.
3 *Popescu v Banff and Buchan District Council* 1987 SLT (Lands Tr) 20 and *Morrison v Stirling District Council* 1987 SLT (Lands Tr) 22. In a later case, however, the tribunal was able to adopt a more flexible or equitable approach where there was uncertainty as to the true extent of the subjects let. See *Quin v Monklands District Council*, 7 February 1989, Lands Tr, unreported.
4 1993 SLT 604.

been concluded, the purchasing tenant objected that the draft disposition prepared in due course by the council did not include a part of the garden which was attached to the house but which had already been sold by the council to the next-door purchasing tenant and refused to proceed without adjustment to the price; the council countered by seeking to have the sale aborted and claimed back rent on the property. The court held that the words apparently allowing the council *carte blanche* in determining the extent of the subjects to be sold could not, on a true reading of the offer, be treated as a 'condition' (against which the tenant might have been expected to appeal) and that, if such a wide-ranging formula was to be inserted as a condition it would be 'instantly challengeable as unreasonable.' The Act did not permit the use of conditions to interfere with its underlying intention which was that it must be exactly the subjects as let which should be conveyed. Interestingly, however, the court did consider that, because the Act had failed to anticipate the real possibility that an authority might exceptionally be incapable of conveying the subjects which had been let (whether because they had been destroyed or because they had been conveyed in error to another person), the appropriate answer might be for the authority to 'append in clear, explicit and unambiguous terms a condition that the subjects to be conveyed were the subjects let *less such part as it was not in their power to convey*, specifying the part.'[1] This might be a departure from the strict intention of statute but was necessary to avoid producing an obligation which was impossible for a selling authority to discharge. An appeal against the reasonableness of such a condition would, in a particular case, lie to the Lands Tribunal.

Finally, conditions to be reasonable must not be vague or ambiguous.[2]

The whole of the discussion so far on the reasonableness or unreasonableness of conditions is based upon the main terms of the Act as interpreted by the Lands Tribunal. However, since an amendment made in 1986, the Secretary of State has the power to intervene by issuing directions (which may be general or addressed to particular landlords or landlords of a particular description) not to include conditions of a particular kind if they appear to him unreasonable. A condition which is included in contravention of such a direction is of no effect.[3]

---

1 Ibid at 610.
2 See *Pollock v Dumbarton District Council* 1983 SLT (Lands Tr) 17; and *Clark v Shetland Islands Council*, 14 June 1982, Lands Tr, unreported.
3 1987 Act, s 78.

E. What is the procedure to be followed?

In addition to the requirement to satisfy the substantive rules as to entitlement to purchase and entitlement to a loan, tenants (and their landlords) have also to observe procedural rules if they are to exercise their rights under the Act. Tenants must make their approach to the landlord in the prescribed way. If they fail to do so, the landlord will not be obliged to respond.

In essence, the procedure to be adopted by both tenant and landlord is remarkably simple and there is no reason why the transaction should not be completed in a quite straightforward manner. Complications can, however, be introduced if disagreements and disputes arise between the parties and the way in which these are to be resolved under the Act must be given some attention. In these notes the following topics will be discussed: (i) the basic procedure. It will be useful first to see how a simple uncontested case is to be dealt with under the Act. This covers events from the first step taken by the tenant to the stage when a contract of sale is completed at which point normal conveyancing practice (which is not covered here), takes over. The Act does, however, foresee complications in the shape, of (ii) disagreements over such matters as conditions to be attached to the sale and deals with their resolution. Further, the Act deals with the situation where (iii) the landlord disputes the tenant's right to purchase and refuses to sell. Alternatively (iv) the landlord may be unwilling or unable to co-operate in the sale procedures at some particular point or generally and this, too, has to be provided for. A final possibility is that instead (v) the tenant fails to proceed with a purchase he or she has initiated. The notes conclude with a reference to (vi) the loans procedure and to (vii) certain miscellaneous matters.

(i) The basic procedure

This consists of three events:

(a) The tenant who wishes to exercise the right to purchase must serve on the landlord an application to purchase. This has to be in the form which has been prescribed by the Secretary of State and is widely available (with comprehensive notes) from landlord authorities and other bodies. The form includes a statement of full details of qualifying periods of occupation and the formal notice of the wish to buy.[1]

---

1 Ibid, s 63(1), SI 1993/2182. A curiosity is the omission from the current form of formal notice of the consent of a spouse.

(b) Within two months, the landlord must, if it does not refuse to sell, serve on the tenant an 'offer to sell.' This is a notice containing:

the market value of the house;
the discount allowable;
the price;
the conditions the landlord intends to impose; and an offer to sell to the tenant (and, where relevant, a joint purchaser).[1]

The procedure where a landlord refuses to sell is discussed in (iii) below. Note that this includes the situation where an islands council refuses to sell a house held for educational purposes and where a landlord refuses, with the Secretary of State's consent, to sell a house provided for elderly people.

(c) If, upon receipt of this offer, the tenant wishes to proceed, he or she must, within two months, serve a 'notice of acceptance' on the landlord.[2] At that point, a contract of sale is constituted between the parties on the terms contained in the 'offer to sell.'[3]

(ii) Disagreement over terms

The simplicity of the basic procedure can be upset if there is disagreement between landlord and tenant as to the terms of the sale. Such disagreements may come at the stage that the tenant receives the offer to sell and considers that a condition contained in the offer is unreasonable. Alternatively a tenant may wish an additional condition in his or her own favour to be included; or may wish to add a joint purchaser (not previously notified) or remove a joint purchaser (originally in the application)—probably following, in either case, the tenant's assessment of his or her ability to pay the price asked without assistance. In all these cases, the tenant may, by notice served within one month, request the landlord to make an appropriate change in the offer to sell. If the landlord agrees to the change, it is required to serve an amended offer to sell within one month of the request. Following such an amended offer, the time-table in the basic procedure is re-applied with the date of the amended offer substituted for the original offer to sell.[4]

1 Ibid, s 63(2).
2 Ibid, s 66(1).
3 Ibid, s 66(2).
4 Ibid, s 65(1).

If, however, the landlord refuses to amend the original offer (either explicitly or by failure to issue an amended offer in time) the tenant has two choices. He or she can either simply accept the original offer unamended within two months after its service (much of which time may well have passed by the time of receiving or failure to receive the landlord's response). Alternatively he or she can, within one month (or with the written consent of the landlord given before the month, two months), appeal by referring the matter to the Lands Tribunal for Scotland for determination.[1] In that event, the Lands Tribunal has full power either to make the adjustment sought by the tenant or not. If the Lands Tribunal's determination of the issue results in a variation of the terms of the original offer, it orders the landlord to issue an amended offer within two months and the tenant then has the standard further period of two months within which to serve a notice of acceptance.[2] If the Lands Tribunal decides that no variation is required, the tenant has two months from the date of that decision within which to accept the offer on the original terms.[3]

It is at this point of intervention by the Lands Tribunal that the 'reasonableness' of conditions proposed by the landlord or tenant can be resolved (see p 117 above). These have given rise to much of the business before the tribunal. It should, however, be noticed that certain of the contents of a landlord's offer to sell are not directly open to challenge by the tenant. No express means of disputing, for instance, the landlord's calculation of the discount is provided although, as we shall see, an offer containing an inaccurate figure may be defective and challenged on that ground.[4]

Notice also that the Lands Tribunal, taking a procedurally strict view of its powers, has held that it cannot intervene to decide upon the reasonableness of any condition until the tenant is formally in a position to be 'aggrieved.' The tenant must wait until the landlord has formally rejected his suggested conditions before appealing. An appeal cannot be lodged at the same time as a request to amend the offer.[5]

However, once the matter is properly before the Lands Tribunal, it is possible for the tribunal to accept either the landlord's or the tenant's view as to what constitutes reasonable conditions for the sale—or the tribunal can accept a compromise version agreed by the parties during the proceedings.[6] The tribunal has also adopted the

1 Ibid, s 65(2).
2 Ibid, s 65(3).
3 Ibid, s 66(1)(b).
4 See p 127 below.
5 See *Marr v City of Aberdeen District Council*, 3 June 1982, Lands Tr, unreported.
6 See eg *Cowie v City of Aberdeen District Council*, 8 June 1982, Lands Tr, unreported.

practice, where necessary, of issuing an interim decision in general terms—leaving until a later date the formulation and approval of the final terms of a complex condition.[1]

(iii) Refusal by the landlord to sell

Two types of refusal have already been considered. One is where the landlord has obtained authority from the Secretary of State not to sell a house designed or adapted for the elderly in which case the tenant is simply unable to proceed further with the application.[2] Re-application could be tried later if the tenant thought there was any reason for the landlord changing its mind and consenting to a sale. The other type of refusal is that of an islands council in relation to a house required for educational purposes in the circumstances already described.[3] Such a refusal must be served within a month of the application to purchase and the refusal must contain sufficient information to demonstrate that the statutory pre-conditions of refusal have been fulfilled in relation to the house.[4]

The Act also provides for the possibility that the landlord may refuse an application on other grounds. On the one hand, the landlord may dispute the accuracy of the information supplied by the tenant in his or her application to purchase. If this is the case (following reasonable inquiry including a reasonable opportunity for the tenant to amend his or her application) and the landlord is of the opinion that the information is incorrect in a material respect, then it must issue a notice of refusal within two months of the application specifying the grounds for the refusal. Alternatively, the landlord, whilst not disputing the accuracy of information supplied, may dispute the tenant's right to purchase on the grounds, for instance, that he or she has an insufficient period of occupancy. In this case, the landlord may serve a notice of refusal within one month of the application—again specifying the grounds for the refusal.[5]

If a notice of refusal is served on the tenant on either of these grounds, he or she may appeal by applying within a month of the refusal to the Lands Tribunal. It is, for example, under this procedure that the cases about purchase by council employees (discussed at p 105 above) have

---

1 See eg *Irvine v Midlothian District Council* 12 May 1982, Lands Tr, unreported. Following an interim decision on 12 May 1982, final orders were issued on 15 December 1982.
2 1987 Act, s 69 and p 104 above.
3 Ibid, s 70 and p 108 above.
4 Ibid, s 70(2).
5 Ibid, s 68. It has been held, in subsequent Lands Tribunal proceedings, that the landlord may rely on additional grounds of refusal. See *Fernie v Strathclyde Regional Council* 1994 SLT (Lands Tr) 11.

come to be decided. The tribunal has the power to make a finding that the tenant has a right to purchase the house on such terms as it may determine.[1] Although this is not expressly stated in the Act, such a finding requires the landlord to issue an offer to sell but one which would be subject to adjustment (including possible further reference to the Lands Tribunal) according to the procedures discussed at p 123 above.[2] One other possibility which may arise if the landlord disputes the tenant's right to purchase is that it may issue a notice of refusal (which may also be challenged before the Lands Tribunal) but at the same time offer a voluntary sale of the house rather than a sale consequent upon the tenant's right to buy.[3] Such a sale may not be quite as satisfactory from the tenant's point of view since it does not automatically carry with it a statutory discount and loan although these facilities can still be made available by a landlord willing to do so.[4]

A limitation on the powers of the Lands Tribunal to determine an application was found in the case, based on peculiar facts, of *Jenkins v Renfrew District Council*.[5] The tenant had applied to purchase two adjoining flats which had, for practical purposes, become a single home. One application had been accepted and the other refused. When he appealed against the refusal, the tribunal took the view that the two flats should be treated as a single dwelling but then refused the appeal on the narrow, technical ground that it related only to one half of a dwelling.

(iv) Refusal by the landlord to co-operate in the sale procedures

The procedure before the Lands Tribunal under sections (ii) and (iii) can be invoked by a tenant who has received an offer he or she does not like or who has been explicitly refused an offer to sell. But what happens if the landlord simply fails to issue either an offer or a refusal within the prescribed periods; or if it issues a defective offer; or fails to follow up a Lands Tribunal determination of terms or finding of a right to purchase with an appropriate offer to sell? These situations of default by the landlord which are clearly incompatible with the Act's assurance to the tenant of a right to purchase are met

1 Ibid, s 68(4).
2 See s 71(1)(b).
3 Ibid, s 68(1)(b) and s 14.
4 Permission (and encouragement) to sell at prices discounted to the level of 'compulsory' sales has been given. See SDD Circulars Nos 30 and 32/1980; and 22 and 23/1983.
5 1989 SLT (Lands Tr) 41.

partly by a special remedy under the Act itself and partly by the general law.

Section 74 of the 1987 Act specifically states that it is the duty of every relevant landlord

'to make provision for the progression of applications . . . in such a manner as may be necessary to enable any tenant who wishes to exercise his rights under this Part [of the 1987 Act] to do so, and to comply with any regulations which may be made by statutory instrument by the Secretary of State in that regard.'

Meanwhile section 71 gives a tenant who is aggrieved by any of the specific landlord failures mentioned above the right to refer the matter to the Lands Tribunal with a statement of the grievance. The Lands Tribunal must then decide whether the tenant's complaint is to be upheld. In doing so the tribunal has taken a very strict view of the time-table it is supervising. It will, for instance, regard an offer which is made only a few days late as one which is not 'timeous' and, therefore, subject to its jurisdiction.[1]

If the tenant's complaint is that he or she has received an offer within the time-limit of two months but that it is defective, and if the Lands Tribunal holds it to be defective, the tribunal will order the issue of a new offer in proper form within a period of not more than two months. Defectiveness may arise from a failure to include within the offer one of the required items (market value, discount, price, conditions and offer itself) or a failure to obtain any item in the specified way.[2] This power to deal with 'defective offers' was introduced by the Local Government and Planning (Scotland) Act 1982 in response to the Lands Tribunal's previous inability to consider the validity of important aspects of an offer which had, on its face, to be regarded as a valid offer under the Act. The tribunal could not look behind the offer to examine the correctness of the description of the land to be sold or at the discount and price.[3] The 1982 Act opened the way for the Lands Tribunal to consider these matters and, as a result, cases have concerned the extent of the subjects to be sold;[4] and the calculation of discount.[5]

---

1 See *Fullerton v Monklands District Council* 1983 SLT (Lands Tr) 15 and *McLaughlin v Motherwell District Council*, 26 July 1982, Lands Tr, unreported.
2 1987 Act, s 71(1)(d).
3 See *Thomson v City of Edinburgh District Council* 1982 SLT (Lands Tr) 39.
4 See eg *Neave v City of Dundee District Council* 1986 SLT (Lands Tr) 18 and *Allison v Tayside Regional Council* 1989 SLT (Sh Ct) 65.
5 See eg *Gliori v Motherwell District Council*, 2 May 1985, Lands Tr, unreported.

If the tenant's complaint is instead that he or she did not receive on time an offer (including a defective one or one required to be made under the procedure just discussed) or a refusal to which he or she was entitled and that complaint is upheld, then it is for the tribunal to undertake the task of issuing relevant notices to the tenant and otherwise completing the sale procedure in place of the landlord. In doing so, the Lands Tribunal has the power to 'give any consent, exercise any discretion or do anything' which the landlord may do in the same circumstances. This includes allowing joint purchasers and, under earlier rules, disregarding breaks in the occupation of a house when calculating the qualifying time for the purposes of the right to buy and entitlement to discount.[1]

Despite the availability to aggrieved tenants of these remedies in Lands Tribunal proceedings, it was the Government's view in the *Tenant's Charter* of 1991 that something more needed to be done. Too many tenants, it said, were still faced with lengthy delays when they wanted to buy their homes. The new remedy to be offered was a financial one which would provide an aggrieved tenant with compensation and, at the same time, impose a penalty on the defaulting landlord. The purchase price eventually to be paid by the tenant would be abated by the amount of rent paid to the landlord during the period of delay. Amendments were made to the 1987 Act by the 1993 Act[2] and these were brought into effect from 27 September 1993.

The abatement of purchase price provisions are divided into two groups. The first deal with delay in the stages *before* a contract of sale is concluded. If, following an application to purchase, delay by the landlord falls into any of the defined categories, the tenant may serve a notice in writing on the landlord requiring him or her to respond, within one month, with the necessary offer (or amended offer) to sell. The categories of delay closely match those already discussed as grounds on which the tenant may apply for relief to the Lands Tribunal:

(a) failure to serve an offer to sell on the tenant within two months;[3]

(b) failure to serve an amended offer (as requested by the tenant) within one month;

---

1 These powers for the Lands Tribunal to give consents etc were added by the 1982 Act. For the previous position see *Fraser v City of Glasgow District Council* 1982 SLT (Lands Tr) 46 and *McDonald v Renfrew District Council* 1982 SLT (Lands Tr) 30. But see also *Henderson v City of Glasgow District Council* 1994 SLT 263.
2 Sections 144–145 inserting new s 66A–66C in the 1987 Act and amending s 72.
3 Or an amended offer under the rent to loan scheme (s 63(3))—see p 137 below.

(c) failure, following an order or finding by the Lands Tribunal, to serve an offer or amended offer to sell within two months or, as appropriate, within the time specified in the order.[1]

If the landlord fails to respond to the tenant's written notice within the one-month period, the imposition of the financial penalty is triggered and the price of the house calculated under the normal rules must be reduced by the amount of rent paid by the tenant between that point and the date on which the offer is eventually served.[2] Although this is not spelt out in the amended Act, failure to adjust the price in accordance with these rules would produce a defective offer, remediable (as above) by reference to the Lands Tribunal.

The second situation in which the price abatement penalty may be applied is where landlord delay arises at the stage following conclusion of a contract of sale (ie after service by the tenant of the notice of acceptance of the landlord's offer). Here the test of whether delay has occurred is not easily formulated by reference to the Act's own requirements and instead the question is whether 'the landlord has failed and continues to fail to deliver a good and marketable title to the tenant in accordance with the contract of sale.' If the tenant believes this to be the case, he or she may serve on the landlord an 'initial notice of delay' which must set out the landlord's failure and then specify:

(a) the most recent action of which the tenant is aware which has been taken by the landlord in fulfilment of its duties under the Act; and

(b) a period, called the 'response period', of not less than a month within which the landlord may serve a counter notice, with the effect of cancelling the 'initial notice of delay.'

The Act is not completely clear about the function of this response period.[3] It is stated that a counter notice may be served by the landlord where there is no action which, at the beginning of the response period, it was for the landlord to take in order to grant a good and marketable title. It is also stated, however, that a counter notice may be served 'during or after the response period' and, especially in the case of a counter notice served after the end of the response period, it is fairly obvious from the general tenor of the provisions that such a counter notice must be permitted to rely on events and circumstances which arise *after* the beginning of the statutory 'response period.'

---

1 1987 Act, s 66A(1).
2 Ibid, s 66A(2).
3 The problem stems in part from late amendments made to the bill prior to the enactment of the 1993 Act.

At all events, if the 'response period' has expired and there has been no counter notice, the tenant may proceed to the next stage and serve what is called an 'operative notice of delay', the effect of which is to reduce the price of the house by the amount of rent paid between the date of the operative notice and the earlier of either the date of service of a counter notice (inevitably outwith the response period) or the date on which a good and marketable title is delivered.

It may, of course, be expected that the tenant will not, in all cases, accept the validity of a counter notice served by the landlord in that he or she does not agree that the landlord is not, as claimed, in default and this situation is provided for by enabling the tenant to refer the matter for consideration by the Lands Tribunal by supplying to the clerk to the tribunal copies of both the initial notice and the counter notice.[1] Where the tribunal upholds the tenant's view and finds that action could have been taken by the landlord, the tenant is entitled to serve an 'operative notice' which then has effect as if no counter notice had been served.

Supplementing these principal rules on price abatement is further provision that, if there is more than one relevant period of delay on the part of the landlord, then these are aggregated for the purpose of calculating the total amount of price abatement.[2] Furthermore, if the period or periods of delay amount to more than 12 months, then the amount by which the price is to be reduced is increased by 50%.[3] Another benefit is that if the tenant sells the house and may be liable to repay a proportion of the statutory discount, the beginning of the period of three years relevant to the operation of the repayment rule is backdated by a period equal to that to which the price abatement related.[4]

In addition to providing the special forms of relief for tenants frustrated by the inactivity or reluctance of landlords under the Act, section 71 preserves other general remedies which may be available against local authorities which default in the carrying out of statutory duties.[5] Most importantly there is a power available to the Secretary of State under the Local Government (Scotland) Act 1973 to declare, following inquiry, an authority to be in default and to order it to rectify the position (behind which stands the possibility of an order from the Court of Session).[6] A failure to comply with statutory duties and with the statutory time-table leading to a failure to 'make provision for the

---

1 1987 Act, s 66B(4).
2 Ibid, s 66C(1).
3 Ibid, s 66C(2). The percentage may be varied by the Secretary of State by statutory instrument.
4 Ibid, s 72(1A).
5 Ibid, s 71(3).
6 1973 Act, s 211 as amended.

progression of applications' could attract default proceedings of this sort. They were first invoked in the case of Dundee District Council when on 23 March 1981 the Secretary of State, following a public inquiry, issued an order declaring the council to be in default (as a result of severe delays) and requiring it to remedy the situation by adhering to time-limits prescribed in the order for responding to applications from tenants under the Act. Other default orders have followed[1] and, more recently, the Secretary of State ordered Glasgow District Council to take steps to reverse the effects of a practice it had adopted under which tenants were required to sign an undertaking not to buy their houses as a precondition of works of improvement or modernisation being carried out.[2]

(v) Tenant's failure to proceed with purchase

Since the object of the Act is to confer on tenants a right to purchase which is enforceable against landlords, the Act's procedural provisions are, in the main, directed against the possibility of obstruction by the landlord. The Act imposes no duty upon tenants to initiate the process towards purchase nor is there any duty upon a tenant, prior to the completion of a contract, to carry through the procedure which he or she has started. If, for instance, the tenant finds the purchase price too high, he or she can simply not accept the offer made. In its original version the 1980 Act imposed a penalty upon a tenant who made an application to purchase and then decided not to proceed. The tenant was not entitled to make a second application for 12 months. This restriction was, however, removed by the Tenants' Rights, Etc (Scotland) Amendment Act 1984.[3]

(vi) Tenant's death after contract but before delivery of disposition

One situation for which no explicit provision is made in the Act is where the purchasing tenant, after service of the notice of acceptance (and, therefore, after the making of a contract of sale between the parties) but before the completion of the conveyancing procedures by delivery of the disposition, dies. Does the right to enforce the contract die with the tenant or does it pass to his or her executor? The question was resolved by the House of Lords in favour of the executor's right to complete the transaction in *Cooper's Executors v City of Edinburgh*

---

1 Against Stirling District Council in 1981 and East Lothian District Council in 1982.
2 27 February 1989.
3 Repealing s 2(10) of the original 1980 Act.

District Council.[1] Despite arguments that such a result effectively denied the right of a qualifying person (if different from the executor) to succeed to the secure tenancy and perhaps to exercise a new right to buy, the court held that the normal rule in conveyancing matters,[2] that contracts for the sale of heritable property are enforceable by and against personal representatives, should prevail.

On the other hand, it has been held in *Jack's Executrix v Falkirk District Council*[3] that, if an executor does proceed to complete the purchase in these circumstances, an early sale by the executor will trigger the provisions requiring repayment of discount. Despite the appeal of reasons of equity and principle to the contrary,[4] because the executor is not the executor of someone who was ever the 'owner' of the house for the purposes of the Act,[5] he or she cannot take advantage of the limited statutory exception from the obligation to repay discount which is available to executors of owners to whom a disposition has been delivered.[6]

(vii) The loans procedure

The question of a tenant's entitlement to a loan has already been considered but it becomes procedurally relevant in two ways.

In the first place, the tenant may wish to contest the total refusal of a loan (which the landlord (or other body) is permitted to do within two months of the application on the ground that information in the loan application is incorrect in a material respect); or, if the loan has been offered, the tenant may wish to challenge the calculation of its maximum amount; or, if neither a refusal nor an offer has been issued, the tenant may wish to challenge the landlord's failure to respond. In any of these cases, the tenant can, within two months, appeal by applying to the sheriff court. In such proceedings the sheriff will, if he considers the tenant to be entitled to a loan under the Act, make a declaration of that entitlement which then has effect as if it were an offer of a loan issued by the landlord.[7] The other procedural consequence of the making of a loan application is that it can affect the date by which the tenant is obliged to accept the landlord's offer to sell. Normally this must occur within two months of the offer (or amended offer or

---

1 1991 SLT 518. But see also *Bradford MCC v McMahon* [1993] 4 All ER 237 for the different approach taken by the English courts.
2 See *Gardiners v Stewart's Trustees* 1908 SC 985, (1908) 16 SLT 200.
3 1992 SLT 5.
4 Ibid at 10 per Lord Coulsfield.
5 1987 Act, ss 73(1) and 338(1).
6 For the general rules on repayment of discount, see p 113 above.
7 1987 Act, s 216(7)–(8).

determination by the Lands Tribunal) but this date can be put back, when there has been a loan application, to a date two months after either that on which the landlord offers or refuses a loan or, where sheriff court proceedings follow, the date of the court's decision.[1] Thus a tenant cannot be obliged either to accept or refuse an offer to sell until he or she has had time to consider the outcome of the application for a loan and so to assess the financial position overall.

(viii) Miscellaneous procedural matters

The Secretary of State has two further groups of powers relevant to purchases by tenants. In the first place, he has the power, on application, to give financial and other forms of assistance to tenants or other purchasers if they are parties, actual or prospective, to proceedings before the Lands Tribunal or sheriff (or some other forms of proceedings but not involving the determination of a market value).[2] Such assistance may, however, be given only when the Secretary of State considers that a 'case raises a question of principle and that it is in the public interest' to give assistance or that there is 'some other special consideration.'[3] The assistance itself may include giving advice or arranging for advice to be given; arranging legal representation; or procuring or attempting to procure a settlement. Any expenses incurred by the Secretary of State are recoverable from a tenant in whose favour an award of expenses is made. In Lands Tribunal proceedings, expenses are not often awarded against tenants who lose but it may be that the Secretary of State's power to give assistance could operate to enable tenants to take 'test cases' in circumstances where they might otherwise have been deterred from doing so.[4]

Another power available to the Secretary of State, when necessary or expedient in relation to the exercise of his other powers, is the power by notice to obtain information from local authorities and other landlords. Officers of a landlord must comply with such a notice.[5]

F. Does the tenant have a remedy if the house is defective?

It has already been explained that all sales under Part III of the 1987 Act are made subject to certain conditions protective of the

1 Ibid, s 66(b)(vi)–(vii).
2 Ibid, s 79.
3 Ibid, s 79(1).
4 Ibid, s 79(4). The powers under s 79 have not been used to date.
5 Ibid, s 81.

purchasing tenant's interests. The tenant must, for instance, receive a good and marketable title. Sales are not, however, made subject to any general guarantee of the physical quality of the house or of its structural soundness. If a house is not in good condition, this is something which the tenant will be expected to discover when the house is surveyed prior to sale and this will be reflected in the price. In some relatively rare circumstances, however, this is not the case. Structural infirmity may not be discoverable at the time of sale and this may be true in particular for some types of prefabricated concrete buildings. The Government was persuaded that this could be a major hardship for a tenant whom it had encouraged to purchase and who then discovered that the house had become unmarketable on account of its type of construction. The Housing Defects Act 1984 was, therefore, passed to provide a remedy for the purchasers of certain defective houses and its provisions have since been incorporated as Part XIV (and Schedule 20) of the 1987 Act. It should be stressed, however, that these provisions do not provide a general remedy for all tenants whose houses turn out to be unsound. They apply to only a limited range of houses and provide specific remedies in relation to them. The provisions are also procedurally complex and will only be summarised here. A much fuller account is available in an SDD booklet, *Housing Defects: Help for Private Owners in Scotland* and in SDD Circular No 31/1984, the attached memorandum, and the Supplementary Information describing the affected houses.

Although it could be extended to any class of house which is defective by reason of its design or construction,[1] Part XIV of the 1987 Act has been applied only to certain types of prefabricated reinforced concrete dwellings designed (but not necessarily built) before 1960.[2] A person (who must be an individual and not eg a company) who claims assistance under the Act must be the owner[3] of a designated house previously sold by a public sector authority before 26 April 1984 (the 'cut-off date') and there must normally have been no further sale of the house after that date. 26 April 1984 is deemed to be the date on which there was general knowledge of the housing defects and sales after that date are deemed to have been made on that

---

1 Ibid, s 257(1).
2 The Housing Defects (Prefabricated Reinforced Concrete Dwellings) (Scotland) Designations 1984 which are annexed to Circular No 31/1984. The designations also prescribe the 'cut-off date' and the period for seeking assistance. Disputes about whether a dwelling is designated are decided by the Secretary of State.
3 Conclusion of missives is not sufficient. See *McSweeney v Dumbarton District Council* 1987 SLT (Sh Ct) 129.

basis. Assistance must be claimed by 1 December 1994 within 10 years of 1 December 1984.[1]

If the defective house is a flat, the owner claiming assistance is entitled to seek repurchase by the selling authority.[2] The entire interest must be acquired; the price is fixed at 95% of the full value ascertained at the time of the repurchasing authority's offer; any discounts originally allowed must be repaid, as appropriate, under the normal rules.[3] Most owners claiming assistance by way of repurchase may also claim the grant of a secure tenancy of a house—which will normally be the defective house itself.[4] Such a tenant has a right to purchase, without the need to requalify by occupation for two years.[5]

If the defective house is not a flat, the owner will be entitled to assistance by repurchase only in cases of hardship where the authority is satisfied that it would be unreasonable for the person to wait for and endure the upheaval of works or reinstatement. In other circumstances, however, assistance is not normally by repurchase but by the making of grant for work to reinstate the dwelling. The value of the work will vary but must be such as to give the dwelling a further life of at least 30 years and to render it suitable as security for a loan in the private sector (which may imply a higher standard of reinstatement).[6] Grants are at 90% (100% in cases of financial hardship) of the value of the work subject to a prescribed maximum per house.[7]

In addition to these principal obligations of authorities, the Act also imposes subsidiary duties. Authorities must take steps to provide information about rights to assistance under the Act. They must give information to those still purchasing defective dwellings to warn them of their lack of entitlement to assistance. The Act also contains provision for the reference of disputes to the sheriff court; for the designation of further defective dwellings under local schemes; and

1   1987 Act, s 259 and the Designations above. Section 260 excludes assistance if remedial work on the house has been carried out.
2   Ibid, ss 265, 266 and 302. For the purposes of this Part of the Act dwellings ('house, flat or other unit') are divided into 'houses' which may include whole buildings or buildings divided vertically into units. Buildings divided horizontally are not treated as 'houses' and, in the text, are described as 'flats'. The reason for distinguishing them is that the problems of a defective flat could never be solved by grant-aided works directed to that flat alone.
3   Ibid, s 275 and Sch 20.
4   Ibid, s 282.
5   Ibid, s 61(3).
6   Ibid, s 266. The section prescribes other conditions to be met.
7   Ibid, s 271. And see SI 1984/1705.

for the protection of those who have lent on the security of defective dwellings.[1]

An amendment was made to these supplementary provisions by the 1993 Act to remove a problem which had arisen in practice.[2] Some tenants who purchased houses after the cut-off date were not warned, as they should have been, that the houses were defective and had brought proceedings in the sheriff court for compensation. Uncertainty had arisen, however, as to the amount of compensation payable, since the local authority concerned had sought to restrict it to the difference between the 'defective' value and the discounted price paid rather than the full market value. The 1993 Act amendment made it clear that compensation should be payable (in proceedings commenced before 1 December 1994, the date on which general assistance under the Act ceases) at the higher level reflecting the difference between the 'defective' value and the full market value.

G. Rent to mortgage

Although the right to purchase rules included, from the start, provision for financial assistance to tenants in the form of discounts and access to a loan, it was the Government's view, as expressed in the *Tenant's Charter* of 1991, that some tenants were deterred from purchase by the financial burden it imposed. To them would be given the possibility of purchase on a 'rent to mortgage' scheme which would enable a tenant to buy the house for a monthly cost close to the amount paid in rent.[3] The necessary statutory changes were made by the 1993 Act[4] and brought into effect on 27 September 1993.[5] The rent to loan scheme (RLS) provisions are grafted on to the right to purchase rules. They define who is entitled to purchase by rent to loan; establish the rules on payment which stipulate an initial capital payment (ICP) at the time of purchase and then a deferred financial commitment (DFC) in respect of the remainder of price which has to be honoured at a later date—normally on the sale of the house; and make some necessary procedural changes.

---

1 Ibid, ss 287–290 and 299.
2 Section 156 of the 1993 Act, adding new sub-ss (4) and (5) to s 299 of the 1987 Act.
3 For research into an earlier pilot scheme, see H Kay and J Hardin *The Rent to Mortgage Scheme in Scotland* Scottish Office (1992).
4 Section 141, inserting a new s 62A; and s 142 inserting a new s 73A–D into the 1987 Act; and s 143 making a number of related amendments.
5 See SI 1993/2163. Scottish Office guidance on the scheme has been issued in Env Circular No 21/1993.

The rules on eligibility for the RLS are straightforward. With only two exceptions all those tenants who have the right to buy may instead use the RLS. The exceptions are (1) where the house concerned is 'defective'; and (2) where a determination has been made that the tenant is entitled to housing benefit (or for whom a claim has been made for housing benefit) at any time during the period starting 12 months before the date of the application to purchase and ending on the day the contract of sale is constituted.[1] A tenant wishing to buy under the RLS must include a statement to this effect in the application to purchase.[2] In response, in the offer to sell, the landlord must include, as usual, notice of the price of the house which, under the RLS, however, is differently calculated. The standard percentage discounts for which tenants are eligible are all reduced by 15%.[3] Also included in the offer to sell must be notice of the minimum amount of the ICP (together with a statement that more may be paid at this stage if the applicant wishes); and the amount of the DFC (as if it were due at the date of the offer to sell), and an explanation of how the amount of the DFC may vary and the procedure for paying it.[4] If the applicant responds by informing the landlord that he or she wishes to pay an ICP larger than the minimum, an amended offer to sell containing the adjusted figures for ICP and DFC must be served (either within the initial two months or, if later, within a month of the landlord's being informed of the tenant's wish).[5] An offer to sell under the RLS must include a condition specifically providing that the tenant will be entitled to ownership of the house in exchange for the ICP.[6]

The ways in which the ICP and then the DFC are calculated are a little complex. The ICP is an amount not less than the maximum amount of loan which could be repaid at the statutory rate of interest[7] over a loan period of 25 years (or, if earlier, to when the applicant—or youngest applicant—would reach pensionable age,[8] but with a minimum loan period of 10 years) by weekly payments each equal to the 'adjusted weekly rent for the house'—an amount equal to 90% of the actual weekly rent at the date of application.[9]

---

1 1987 Act, s 62A.
2 Ibid, s 63(1)(d).
3 Ibid, s 73A(a).
4 Ibid, s 63(2)(cc).
5 Ibid, s 63(3).
6 Ibid, s 73A(3).
7 Defined by reference to s 219(4) of the 1987 Act. See p 217 below.
8 Within the meaning of the Social Security Act 1975 ie currently 60 for women and 65 for men.
9 1987 Act, s 73B.

The DFC starts off simply as the difference between the amount paid as ICP and the price of the house but is subject to adjustment over time. The means by which it is calculated, and the date at which it becomes payable is determined, are best seen as a process consisting of a number of stages:[1]

Stage 1
Calculating the difference between the price of the house at the time of the initial sale and the ICP.

Stage 2
Expressing that difference as a percentage of the *market value* of the house at the same time.

Stage 3
Reducing that percentage figure by 7 (or other prescribed figure).

Stage 4
Where relevant, further reducing the percentage figure, where an additional payment has subsequently been made by the purchaser with a view to reducing his or her eventual liability to pay the DFC, by the amount of that payment, expressed again as a percentage of the initial market value of the house. These 'payments on account' may be made at any time, but not within a year after a previous payment. They may also be of any amount save that each one must not be of less than £1,500 (or other prescribed figure) and must not exceed the 'statutory maximum'— the amount which would reduce the percentage figure calculated under stages 1–3 to 7.5% (or other prescribed figure). These restrictions are designed to avoid the administrative problems which would accompany trivial payments or payments which leave trivial amounts outstanding. The *full* DFC may be repaid at any time.

Stage 5
Finding the sum which is equal to the percentage resulting from stages 1–4 of the resale value of the house, as at the date of calculating the DFC. This will normally be done at the time when the DFC formally becomes payable which is either when the purchaser sells or otherwise disposes of the house or on the purchaser's death. The 'resale value' is thus normally the actual price of the house if it is being sold on the open market with vacant possession and a good and marketable title or, alternatively, its value for the purpose of confirmation to the purchaser's estate. If, however, the DFC is being paid voluntarily or the house is being disposed of other than on the open

1 Ibid, s 73C(1).

market, or the DFC has, for some other reason, to be calculated, it is an amount agreed between the purchaser and the 'original seller'— the landlord (or successor body) which originally sold the house and to which payment of the DFC is made. Failing agreement, the resale value is to be determined by an independent valuer, on the assumption that the house is for sale on the open market on a date as near as may be to the date when payment of the DFC is to be made.[1] In all the calculations of the resale value, no account is to be taken of:

(a) anything done by the rent to loan purchaser (or any predecessor secure tenant of the house) which has added to the value of the house, or

(b) any failure by him or her (but not by a predecessor tenant) to keep the house in good repair (including decorative repair).[2]

In some circumstances, special rules govern the duty to pay the DFC and the way in which it is calculated. In the first place, the date on which the DFC becomes payable is deferred if the house passes, whether on sale or death, to the purchaser's spouse. Thus, if the purchaser does sell or otherwise dispose of the house to his or her spouse (or person with whom they are living as husband and wife) and the house is, at that time, that person's only or principal home, then the DFC does not become payable on that disposal but instead on a subsequent disposal by (or on the death of) the spouse. The same rule applies where, on the original purchaser's death, the house passes 'by operation of the law of succession' to any person (or persons) for whom (or for one or more of whom) the house was, for the period of 12 months immediately preceding the death, their only or principal home; and also where the original purchase was a joint purchase and, on the death of one of them, the house was, at that time, the only or principal home of one or more of the survivors. Where, in these last instances, there has been more than one successor survivor, the duty to pay arises, if there is no prior disposal, on the death of the last of them for whom the house was, both at the time of the succession or survival and at the time of the death, his or her only or principal home.[3]

The other special circumstance arises in the event of the destruction of the house or damage to the house by fire, tempest, flood or any other cause against which it is normal practice to insure. In such a case

1 Ibid, s 73C(8).
2 Ibid, s 73C(9).
3 Ibid, s 73D(1)–(2). Does this rule leave unclear the position if eg the last survivor dies but only after moving away from the house and ceasing to occupy it as his or her only or principal home?

the DFC must be paid 'as soon as may be' after the destructive event—but not if the house is rebuilt or reinstated, in which case the normal rules apply.[1] While it remains outstanding, no interest accrues on the DFC.[2] It must be secured by a standard security over the house[3] which[4] has priority *before* a security securing repayment of discount in the event of an early resale[5] but immediately *after* one securing a loan from a 'recognised lending institution'[6] to enable payment of the ICP (or payment on account of the DFC) or for the improvement of the house or both.[7]

Stage 6
Reflecting the rules which apply under the ordinary right to buy,[8] 'cost floor' provisions operate to increase the amount of the DFC, calculated under stages 1–5, in appropriate cases.

A 'worked example' of the application of these rules was provided in initial Scottish Office guidance on the scheme:[9]

> Assuming a house with a market value of £31,500 and a tenant with 15 years in public sector housing produced a purchase price of £22,050.
> Assuming a weekly rent of £26.50 and a loan period of 15 years then produced a minimum ICP of £13,100 and a DFC (at date of offer) of £6,744, with calculated adjustments thereafter according to amounts paid and eventual market value.

1 Ibid, s 73C(5)–(6).
2 Ibid, s 73C(2).
3 Ibid, s 73A(4).
4 Notwithstanding s 13 of the Conveyancing and Feudal Reform (Scotland) Act 1970.
5 See p 113 above.
6 See ss 222–224 of the 1987 Act.
7 1987 Act, s 73C(7). Together, in all cases, with any interest and expenses. With the consent of the original seller, the DFC security may also be ranked after a security over the house in respect of any other loan.
8 See p 112 above.
9 Env Circular 21/1993 above.

CHAPTER 9

Other public sector sales

1. INTRODUCTION

Whatever view is taken of its desirability there can be no doubt about the general significance of conferring in 1980 the right of secure tenants to buy their own houses. It has been the Government's major thrust towards owner-occupation and the lessening of the role of public sector landlords, especially local authorities. New fronts have, however, been opened up against public sector landlords and they have been given statutory form in Part III of the Housing (Scotland) Act 1988 and in amendments made by the Housing Act 1988 to the Housing (Scotland) Act 1987. Their purpose is not to turn public sector tenants into owner-occupiers but to make them tenants of different landlords, in particular landlords in the 'independent sector.' The Government's policy aims were articulated in 1987 in the White Paper, *Housing: The Government's Proposals for Scotland.*[1] The paper spoke of 'difficulties arising from the excessive dominance of the public sector.' It had become a 'negative factor' in some parts of Scotland. It constrained choice and, in some areas, produced major problems of 'unsuitable house types, disrepair and management failure.' Landlording operations on a vast scale brought the 'inevitable risk that they become too distant and bureaucratic to respond well to individual tenants' 'wishes or needs.'[2] These and other related considerations had led the Government towards a commitment to local authorities as *enablers* as much as providers.[3] More specifically it was 'necessary to increase the capacity of those other than housing authorities, particularly the private sector, to make a contribution to an improved housing service.' Partnerships between housing authorities, housing associations, private landlords and developers which might be facilitated by (or directly involve) Scottish Homes

---

1 Cm 242.
2 Ibid, paras 1.11–1.13.
3 Ibid, para 1.22.

were needed. The progressive withdrawal of rateborne subsidies to local authorities' housing revenue accounts was also important.[1]

Prominent in the Government's proposals was the introduction of a 'tenant's right to choose a new landlord.'[2] This was the origin of Part III of the Housing (Scotland) Act 1988. The other main statutory initiative is an expansion of the rules governing the 'voluntary' disposal of housing accommodation by local authorities and, less significantly in numerical terms, other public sector landlords. The two changes will be discussed in turn.

2. TENANT'S CHOICE OF LANDLORD

The 1987 White Paper contained the proposals for 'new rights for tenants to transfer' to another landlord. Dissatisfied tenants should not have to wait for their public sector landlords to make improvements. They should have a new right to choose to transfer their tenancy to other landlords. Tenants would be able, the paper proposed, to decide, if they wished to transfer, to set the process in hand at a time of their own choosing. The landlords to whom such tenants could transfer might be housing associations or commercial landlords or the tenants themselves as a co-operative. In all cases the new landlords would require to be approved by Scottish Homes on the basis of their suitability and viability.[2]

Translated into the language of Part III of the Housing (Scotland) Act 1988, the scheme took a form rather different from that implied by the White Paper. It is very closely modelled on the tenant's right to buy provisions in the 1987 Act but it is now the new landlord who has the right to acquire a house under the conditions laid down in the Act. The tenant's 'right to choose' a landlord becomes, in Part III, formally the right to refuse consent to an approach proposed by a landlord wishing to exercise the right to acquire. The procedure to be adopted may be summarised by considering four salient aspects:

1. Who has the right to acquire as landlord a house under Part III of the Housing (Scotland) Act 1988?
2. From whom?
3. Which houses may be acquired?
4. How is an application made, considered and determined?

---

1 Ibid, paras 6.6–6.8.
2 Ibid, paras 6.9–6.10.

Because much of the process is so closely based on the 'right to buy' provisions, the details need not all be repeated.

1. Who has the right to acquire?

The right to be an acquiring landlord (ie a person whom a tenant may choose as a landlord) is confined to Scottish Homes itself and to persons approved by Scottish Homes.[1] Since one of the purposes of the new rules is to move tenants out of the public sector, it has always been unlikely that Scottish Homes would, in practice, exercise its own right to acquire. The intention is that 'approved persons' will normally be the acquiring bodies. No 'public sector landlord' can be approved. For these purposes, a public sector landlord is a district or islands council, a new town development corporation, or the Housing Corporation. (Scottish Homes is also itself a public sector landlord but, as already stated, it may, in appropriate instances, also be an acquiring body.) No regional council may be approved.[2] These exclusions apart, Scottish Homes has a general power to approve either particular persons (bodies) or persons of a particular description; an approval may relate to a particular acquisition, area or period or may be made generally; an approval may specify a maximum number of houses to be acquired; and an approval may be given subject to conditions.[3] An approval may be revoked.[4] There is no statutory regulation of the procedure for approval, or indeed for revocation. It should, however, be borne in mind that in this function as in others, Scottish Homes must comply with any directions it is given by the Secretary of State.[5] The White Paper anticipated that Scottish Homes would be giving approvals on the basis of 'suitability and viability'[6] and these have been the principal guiding criteria in practice.

2. From which landlords are the houses to be acquired?

The answer here is the 'public sector landlords' as defined above—ie islands or district councils, new town development corporations, Scottish Homes and, although it may scarcely ever arise, the Housing

1 Housing (Scotland) Act 1988, s 56(1) and s 57.
2 Ibid, s 56(3) and s 57(1).
3 Ibid, s 57(2).
4 Ibid, s 57(3).
5 Ibid, s 2(10).
6 Cm 242, para 6.10.

Corporation.[1] Regional councils are not, for these purposes, 'public sector landlords.'

3. Which houses may be acquired?

In general any house (and connected property) of which a public sector landlord is the owner (heritable proprietor) and which is occupied by a 'qualifying tenant' may be acquired.[2] 'Qualifying tenant' means a secure tenant provided the tenant is not already or about to be required to give up possession of the house by order of a court.[3]

There are, as with the right to buy, limited exceptions in the case of sheltered or special needs housing,[4] and houses in an area designated, on application by the islands or district council, by the Secretary of State as a rural area. The same criteria and the same procedure apply to such a designation as they do in relation to the power to impose conditions on right to buy applications.[5] Another parallel is the exception of school houses owned by islands councils where the council is not likely to be able reasonably to provide other suitable accommodation for the tenant.[6]

4. Application

Formally, the initiative has to be taken by the 'approved person', the would-be new landlord, to apply to the public sector landlord to exercise the right to acquire. The application must be in the prescribed form and, most importantly, must be accompanied by the consent in writing of the qualifying tenant to an approach being made to his or her existing landlord.[7] This requirement of the consent of the qualifying tenant (which, for this purpose, includes a spouse or person living with the tenant as husband or wife occupying the house as his or her only or principal home)[8] is significant at a number of points. It is the device which is supposed to ensure a measure of 'choice' by the tenant. An application must not only be accompanied

---

1 Housing (Scotland) Act 1988, s 56(1) and (3).
2 Ibid, s 56(1)–(2).
3 Ibid, s 56(4).
4 Ibid, s 56(5)(a), (b).
5 Ibid, s 56(5)(c) and (7)–(9).
6 Ibid, s 56(6).
7 Ibid, s 58(1). For the prescribed form, see SI 1989/423 and, for guidance on the procedure in general, see SDD Circular No 10/1989.
8 Ibid, s 58(2).

by the written consent but will cease to have effect if that consent is subsequently withdrawn by notice to the landlord.[1] If the landlord responds to the application by serving an offer to sell, a copy must go to the tenant.[2] Finally, the purchaser's notice of acceptance must be preceded by the conclusion of a lease between tenant and purchaser for the period subsequent to the sale.[3] The affected tenant is, therefore, from initial consent to an 'approach' to conclusion of the new lease formally kept involved in the acquisition process. The underlying expectation of the Government is, however, that the whole process may in practice be initiated by the tenant rather than the acquiring landlord or through collaboration between the two, with a promotional role of introducing the one to the other lying with Scottish Homes in appropriate cases.[4]

Before leaving the participation of the tenant in the acquisition process, it should be recalled why the change of landlord and, therefore, his consent is of such importance. It may be that the tenant changes landlord in the general hope of improved conditions. What also occurs, however, in the move from public sector to private sector (which includes housing associations) is a move from a secure tenancy to an assured (or short assured) tenancy; from rent setting by a public authority to rent setting by a private landlord uncontrolled by statute; and the loss of a statutory right to buy. This is not preserved, in contrast with the case of 'voluntary' disposals where the consent of each individual tenant is not required.[5] There is, however, one further form of protection given to the tenant who 'chooses' a new landlord in that there is some control of a further disposal by that landlord which might be detrimental to the tenant's interests. A second disposal may be made only with the written consent of Scottish Homes. Such consent may be particular or in relation to a class or description of disposals, with or without conditions. Before giving its consent, Scottish Homes must satisfy itself that the disposing landlord has taken appropriate steps to consult the tenant or tenants of affected houses and must have regard to the response of tenants to the consultation. Once again, Scottish Homes must act in accordance with any directions given by the Secretary of State.[6]

The account of the change of landlord procedures viewed from the point of view of affected tenants has already indicated some of their

1 Ibid, s 58(4).
2 Ibid, s 58(9).
3 Ibid, s 60(2).
4 Cm 242, para 6.10.
5 See p 150 below.
6 Housing (Scotland) Act 1988, s 63 (as amended by the insertion of sub-s (2A) by the Housing Act 1988, Sch 17, para 89).

other features and especially their similarity with the right to buy. The application served by the acquiring landlord must be followed either by a refusal (appealable to the Lands Tribunal)[1] or an 'offer to sell notice.'[2] Such a notice must include a statement by the public sector landlord of the 'market value' of the house and of conditions it intends to impose. The market value (determined by an agreed qualified valuer or the district valuer, at the option of the selling landlord) is to be calculated by reference to the price the house would realise if sold on the open market by a willing seller upon the assumptions (a) that it was subject to the tenancy of the qualifying tenant but otherwise with vacant possession; (b) that it was to be conveyed with the same rights and burdens as would apply to this acquisition procedure; (c) that the only prospective purchasers were Scottish Homes or an 'approved person'; and (d) that the applicant (purchaser) would, within a reasonable period, carry out works to put the housing into the state of repair required by the selling landlord's repairing obligations. The statutory scheme recognises that some houses would not, on the basis of these assumptions, sell. They would not have a positive market value and would, therefore, have either a market value of nil or indeed a negative market value—which would impose upon the selling landlord the obligation to pay the 'price'.[3] Any conditions attached to the offer to sell must be reasonable (subject to reference to the Lands Tribunal)[4] and must not reduce the 'tenant's enjoyment and use of the house' in the change from one landlord to the other. Conditions must also ensure that the acquiring landlord receives a good and marketable title to the house.[5] No condition may require either the purchaser or the tenant to pay any expenses of the selling landlord.[6]

As already indicated, the transaction is concluded, with a contract of sale of the house, when the acquiring landlord serves notice of acceptance of the offer to sell (or amended offer to sell) after, if necessary, any relevant finding or determination of the Lands Tribunal. This must normally follow within two months of the offer to sell.[7] As with the right to buy, the acquiring landlord may refer to the Lands Tribunal the same kinds of failure by the selling landlord to progress the application.[8]

1 Ibid, s 61.
2 Ibid, s 58(5).
3 Ibid, s 58(6)–(8).
4 Ibid, s 59.
5 Ibid, s 58(10).
6 Ibid, s 58(12).
7 Ibid, s 60.
8 Ibid, s 62.

3. VOLUNTARY TRANSFERS OF PUBLIC SECTOR HOUSING

The arrangements just described are for disposals by public authorities which may, in principle, be compelled to sell to a private sector body which, with the consent of the tenant, applies to buy. They required a substantial new statutory procedure. The second Government initiative was to encourage voluntary transfers— 'voluntary' in the sense that the authority cannot (directly, at least) be compelled to sell but has the opportunity to do so if it wishes. Its primary target was local authority housing and, in particular, the larger schemes. For this, no new statutory powers were required since local authorities already had powers (with the approval of the Secretary of State) to dispose of housing stock. As explained in an SDD 'Information Paper', *Voluntary Transfers of Local Authority Housing to Private Bodies*,[1] the point of new measures (contained in the Housing Act 1988 as amendments to the Housing (Scotland) Act 1987) was, in the Government's view,

'to protect and safeguard the interests of tenants by clarifying various factors which the Secretary of State will be entitled to take into account before reaching his decision on any proposed disposal, and the conditions he may impose on consents given.'

The powers of local authorities to sell land held for housing purposes and the houses erected on it were consolidated from earlier legislation in section 12 and subsequent sections of the Housing (Scotland) Act 1987. A power to sell is granted and sales may be made subject to conditions imposed by the authority.[2] However, that power to sell is made subject to the consent of the Secretary of State in the case of houses on the housing revenue account ie all the normal stock of a housing authority.[3] This requirement of consent and the varying degrees of ministerial enthusiasm with which consent was granted was an important regulator, in the period prior to the Tenants' Rights, Etc (Scotland) Act 1980, of sales of council houses. Since the 1980 Act, sales under its 'right to buy' provisions (and their successors in Part III of the 1987 Act) became exceptions to the normal rule requiring the consent of the Secretary of State.[4] Another exception is the sale of a house which is unoccupied and, in the opinion of the authority, either

1 Issued 27 September 1988.
2 1987 Act, s 12(1).
3 Ibid, s 12(7) as amended by the Housing Act 1988.
4 Ibid, s 12(7) and s 14(1) and (2)(a).

surplus to requirements or difficult to let.[1] These exceptional cases have been joined by a third—sales under the 'change of landlord' provisions in Part III of the Housing (Scotland) Act 1987 just described.[2] Those sales require no further consent by the Secretary of State.[3] Thus, the position prior to the changes of 1988 was that the necessary minimum legislation was in place to enable but not directly to compel local authorities to accede to the Government's wish to see a major diversification of tenure. Local authorities had the power to sell, subject to the Secretary of State's consent which would be willingly given in normal cases. Two main further purposes, or groups of purposes, had to be pursued by the Government. In the first place, it had to act in the knowledge that only those authorities ideologically aligned with itself (ie very few in Scotland) would respond enthusiastically to the Government's encouragement towards diversification. Most authorities, therefore, would be unlikely to volunteer disposals beyond the small numbers (to special needs or co-operative housing associations and others) which might suit them from time to time. The Government's response to this appears to have taken two forms, neither of them directly involving statutory measures. One was to wage a war of persuasion through words. Much of the material surrounding the proposals for Scottish Homes was aimed at defining a new role for local authorities.[4] The other response has been financial. The Government's commitment to removing rate-borne (and then poll and council tax-borne) subsidies[5] for council housing and its use of the power to control capital allocations[6] to local authorities may, over time, make it increasingly difficult for some authorities not to 'volunteer' some disposals in order to finance their remaining operations.

The second purpose was to expand upon the rather skeletal provisions in sections 12 and 13 of the Housing (Scotland) Act 1987— both to spell out the Secretary of State's powers and to offer certain safeguards to tenants affected by a disposal. Four changes were made by the Housing Act 1988:[7]

---

1 Ibid, s 14(2)(*b*).
2 Ibid, s 14(2) as amended.
3 The absence of a need for ministerial consent does not remove the general need for a local authority to obtain the best selling price. See Local Government (Scotland) Act 1973, s 74(2).
4 See, in particular, *Scottish Homes* and the White Paper *Housing: The Government's Proposals for Scotland*, Cm 242.
5 Cm 242, para 6.8 and see p 14 above.
6 See p 9 above.
7 A further amendment made by the 1989 Act made it clear that a housing authority need not own *any* housing stock—thus permitting a total sell-off.

1. The Secretary of State's consent

When deciding whether to give his consent to a sale and, if so, subject to what conditions, the matters to which the Secretary of State may have regard are now specified and must include (a) the extent to which the intending purchaser may be dependent upon, controlled or influenced by the selling authority (or any of its members or officers); (b) the extent to which the intending purchaser might become the predominant or a substantial owner of tenanted property in the area; (c) the terms of the proposed sale and (d) any other matters whatsoever that he considers relevant.[1] If the Secretary of State does give his consent to a disposal he may give directions as to the use of any capital monies received.[2] Guidance on how the matters in (a)–(d) would be interpreted by the Secretary of State was provided in the SDD Information Paper referred to.

2. The requirement of consultation

New duties were imposed on local authorities and the Secretary of State where a disposal is a sale of houses let on secure tenancies to a private sector landlord. An application from a local authority for consent must be accompanied by a certificate to the effect that consultation with tenants has taken place. Such consultation has to include service of notice in writing on all tenants informing them of details of the proposed sale including the identity of the purchaser; the likely consequences for the tenant; and the effect on the right to buy. The notice must invite representations (within a period of not less than 28 days) and the authority must then consider representations before making its application for consent. Tenants must be informed of resultant changes made to the proposal and given a further opportunity to object to the Secretary of State. The Secretary of State may require further consultations to be carried out. He must not give consent to a disposal if it appears to him that a majority of tenants object to the proposal. He has a 'general discretion' to refuse on grounds of lack of support by tenants or on other grounds.[3] The statutory rules do not themselves require a ballot of tenants, but the Secretary of State has indicated that this should be normal practice.[4]

---

1 1987 Act, s 13(2) inserted by Housing Act 1988.
2 Ibid, s 13(3) inserted by Housing Act 1988.
3 Ibid, s 81B and Sch 6A inserted by Housing Act 1988.
4 See SDD Information Paper of 27 September 1988.

3. The preservation of the right to buy

In the absence of specific statutory provision, it would follow that, on the disposal of a house to a private sector landlord, the tenant would become an assured rather than a secure tenant. This would carry with it a number of consequences, and, although this may not be of great practical importance in many cases, the right to buy would be lost.[1] This position was reversed by a new section 81A of the 1987 Act which ensured that the right to buy provisions continued to apply to such tenants in accordance with regulations to be made by the Secretary of State. Current regulations[2] provide that the right to buy (but not the rent to mortgage) rules apply where there has been a sale to a private sector landlord except where the choice of landlord provisions have operated or where the sale was to a co-operative (fully mutual) housing association. The preserved right to buy is extended to include a house made available as 'suitable alternative accommodation' where the landlord repossesses the original house specifically on the grounds that such accommodation will be provided.[3]

4. Subsequent disposals

A final matter which has received specific statutory attention is the question of the 'second disposal'—the disposal by a first private sector landlord to another, with further consequential risks for affected tenants. At this stage, the Secretary of State's further consent is now explicitly required for the disposal. Such a consent may relate to a class or description of disposals and conditions may be attached. Once again, consultation with affected tenants is required, although the procedure to be adopted is less elaborate and less rigid than at the stage of the first disposal. The Secretary of State is not bound to refuse his consent on account of a majority of opposed tenants. There is no statutory guarantee of the survival of a right to buy, although an equivalent right could presumably be made a condition of the sale and be enforceable on a contractual basis.[4]

---

1 For the right to buy in general, see Chap 8.
2 The Housing (Preservation of Right to Buy) (Scotland) Regulations 1993, SI 1993/2164 (replacing SI 1992/325).
3 Reg 7. See 1988 Act, Sch 5, ground 9.
4 1987 Act, s 12A inserted by Housing Act 1988.

CHAPTER 10

Homelessness

1. INTRODUCTION

Whilst local authority powers of housing provision are, on the whole, general in the sense that they are directed not towards any particular population group but towards the needs of all the people of each area, the most significant exception in recent years, both in terms of social and political pressure and legislative response, has been the treatment of homeless people.

One consequence of the 1975 reorganisation of local government which attracted adverse criticism was the separation of the housing and social work functions by their allocation to the district and regional councils respectively. In particular this meant that while districts were given the principal function of housing provision the only specific duty to provide temporary housing for homeless people was, in terms of sections 12 and 94 of the Social Work (Scotland) Act 1968, imposed upon the regions. This position was completely changed by the Housing (Homeless Persons) Act 1977 which came into force in Scotland on 1 April 1978, repealed the former minimal obligation under the 1968 Act and replaced it with an elaborate procedure imposing new and potentially far-reaching duties upon housing authorities combined with new duties of co-operation imposed upon other public bodies. The 1977 Act was amended in technical ways when housing law was consolidated in England and Wales in the Housing Act 1985. Small but important amendments were later made by the Housing (Scotland) Act 1986[1] and the whole of the 1977 Act as amended was consolidated in Part II of the Housing (Scotland) Act 1987.[2]

---

1 Section 21.
2 The Act has since been amended by the Law Reform (Miscellaneous Provisions) (Scotland) Act 1990 which added s 24(2A) and (2B) and is to be read subject to the terms of the housing provisions (ss 4–5 and Sch 1) of the Asylum and Immigration Appeals Act 1993.

Even when passed in 1977, the homeless persons legislation (which resulted from a Private Member's Bill[1]) was controversial. For some, it was an inadequate response to a growing problem. For others, resentful of the aims and likely cost of the legislation, it was the target of hostile criticism. The Government has, at some points, shown signs of wishing to dilute the impact of the equivalent legislation in England and Wales although this wish seems to be less directly evident in Scotland.[2] On the other hand, those concerned about housing provision for homeless people did not derive much encouragement from the Government's treatment of homelessness as a merely 'residual problem' in the 1987 White Paper[3] nor from the general reduction in the role of local authorities as housing providers which that paper and subsequent legislation suggested.[4] A fuller critique of the past and likely future impact of the homelessness legislation may be found elsewhere.[5] So too may much more detailed analyses of the legal rules themselves in an area which has generated much litigation and many reported cases both north and south of the Border.[6]

What follows is a summary of the duties imposed upon housing authorities and the procedures according to which they must be carried out. They are divided into the preliminary duties (mainly inquiries into the circumstances of someone claiming to be homeless); and the principal duties (mainly to house certain categories of homeless people). A note on procedures and the enforcement of duties concludes the chapter. Frequent reference is made throughout to *Homelessness: Part II of the Housing (Scotland) Act 1987 Code of Guidance— (Scotland)* (the *Code*) which is a publication issued by the Secretary of State under section 37 of the 1987 Act which requires that housing and other authorities 'shall have regard in the exercise of their functions to such guidance as may from to time be given by the Secretary of State.' The *Code* contains such guidance and, whilst it is not to be treated as of binding legal authority, it throws light upon the interpretation of the Act itself as well as providing

---

1 For a useful discussion of the background to and legislative passage of the Bill, see Partington, *The Housing (Homeless Persons) Act 1977*, Sweet and Maxwell, 1978.
2 But see p 153, n 1 below.
3 *Housing: The Government's Proposals for Scotland*, Cm 242, para 1.1.
4 Ibid, Chap 6.
5 See especially Watchman and Robson, *Homelessness and the Law in Britain*, Planning Exchange (2nd edn) 1989.
6 Ibid. The emphasis in what follows is upon cases decided in Scottish courts and English cases adopted or endorsed by them.

a central government view of the way in which the powers in the Act should be deployed.[1]

Although the principal powers and duties in relation to homelessness are to be left intact, the Local Government Etc (Scotland) Bill 1994 will require a number of changes (effective from April 1996) made necessary by the creation of a single-tier structure of local authorities.

2. THE PRELIMINARY DUTIES OF HOUSING AUTHORITIES

Under section 28 of the Act, the first obligation of a housing authority arises when a person, whom the authority has reason to believe may be homeless or threatened with homelessness, applies to the authority for accommodation or for assistance in obtaining accommodation. The application may be a totally informal request and, as the *Code* points out, it may be to any section of the authority.[2] The authority may (indeed) be approached by homeless people who are quite unaware of any legal obligation owed to them; they may be disabled; and they may lack fluency in English. They may be in very urgent need of help. For all these reasons, authorities are encouraged to provide arrangements which are as accessible and well-publicised as possible. They should, in particular, have a 24-hour emergency contact service.[3] The authority's duty is to respond to an approach for help by making what the Act calls appropriate inquiries. 'Homeless', 'threatened with homelessness' and 'appropriate inquiries' are all terms of art in this context. They are statutorily defined and require with others mentioned below, some discussion. The term 'person', although not statutorily defined, also requires attention.[4]

1 See also p 162 below. The *Code* is in its second edition which superseded the first, published in September 1980. It is currently being amended to include reference to the Asylum and Immigration Appeals Act 1993 (see p 174 below) and is also subject to more general revision in preparation for a new edition. No doubt, a further new edition will be required to accompany local government reorganisation in 1996. It is quite possible that more wide-ranging changes of both the legislation and the *Code* may be introduced if proposals are made for Scotland to parallel those already made by the DoE for England in *Access to Local Authority and Housing Association Tenancies* (January 1994).
2 *Code* para 4.1.1.
3 Ibid, paras 4.1.2–4.1.3.
4 1987 Act, ss 24 and 28.

(i) Homeless

A person is said to be 'homeless' if he or she has no accommodation in Scotland or England and Wales[1] and a person is to be treated as having no accommodation if there is no accommodation which the person (along with other persons recognised as normally residing with him or her) either (a) is entitled to occupy whether by virtue of an interest in it or by virtue of an order of a court; or (b) has a right or permission (express or implied) to occupy;[2] or (c) occupies as a residence by virtue of an enactment or rule of law giving the person the right to remain in occupation or restricting the right of any other person to recover possession. The 'other persons' recognised by the Act as normally residing with the person who claims to lack accommodation fall into two groups. One consists of members of the person's family. Originally, there was some doubt about who this might include, although the first edition of the Code contained some suggestions. With the passing of the 1987 Act, however, section 83 extended, perhaps inadvertently, the definition of members of a person's family originally used only in relation to the right to buy to the whole of the Act's provisions including the homeless persons sections in Part II. Thus a person is a member of another's family if he or she is either the spouse of that other person (or if they cohabit as husband and wife) or that person's parent, grandparent, child, grandchild, brother, sister, uncle, aunt, nephew or niece regardless of whether the relationships are by blood or by marriage; or of the half-blood or whole blood. A child is so treated if a stepchild or a child of parents who are not married. The other group of people are those who normally reside with the person claiming to be homeless 'in circumstances in which the local authority consider it reasonable' for them to reside with him or her. The Act does not expand on what is 'reasonable' here but the Code suggests that it would include circumstances in which elderly or disabled persons are accompanied by housekeepers or other companions and where foster children are living with their foster parents.[3] It also suggests that householders separated for no other reason than that they have no accommodation in which they can live together should be regarded as homeless.[3]

1 The extension of homelessness legislation to Northern Ireland by the making of the Housing (Northern Ireland) Order 1988, SI 1988/1990 (which includes as Part II 'Housing the Homeless') has not affected the territorial scope of the definition in the 1987 Act.
2 For discussion of occupancy rights under the Matrimonial Homes (Family Protection) (Scotland) Act 1981 as an implied right to occupy, see *McAlinden v Bearsden and Milngavie District Council* 1986 SLT 191.
3 Para 4.3.3.

It may not always be obvious when a person's entitlement or permission to occupy a house comes to an end for the purpose of establishing homelessness. In *Stewart v Inverness District Council*[1] the local authority had decided that someone to whom notice to quit had been given and against whom possession proceedings had been taken and decree obtained was only 'threatened with homelessness' as long as the landlord (in this case the authority itself) did not then take steps to actually enforce the decree. The court held this to be wrong and that, whatever might be the correct view of the position before the court's decree was formally extracted, once that had happened the person's occupation was precarious and, therefore, the person was, for the purposes of the Act, homeless. No account should be taken of the fact that the landlord had not yet enforced the decree.[2]

The Act also includes within the definition of a homeless person someone who has accommodation in the sense that he or she is entitled to occupy it but who is prevented from using it because either (a) the person cannot secure entry to it—which should include, according to the *Code*, the situation where illegally evicted tenants cannot immediately be restored to occupation of their home; or (b) the accommodation consists of a mobile caravan or houseboat but there is no place where the person is permitted to put it and reside in it; or (c) it is probable that occupation of the accommodation will lead to violence or threats of violence (likely to be carried out) from some other person in it or from a person who previously resided with the person, now treated as homeless, whether in the accommodation or elsewhere.[3] The *Code* asks housing authorities to respond sympathetically to people (usually women) in fear of violence. In particular, authorities are reminded that the lack of actual violence in the past does not, on its own, suggest that it is not likely to occur and that evidence of potential violence may have to be confined to the woman's own fears. Police or other evidence may well not be available and authorities are urged that they should, in no circumstances, require an applicant to provide evidence supplied by the person alleged to be violent. Nor should

1 1992 SLT 690.
2 Ibid at 693. It is interesting to note further that the judge went on to hold that the failure to distinguish between a 'homeless' and a 'threatened with homelessness' situation left him with no alternative but to reduce the authority's decision, even if it could have been shown that no practical consequences would have flowed from the failure ie because intentionality could be established.
3 See 1987 Act, s 24(3)(bb) inserted by the Law Reform (Miscellaneous Provisions) (Scotland) Act 1990.

authorities rely upon an interdict issued by a court to guarantee that the person against whom it is made will be restrained.[1]

Finally, a person is homeless even if he or she has accommodation but it is overcrowded and may endanger the health of the occupants. For these purposes, the test of whether accommodation is over-crowded is stated to be that contained in section 135 of the 1987 Act. This defines a house (presumably, but unsatisfactorily, the equivalent of 'accommodation') as overcrowded by reference to the 'room stand-ard' and the 'space standard' discussed in Chapter 11 below.[2] Until the passing of the Housing (Scotland) Act 1988, it was arguably correct to assume that the qualification made by section 151 of the 1987 Act to the definition of a 'house' for the purposes of section 135 also extended to qualify 'accommodation' for the purposes of the homeless persons provisions in Part II. This qualification, since repealed by the Housing (Scotland) Act 1988, restricted the meaning of 'house' to one having a rateable value of under £45![3]

It is important to appreciate that the inclusion within the category of homeless persons of people who have accommodation which is overcrowded and which may endanger the health of the occupants results from the main amendment (see also the related amendment below)[4] made to the homeless persons legislation since its enactment. The amendment was made by the Housing (Scotland) Act 1986 in (partial) response to a notorious decision made by the House of Lords in the case of *Puhlhofer v Hillingdon London Borough Council*.[5] Prior to the 1986 amendment, there was virtually no statutory guidance on the standard to which accommodation would have to fall before a person was to be regarded as homeless. When would accommodation cease to be a home? In *Puhlhofer* the House of Lords held that a family were reasonably regarded as not homeless despite the overcrowded conditions in which they lived. The court accepted that conditions could sink to quite a low level before it would find an authority to be legally at fault in denying an applicant's homelessness; the criteria introduced by section 17 of the 1977 Act (now, for Scotland, section 26 of the 1987 Act) (especially that of 'whether it would have been reasonable for a person to continue to occupy accommodation') in relation to 'intentional homelessness' (to be considered below) were not relevant

---

1 *Code* para 4.3.6.2.
2 See p 193.
3 There had been an unsuccessful attempt to achieve the repeal of the rateable value restriction during the consolidation leading to the 1987 Act. It was eventually made by the 1988 Act, Sch 10.
4 See p 169.
5 [1986] 1 All ER 467.

to establishing homelessness itself. Accommodation could be unsatisfactory to the extent that it would not be unreasonable to leave it but still be 'accommodation.' The statutory references to overcrowded accommodation imposed some standards in this area.

In addition, an important change further undoing the effect of *Puhlhofer* was made in 1990 when a general rule was introduced that a person is not to be treated as having accommodation at all unless it is accommodation which it would be reasonable for the person to continue to occupy.[1] The meaning of 'reasonable' in this context is further explained in the Act and additional advice is offered by the *Code*. The Act provides that, in determining whether it would be reasonable for a person to continue to occupy accommodation, regard may be had to the general circumstances prevailing in relation to housing in the area of the local authority.[2] As the *Code* says, this means that there can be no standard definition of reasonableness applied across the board. Examples of unreasonable accommodation may include a house which in an immediate and important way falls below the tolerable standard[3] or inadequate bed and breakfast or hostel accommodation.[4]

Two further points of relevance to overcrowding as an indicator of homelessness were raised in *Stewart v Inverness District Council*[5] already mentioned above. First, the court held that there should be no objection to a finding that a mobile home, caravan or even a boat was 'overcrowded' even if such types of accommodation did not easily fit within the statutory definition of overcrowding.[6] More generally, the court insisted that in all situations it was for the local authority to make its decision on whether an applicant's accommodation was reasonable or overcrowded, even where the applicant did not raise the issue and might indeed have been quite happy with the accommodation and wished to return to it.[7]

(ii) Threatened with homelessness

The Act says that a person is threatened with homelessness if it is likely that he or she will become homeless within 28 days. Although this is the statutorily defined period (corresponding to that within which

---

1 1987 Act, s 24(2A) inserted by the Law Reform (Miscellaneous Provisions) (Scotland) Act 1990.
2 Ibid, s 24(2B).
3 See p 181 below.
4 *Code* para 4.3.5.
5 1992 SLT 690.
6 Ibid at 695–696.
7 Ibid at 695.

many notices to quit may become effective) during which housing authorities' duties arise under the Act, they are encouraged to be ready to advise and assist people where the possibility of their becoming homeless is known to the authority more than 28 days in advance. Early action may avert the threat.[1]

(iii) Appropriate inquiries

These are defined as such inquiries as are necessary to satisfy the authority whether the applicant is homeless or threatened with homelessness and, if so, further inquiries necessary to satisfy it as to whether he or she has a 'priority need for accommodation' or whether he became 'homeless or threatened with homelessness intentionally.'[2] This raises two further points which are the subject of statutory definition.

(iv) Priority need for accommodation

The Act distinguishes between those persons who are homeless or threatened with homelessness and can also show a priority need for housing and those who cannot. A housing authority's duties vary according to the category into which an applicant falls. An applicant has a priority need when the authority is satisfied that he or she is in one of the following categories:

(a) a person who has dependent children who are residing with him or her or who might reasonably be expected to reside with him or her;

(b) a person who is homeless or threatened with homelessness as a result of an emergency such as flood, fire or any other disaster;

(c) a person (or any person with whom such a person resides or might reasonably be expected to reside) who is vulnerable as a result of old age, mental illness or handicap or physical disability or other special reason.

Also defined as having a priority need is a pregnant woman or someone who might reasonably be expected to reside with a pregnant woman.[3]

---

1 *Code* para 4.3.7. For the importance of distinguishing 'homeless' from 'threatened with homelessness' see *Stewart v Inverness District Council* 1992 SLT 690.
2 For comments on the extent of inquiries required, see *Mazzaccherini v Argyll and Bute District Council* 1987 SCLR 475. See also p 166 below.
3 1987 Act, s 25.

Clearly the definitions of the categories of priority need are not absolutely precise and leave some room for local authority discretion in each case. The Secretary of State has issued in the *Code* some guidance on the more important matters. The *Code* points out, for instance, that the term 'dependent children' is not defined in the Act but urges that it should include all children of 15 or less together with others of 18 or less who are in full-time education or training or who are otherwise unable to support themselves. Dependants need not necessarily be the applicant's children but may either be related more distantly or may be adopted or foster children. One-parent families are clearly included. The *Code* also stresses that the children need not actually be living with the applicant at the time of the application—they may, for instance, be with relatives or in care—and insists on the need for a housing solution which does not split families.

The *Code* also urges some flexibility in the interpretation of vulnerability under the Act. People should be treated as vulnerable if they are over 60 or if, approaching that age, they are, for instance, particularly frail or in poor health. Mental illness or handicap, the *Code* stresses, may not be immediately recognisable as the cause of vulnerability and homelessness officers should be alert to this possibility. Physical disability will usually be more readily ascertainable but vulnerability will depend on the applicant's circumstances. Other 'special reasons' giving rise to vulnerability will obviously vary but the *Code* provides, as examples of possibly vulnerable people: young people of 16 or 17; other young people otherwise at risk of sexual or financial exploitation or involvement in serious drug or solvent abuse; chronically sick people (including people with AIDS or HIV related illnesses); people recently discharged from local authority care or hospital or prison; women suffering or in fear of violence (even if without children); refugees and asylum seekers;[1] people who have 'exceptional leave to remain in this country'; and people at risk of racial harassment.[2]

The *Code's* encouragement to authorities to take a generous view of vulnerability has also received some support in the courts. The case of *Kelly v Monklands District Council*[3] concerned the rejection by the council of the claim by two women aged 16 to be treated as being in priority need on the grounds of vulnerability as a result of some 'other special reason.' After hearing about the circumstances of the first petitioner, Lord Ross said:

1 But see p 174 below.
2 *Code* para 4.4.
3 1986 SLT 169.

'I am not persuaded that every 16-year-old is vulnerable within the meaning of the Act. However, when you find a girl of 16 who has no assets, no income and nowhere to go and who has apparently left home because of violence, I am of opinon that no reasonable authority could fail to conclude that she was vulnerable. A girl of that age and with that background is bound to be less able to fend for herself than a less vulnerable girl; being less able to cope, such a person is liable to injury or harm . . . exploitation does not have to have occurred before exploitation can reasonably be apprehended.'

In a case decided in the English Court of Appeal (and cited with approval by Lord Ross) a housing authority was held to have adopted the wrong approach to vulnerability when it refused to treat a man of 59 (and not, therefore, vulnerable on grounds of age alone) who was both an alcoholic and brain-damaged as being in priority need.[1] The man was described as being disorientated and in a confused state. The council's mistake was to focus narrowly upon whether the man was (in the terms of the English Code) 'substantially disabled mentally or physically.' This had led it to ignore the man's overall vulnerable condition which was the product of many factors. To rather similar effect, in *Wilson v Nithsdale District Council*[2] it was held that the approach to vulnerability was one of general comparison. The question to be asked was not whether a person was 'at great risk' but whether, because of the person's particular problems, he or she was at greater risk of harm and less able to cope with homelessness. The appropriate comparison had to be with 'some assumed average or normal or run-of-the-mill homeless person'![3]

(v) Intentional homelessness

The inclusion in the Act of the distinction (which again affects a local authority's duties) between those who are simply homeless (or threatened with homelessness) and those who are homeless intentionally was highly contentious at the time of the passage of the 1977 Act and has been one of the most troublesome aspects of the legislation ever since its implementation. The original Bill did not refer to intentional homelessness but the term was introduced to meet objections from those who argued (apparently against the force of existing evidence[4]) that rights conferred under the Act would be exploited by people who quite deliberately brought homelessness upon themselves.

1 *R v Waveney District Council, ex p Bowers* [1982] 3 All ER 727.
2 1992 SLT 1131.
3 Ibid at 1136 and 1134.
4 See *Partington* above at 48/3.

Thus a person is defined as homeless intentionally

'If he deliberately does or fails to do anything in consequence of which he ceases to occupy accommodation which is available for his occupation and which it would have been reasonable for him to occupy.'

The Act also requires, however, that 'an act or omission in good faith on the part of a person who was unaware of any relevant fact is not to be treated as deliberate.' It also states that, in determining the 'reasonableness' of a person's continued occupation of accommodation, regard may be had to the general circumstances prevailing in relation to housing in the area.[1] Even with these qualifications, however, decisions on the intentionality of a person's homelessness are bound to involve difficult questions of interpretation. The *Code* offers some guidance. It stresses that, for intentionality to be established, the three elements of deliberateness of action, reasonableness of continued occupation and awareness of all facts must be combined and that the onus is upon the authority rather than the applicant to make its case.

The *Code* does not attempt to itemise the categories of homeless persons who should be branded with intentionality and those who should not but it does make some suggestions. A person who chooses to sell his or her home or who has lost it because of wilful and persistent refusal to pay rent would, in most cases, be regarded as intentionally homeless. On the other hand, the deliberate act or failure must have been that of the applicant and not, for instance, that of his or her partner. If the partner is found to have been at fault, the applicant who is not, therefore, intentionally homeless must be helped even if the partner would also benefit from the rehousing.[2] Further, the test of the deliberateness of the applicant's act or omission is whether *that person* knew—not whether some hypothetical reasonable person ought to have known—that it would result in homelessness.

A person who becomes homeless as a result of losing tied accommodation should not normally be considered as intentionally homeless. Nor should a person be expected to continue in employment if it would not be considered reasonable to do so simply in order to keep tied accommodation.[3]

In general, the *Code* continues, authorities should not treat as intentionally homeless those who have been driven to leave their

1 1987 Act, s 26.
2 See *Hynds v Midlothian District Council* 1986 SLT 54.
3 *Code* para 4.5.10.

accommodation because conditions have degenerated to a point where they could not in all the circumstances have been expected to remain, whether because of overcrowding, lack of basic amenities or severe emotional stress. The fleeing victim of domestic violence should never be regarded as having become homeless intentionally.

It is the Secretary of State's view, again as expressed in the *Code*, that a prime consideration in assessing intentionality should be the immediate cause of homelessness rather than events which may have taken place previously. He also urges that individuals once considered intentionally homeless should not be so considered for all time. A periodic review should be undertaken following which a different conclusion may be reached.[1]

Reading the *Code of Guidance* as an interpretation of the terms of the Act, one should be careful not to attribute to it too much authority. As the English Court of Appeal has pointed out, the *Code* is not binding upon local authorities which are simply obliged to have regard to it.[2] This view was trenchantly endorsed by Lord Jauncey in a Scottish case in 1987 when he said:

'it must be inconceivable that the Secretary of State intended the Code of Guidance to be a queue-jumper's charter and if a housing authority considers that in a particular case the circumstances do not merit the rigid application of a part of the code, I do not consider that they could be faulted in law or said to have acted unreasonably.'[3]

There have also been signs that some Scottish local authorities, at least, have interpreted intentionality against applicants more strictly than the *Code* might suggest[4] and a warning has been given that, whilst a local authority was perfectly entitled to remain completely silent as to whether it had actually considered the *Code* when making its decision in a case, if that decision was unexplained, then the presumption that the authority had indeed consulted the *Code* would be readily displaced by even slight indications to the contrary.[5]

As might have been expected, the issue of intentionality has given rise to many disputes between applicants and local authorities and these have led to challenges in the courts and to an overall legal position of some complexity. Some cases have focussed upon the initial circumstances of the alleged intentional homelessness itself. The Act

---

1 Para 4.5.11.
2 *De Falco v Crawley Borough Council* [1980] 1 All ER 913. See also *Kelly v Monklands District Council* 1986 SLT 169, discussed further below.
3 *Mazzaccherini v Argyll and Bute District Council* 1987 SCLR 475 at 478.
4 *See Watchman and Robson*, above, Chap 5.
5 *Wilson v Nithsdale District Council* 1992 SLT 1131 at 1134.

operated, for instance, in what may seem to be a harsh manner when it was held by the House of Lords that a family who left their home for temporary accommodation at a time when their eviction for non-payment of rent was imminent had brought their eventual homelessness upon themselves 'intentionally.' They had left their home before a court order had been obtained against them and their homelessness was, therefore, a direct consequence of a move they had not been forced to make.[1] On the other hand, in a later case in the English High Court, it was held not to be intentional homelessness where the applicants gave up accommodation which they had obtained from their landlord by deception when the landlord discovered their deception. It was at that point unreasonable for the applicants to continue to occupy the accommodation.[2] In a case of a different sort, the House of Lords reversed a very tough judgment of the English Court of Appeal. That court had held that, when a man originally from Bangladesh arranged to be joined in Britain by his wife and four children, they became intentionally homeless as a result of their abandonment of his single (shared) accommodation in London and his family's house in Bangladesh. The Lords held that there had been no intentional homelessness since no accommodation available for the family as a whole had been given up.[3]

The need to look to the interests of the family unit as a whole also arose in the case of a man who voluntarily gave up both his job and, with it, his tied house. It was held that neither he *nor his wife* could apply successfully for full assistance under the Act because of the deliberateness of his action.[4] On the other hand, Lord Ross pointed out in *Hynds*[5] that viewing people as 'family units' should not be taken too far. It may be appropriate in some circumstances but it should also be remembered that, under the Act, it is individuals who are, in the first place, homeless and who apply for accommodation.

This is an important point to bear in mind as we turn to the other principal type of case which has arisen in relation to intentionality. This is concerned not with the 'intentional' act itself but whether it is relevant to the case before the court. The applicant may wish to rely on his or her immediate homelessness resulting from an 'unintentional' act on his or her part. On the other hand, the authority may deny neither the homelessness nor the lack of immediate intentionality but

1 *Din v London Borough of Wandsworth* [1981] 3 All ER 881.
2 *R v Exeter City Council, ex p Gliddon* [1985] 1 All ER 493.
3 *Islam v London Borough of Hillingdon* [1981] 3 All ER 901.
4 *Lewis v North Devon District Council* [1981] 1 All ER 27.
5 *Hynds v Midlothian District Council* 1986 SLT 54.

may seek to rely on an earlier intentional act whose eventual consequence is the applicant's homelessness. The adoption of this latter approach in appropriate circumstances has been approved by courts on both sides of the Border. In one such case, the English Court of Appeal did not interfere with an authority's decision to look back to the original circumstances in which a family left Italy for the United Kingdom to determine the intentionality of their eventual homelessness rather than relying upon the family's departure from the home of relatives in England as the event leading most immediately to their loss of accommodation.[1] In *Hynds*, Lord Ross held that the petitioner's original intentional abandonment of the family home, despite successive subsequent moves leading to homelessness, left her unable to claim full assistance under the Act. This was in spite of an argument promoted on her behalf that her changed circumstances (she and her husband had separated since the original move) had led to a necessary break in the chain of causation between past intentionality and present homelessness. The change in the composition of the family unit was, in these circumstances, 'neither here nor there.'[2] A similar approach to the chain of causation was adopted in *Mazzaccherini v Argyll and Bute District Council*[3] in which the earlier abandonment by the petitioner of a secure tenancy in Glasgow to enable her to seek employment in Dunoon was treated as intentional, although her eventual eviction from premises in Dunoon was involuntary.

An important contribution to the interpretation of intentionality came, in very different circumstances, in the case of *Wincentzen v Monklands District Council*.[4] There a young woman whose parents had separated left accommodation with her father to live for a while with her mother. At the time of her departure her father told her that, if she went to live with her mother, he would never permit her to return. When eventually the woman claimed to be homeless, the local authority took the view that her loss of accommodation with her father had been intentional. As already noted, however, the Act provides that 'an act of omission in good faith on the part of a person who was unaware of any relevant fact shall not be treated as deliberate'[5] and it was successfully argued on behalf of the woman that her father's

---

1 *De Falco* [1980] 1 All ER 913. See also *Dyson v Kerrier District Council* [1980] 3 All ER 313.
2 1986 SLT 54 at 57. See also *Lambert v Ealing London Borough Council* [1982] 2 All ER 394.
3 1987 SCLR 475.
4 1987 SCLR 712, 1988 SLT 259 (OH) upheld on appeal by the First Division at 1989 SCLR 190, 1988 SLT 847.
5 1987 Act, s 26(3). See also *Robson v Kyle and Carrick District Council* 1994 SLT 259.

intentions, his state of mind, could be treated as a 'relevant fact' for these purposes. She had, in good faith, simply not believed that her father would not permit her return although, as a 'fact', he did indeed intend never to permit it. She was 'unaware' of this 'fact' and, therefore, not intentionally homeless.

(vi) Local connection with the area of another housing authority

Another factor which can, in some circumstances, affect an authority's duties under the Act is the extent to which the applicant has connections with the area of another housing authority. The idea is that an applicant from some other part of the country should not automatically be able to claim accommodation under the Act in the area in which the person happens to find him or herself. The duty, if any, to house the person should transfer to his or her native authority. The Act provides, therefore, that, at the stage of making 'appropriate inquiries', an authority may, if it thinks fit, inquire as to whether the applicant has a 'local connection with the area of another housing authority' in case this becomes relevant at a later stage. Under the Act a person is defined as having a local connection with an area (a) because he or she is or in the past was normally resident in it and his or her residence is or was of his or her own choice; or (b) because he or she is employed in it; or (c) because of family associations; or (d) because of any special circumstances.[1]

(vii) The 'persons' who may apply

Although it might appear that the question of who is to be regarded as a 'person' for the purposes of the Act is of such primary significance as to require to be taken ahead of the matters so far discussed, it is taken at this stage because it has in practice, not in general, been troublesome and the particular issues which have been raised are better understood in the light of the earlier discussion. (See also the issue of 'illegal immigrants' discussed later in this chapter.[2])

Two important matters were decided by the House of Lords in the English case of *Garlick v Oldham Metropolitan Borough Council*.[3] The first is that, although there is no explicit indication to this effect in the Act itself, the 'person' who may apply to a local authority cannot be a

---

1 Ibid, s 27. See p 172 below.
2 See p 175.
3 [1993] 2 All ER 65.

dependent child applying on the strength of his or her own vulnerability on grounds of age. As in *Kelly v Monklands District Council*[1] a young person may indeed be vulnerable and, if not dependent on others, may be fully entitled to apply for accommodation. A dependent child, however, and especially a child dependent on parents whose own application for assistance has already been rejected on grounds of intentional homelessness, is not entitled to make an application on his or her own behalf. This would by-pass the rule on intentionality, something for which Parliament would have made express provision if it had wished to do so.

The second part of the decision in the case (with Lord Slynn dissenting) was less obvious from the logic of the Act and may be regarded as rather harsh. The House of Lords held that someone who would not have the capacity to understand and respond to an offer of accommodation or undertake the responsibilities resulting from accepting accommodation could not personally be an applicant. In *Garlick*, the person was someone who lacked hearing, speech and education. A carer might be able to apply separately on the strength of the vulnerability of the disabled person but an application could not be made in the name of that person. Furthermore, the decision of an authority that a person did not have the capacity to apply was one which could be challenged by judicial review only on the grounds that it was irrational.[2]

These, then, will be the main concerns of an authority when it makes 'appropriate inquiries' as an initial response to an application. It must determine whether or not the person is homeless (or threatened with homelessness); whether or not he or she has priority need for accommodation; whether, if homeless, he or she is intentionally so; and, where relevant, whether he or she has a local connection elsewhere. The *Code*, in addition to offering the guidance already discussed on these specific issues, also makes general suggestions about the inquiries themselves. Flexibility of approach, speed and an eye to the urgency of the plight of the applicant and any consequent stress are mentioned. The extent of the inquiries should include

'the size and structure of the household; the nature and location of the accommodation last occupied; the reasons for leaving it and the prospects of return; the availability of accommodation elsewhere; any special problems such as illness or disability; the need for accommodation located some distance from a violent partner, or from any person alleged to have behaved violently; any

1 1986 SLT 169. See above.
2 [1993] 2 All ER 65 at 72.

immediate danger of abuse; financial circumstances and/or problems; nature of threatened homelessness; and the length of time the applicant expects to stay in the area. Other relevant information will often include the place and type of employment, family connections, or attendance at hospitals, day centres and schools.'[1]

The *Code* also makes reference to section 40 of the Act which creates the offence of making false statements to a housing authority when they are made knowingly or recklessly. Knowingly to withhold information is also an offence as is a failure subsequently to inform an authority of changes of facts material to the applicant's case. The section is there to prevent abuse of the Act but the *Code* urges sensitive implementation.[2]

The *Code* further stresses the importance of authorities using staff, for assessment of applications and making inquiries, who are trained in the requirements of the legislation and of the *Code* and who are skilled in interviewing. It is undesirable for elected members to be directly involved in assessment.[3]

On the completion of its inquiries into the case, the authority must notify the applicant of the outcome and, in the case of an 'adverse' decision, must give reasons. This and other procedural matters are mentioned in section 5 of this chapter.

(viii) *Temporary accommodation*

As well as requiring authorities to respond to applications by making the necessary inquiries about applicants and their circumstances, the Act recognises that, even before the outcome of these inquiries, there may be an urgent need for accommodation. It requires that if an authority has reason to believe that the applicant may be homeless and may have a priority need then it must ensure that accommodation is made available pending the outcome of the authority's inquiries. This duty applies whether or not the applicant has a local connection with the area of another authority.[4] At the same time the authority becomes bound to take steps to protect the moveable property of the applicant (but recovering a reasonable charge where appropriate) if there is a danger of loss or damage to the property and no other suitable arrangements have been made for its protection.[5]

1 Para 4.2.2.
2 Para 4.2.7.
3 Para 4.2.1.
4 1987 Act, s 29.
5 Ibid, s 36.

3. THE PRINCIPAL DUTIES

Depending upon the outcome of its preliminary inquiries, the Act imposes different levels of obligation upon the authority.

If, in the first place, the authority is satisfied that the applicant is neither homeless nor threatened with homelessness as these terms are defined under the Act, then the applicant has failed to get over even the first hurdle and the authority is under no obligation whatever towards him or her. Applicants who clear it, however, then face further tests.

The second type of applicant is the person who is homeless (or threatened with homelessness) but about whom the authority either is not satisfied that he or she has a priority need, or while satisfied of that, is also satisfied that the person became homeless (or threatened) intentionally. In this case the authority does not normally come under any duty to find accommodation for the applicant, but it is obliged simply to furnish the applicant with advice and appropriate assistance.[1] 'Advice' is not defined in the Act but 'appropriate assistance' is defined as such assistance as an authority considers it 'appropriate in the circumstances to give him in any attempts that he may make to ensure that accommodation becomes or does not cease to be available for his occupation.'[1] The *Code* offers some guidance as well as asking authorities to respond as helpfully and constructively as they are able. Advice and assistance, it says, should always be positive. It should at least include advice on housing, financial, legal and social matters, as appropriate, or information on where to get such advice. Beyond that, the *Code* recognises that appropriate advice and assistance will vary according to circumstances but urges that authorities keep themselves prepared to offer help by maintaining comprehensive information about housing possibilities in all sectors in their areas.[2]

There is one sub-group of these applicants normally entitled to only advice and appropriate assistance who can claim a rather higher level of help. For applicants who are actually homeless and do have a priority need but who became homeless intentionally an authority must ensure that accommodation is made available for such period as it considers will give them a reasonable opportunity to find their own accommodation.[3] There is no precision about the length of time for which accommodation has to be provided but the *Code* advises that

---

1 Ibid, s 31(3)(b) and (4).
2 *Code* Chap 6.
3 1987 Act, s 31(3)(a).

authorities should not arbitrarily nor too quickly withdraw the provision of accommodation. As far as possible, people in priority need particularly where children are involved should not be left without a house.[1] The type of accommodation to be provided may vary—as it does when a longer term commitment is involved and this is discussed below. It has been held that such accommodation provided on a temporary basis need not be of the standard normally to be expected of permanent accommodation.[2]

The highest level of duty is owed to an applicant who is homeless and who has a priority need but did not become homeless intentionally. For such an applicant, who is the main beneficiary of the Act, an authority must ensure that accommodation becomes available for his or her occupation. For an applicant satisfying the same conditions but who is, as yet, only threatened with homelessness, an authority must take reasonable steps to ensure that accommodation does not cease to be available for his or her occupation.[3] Once again the reasonableness of the steps to be taken is not further specified and again much will depend on the circumstances. The *Code* does not address itself directly to this question but it does devote a chapter to the 'Prevention of Homelessness.'[4] It discusses the ways in which people may risk losing their homes and the steps which may be taken to prevent this whether they are private or public sector tenants, owner occupiers, a family in dispute, or people leaving hospitals or prisons or being displaced by redevelopment schemes. Whatever 'reasonable steps' are taken to avoid the threat of homelessness are taken against a background of the near certainty that, if they fail, an authority's obligations do not, as a result, cease but instead change to the need to secure new accommodation to replace the person's former home.

As to the obligation to secure that accommodation becomes available the Act does spell this out a little further. In the first place, since another post-*Puhlhofer* amendment,[5] the accommodation to be provided must not be accommodation which is overcrowded or which may endanger the health of the occupants.[6] Although these standards are arguably slightly higher in the form consolidated in the 1987 Act than they were previously, the precise standard required is not completely clear. It might be thought that accommodation should be

1 Para 5.1.3.
2 *R v Exeter City Council, ex p Gliddon* [1985] 1 All ER 493.
3 1987 Act, s 32.
4 Chap 3.
5 See p 156 above.
6 1987 Act, s 32(5).

'suitable'[1] or that it should be 'reasonable' (to parallel the way in which accommodation must fail a test of reasonableness if a person occupying it is to be held to be homeless in the first place). Neither of these qualities is, however, required by the Act itself and it has recently been held that they are not to be implied.[2] This creates the paradox that rehousing a person held to be homeless on account of the 'unreasonableness' of his or her first accommodation in a similarly unreasonable house will nevertheless satisfy the Act's terms—producing the absurdity of a potentially endless merry-go-round of rehousings and findings of homelessness.

Secondly, it is made clear that the provision of a council house is not the sole approach.[3] As alternatives, ensuring that the applicant obtains accommodation from some other person and even giving advice and assistance to ensure that such accommodation is obtained will suffice. Elaborating on these statutory possibilities the *Code* asks authorities to have available advice, not only on council housing, but on house purchase for those who (perhaps with the aid of a local authority loan) may be able to afford it; the private rented sector; other housing authorities; new towns; housing associations; and mobile homes—'Wherever possible housing found should be reasonably convenient and avoid undue disruption of education, employment or other personal or social ties.'[4] The *Code* does, however, recognise that, in some situations, interim arrangements may have to be made before permanent accommodation can be found. These might include the temporary occupation of property awaiting demolition or improvement; hostels and refuges; and, as a last resort, accommodation in guest houses or hotels. In whatever way accommodation is made available for an applicant, the Act itself provides that the authority can charge for it. An authority may require such reasonable amount as it may determine towards the rent whether the house is the authority's own or is paid for by it.[5] As in the case of applicants temporarily provided with accommodation pending the outcome of inquiries, there is a duty upon any authority required to provide further temporary or permanent accommodation (or to ensure the continued availability of accommodation) to provide also for the

---

1 The term used in the parallel legislation for England and Wales in s 69 of the Housing Act 1985.
2 *Bradley v Motherwell District Council* 1994 SCLR 160 (Notes).
3 1987 Act, s 35.
4 Para 5.1.6 and Chap 5 generally.
5 1987 Act, s 35(2). Temporary lets to homeless people do not become secure or assured tenancies.

protection of an applicant's property. Reasonable conditions may be attached including the power to recover reasonable charges and to dispose of the property if unclaimed.[1]

Although the main impact of the Act is to impose the principal duty upon the local authority to which application is made by an appropriate applicant, the burden, or some of it, can sometimes shift to others. In the first place, the Act imposes a standing obligation upon housing authorities at large as well as social work authorities to co-operate in the discharge of duties under the Act. Thus, if a housing authority requests assistance from another housing authority, a new town corporation, a registered housing association or Scottish Homes or if it asks a social work authority (regional council) to exercise any of its functions in relation to a particular case, then such an authority or body must co-operate in rendering such assistance as is reasonable in the circumstances.[2] In the *Code* the Secretary of State says that such co-operation is vital if the effective implementation of the Act is to be achieved.[3] Other bodies with housing responsibilities may be able to help where they have accommodation which is useful because it is in another area (eg away from domestic violence) or because it caters for special needs.

Of particular importance is the assistance which may be required of social work authorities. The general consequences of the division between social work and housing responsibilities and the remedial proposals of the Morris Committee were mentioned earlier,[4] and nowhere is co-operation between authorities both on individual cases and in terms of formal structures for liaison more important than in the case of homelessness. The *Code* suggests that co-operation may be particularly necessary and helpful in the areas of preventive action— the stage of initial inquiries into a case and the provision of emergency services and special supportive accommodation. It may be assumed that, for the most part, the general duty of different authorities to co-operate in the discharge of their functions under the Act will not be one to be enforced by the courts but the *Kelly v Monklands District Council* case illustrates one way in which it may be judicially considered. In that case, one of the grounds on which the authority's decision was faulted was that its officers had failed to have due regard to the *Code of Guidance* and had failed to take into account material

1 Ibid, s 36. See *Code* Chap 7.
2 Ibid, s 38.
3 Para 2.9 and Chap 2 generally.
4 See p 39 above.

which they ought to have taken into account. They had failed to cooperate with the social work authority in that they had taken no account at all of that authority's views on the vulnerability of the applicants.[1]

In some cases, responsibility for discharging duties under the Act is not only to be shared with other authorities but may be formally transferred from one housing authority to another and this brings us back to the question of 'local connection.' If an applicant is found to be homeless, in priority need and not intentionally homeless—circumstances which would normally require the provision of accommodation by the authority applied to—the authority does not become subject to the principal duty:

(a) if it is of the opinion that
    (i) neither the applicant nor a person reasonably expected to reside with him or her has a local connection with its area and
    (ii) the applicant does have a local connection with the area of another housing authority and
    (iii) he or she will not run the risk of domestic violence in that other area; and
(b) if it notifies the other authority of the application and of its own opinion as above. In this case the duty to secure the availability of accommodation passes to the 'notified' authority—provided that the opinion of the 'notifying' authority turns out to be correct.[2]

What is to be regarded as a 'local connection' for the purpose of the Act is not without difficulty and has given rise to actions in the courts. In the important case of *Eastleigh Borough Council v Betts*[3] decided in the House of Lords, the application of the local authority's internal guideline on local connection was challenged. This provided that a local connection with its area would be achieved only after six months' residence in it. The challenge was on the basis that any period of normal residence in the area should establish a local connection but this was rejected on the grounds that local connection flowed from a range of factors of which residence was only one; it was not unreasonable for an authority to establish an internal guideline on its normal requirements as to residence, and, provided this guideline was not applied inflexibly, a decision based on it could not be faulted by the courts. Another point of difficulty arose in *R v Newham London Borough Council, ex parte Tower Hamlets London Borough Council*[4]

---

1 1986 SLT 169.
2 1987 Act, s 33.
3 [1983] 2 All ER 1111.
4 [1992] 2 All ER 767.

where an applicant arriving from Bangladesh was turned down by one local authority on grounds of intentionality. On application to a second authority, however, that authority found, by reference to conditions in its own area rather than that of the first authority, no intentionality but referred the applicant back to the first authority on grounds of local connection. The referral was flawed because, at both points of decision, conditions in the first authority had not been taken into account. Lord Donaldson MR insisted that

'good administration and comity between local authorities demand that . . . the authority should take full account of the general circumstances prevailing in relation to housing in both their areas and should give serious consideration to whether, notwithstanding that the conditions of referral are satisfied . . . the public interest requires that the rehousing should be undertaken by it rather than by the other authority.'[1]

The court went on to repeat criticisms made in earlier cases[2] of the statutory mechanisms themselves and called for legislative reform.[3]

In the meantime the handling of cases involving notification of another housing authority may clearly be the cause of some disagreement both between the authorities themselves (primarily because of the administrative and financial burden of the duty to be discharged) and between the original authority and the applicant who may have strong views. The interpretation of the relevant terms of the Act will not always be straightforward and this is acknowledged by the provision of machinery for the settling of disputes. The Act assumes that, in the first place, any questions arising will be settled by agreement between the two authorities. Failing that, there has to be resort to 'appropriate arrangements' prescribed by the Secretary of State. According to these, the matter in dispute is referred to an individual arbiter appointed from a panel drawn up by COSLA with power to inquire into and determine the issue.[4] COSLA has also adopted a nonstatutory code of procedure designed to assist authorities to resolve disputes without recourse to the formal arrangements for arbitration.[5] The *Code* briefly considers the transfer of duties under the Act and reminds authorities that the transfer procedures apply only where the 'other' authority and area are within Great Britain.[6] Thus, whilst it is

1 [1992] 2 All ER 767 at 778.
2 See especially Lord Templeman in *R v Slough Borough Council, ex p Ealing London Borough Council* [1981] 1 All ER 601 at 617.
3 [1992] 2 All ER 767 at 776, 783 and 784.
4 SI 1978/661.
5 The procedure has also been adopted jointly by relevant local authority associations in England and Wales. See *Agreement on Procedures for Referrals of the Homeless.*
6 Para 4.6 and Annex B.

perfectly possible for a local connection to be established with an English local authority, this does not apply, for instance, to an authority in the Irish Republic as *R v Bristol City Council, ex parte Browne*[1] made clear. In that case the applicant came originally from Tralee but had escaped domestic violence there and arrived in Bristol. When the city council's decision not to provide accommodation in Bristol was challenged, it was recognised that it could not rely upon the formal transfer procedure to pass the responsibility back to Tralee. The court also accepted, however, that it was competent for the council to give assistance to secure 'accommodation from some other person' by arranging for such accommodation in Tralee through the community welfare officer there—despite the applicant's wish to avoid returning (even to a house away from her husband) because of her fear of continuing domestic violence.

4. IMMIGRANTS TO THE UNITED KINGDOM

It will be noted that, although some of the cases referred to (especially on intentional homelessness) have arisen out of circumstances involving people moving to the United Kingdom from other countries, no general distinction is drawn by the 1987 Act between applicants for housing on grounds of their country of origin. Two fairly recent developments in the law, perhaps rather invidiously grouped together in this account, deserve some attention.

Asylum-seekers and their dependants

New rules enacted in the Asylum and Immigration Appeals Act 1993 have affected (since they came into force on 26 July 1993[2]) both local authority procedures on how to handle applications from people who are or may be asylum-seekers or their dependants (spouse or child under 18) and its duties to house asylum-seekers under the 1987 Act.[3] An asylum-seeker and dependants of an asylum-seeker[4] are defined as people whose claim (or the claim of the person on whom they are

---

1 [1979] 3 All ER 344.
2 See SI 1993/1655.
3 The *Code* (which in its 1991 version (para 4.4.4.6) recorded that 'Refugees and asylum seekers may be vulnerable if they are still subject to physical or psychological effects of trauma or persecution suffered before entering Britain') is also being modified to take account of the statutory changes.
4 Somewhat ironically termed 'qualifying persons' in Schedule 1 to the 1993 Act.

dependent) for asylum has been recorded by the Secretary of State (in practice, the Home Office Immigration and Nationality Department[1]) and it is the duty of a housing authority which has reason to believe that an applicant is an asylum-seeker to include in its inquiries such inquiries as are necessary to satisfy itself as to whether the applicant is indeed an asylum-seeker and, if so, whether any duty is owed to him or her.[2] If the applicant's status is established as an asylum-seeker (or dependant)—principally by reference to documentation supplied by the Home Office—the duties owed to him or her are much less than those owed to other applicants. Thus, if the person has (or has available) any accommodation that it would be reasonable for him or her to occupy, nothing shall require the authority to secure that other accommodation should be made available.[3] In assessing the 'reasonableness' of accommodation, regard is to be had to the 'general circumstances prevailing in relation to housing' in the district of the authority.[4] If such accommodation is found not to be available to the applicant and a duty to secure the availability of accommodation is established, it is a duty which continues only so long as the person is an asylum-seeker, and the person's needs are, therefore, to be regarded as temporary only.[5] If a person treated as an asylum-seeker is subsequently given leave to remain in the United Kingdom, any application under the 1987 Act must be treated as a fresh application in relation to which new inquiries must be made.[6]

Illegal immigrants

The 1987 Act does not explicitly qualify its reference to the persons who may be applicants for housing in any way to exclude people who are illegal immigrants to the country. In the recent case of *R v Secretary of State, ex p Tower Hamlets*[7] decided by the English Court of Appeal it was, however, made clear (reaffirming decisions in earlier cases) that the definition of persons must be assumed to exclude those who were illegally in the country—whether they had unlawfully by-passed immigration control completely or had obtained leave to enter on the

---

1 Asylum and Immigration Appeals Act 1993, s 5.
2 Ibid, Sch 1, para 2.
3 Ibid, s 4(1).
4 Ibid, s 4(2).
5 Ibid, s 4(3).
6 See ibid, s 4(4). Other procedural provisions concerning asylum-seekers are contained in Sch 1 to the Act—including a substituted rule on the referral of applications to another housing authority.
7 [1993] 3 All ER 439.

basis of a misrepresentation (including representations as to the availability of accommodation in the United Kingdom). This in itself may be regarded as a relatively uncontroversial conclusion. However, what the Court of Appeal also decided and for which it has attracted sharp criticism[1] is that a person may be treated as an illegal immigrant before the immigration authorities have decided this to be the case and before any court has determined the correctness of their view. 'A person who steals my purse is a thief, whether or not he is prosecuted, convicted or sentenced. So it is with an illegal immigrant.'[2] In particular, therefore, the court held a housing authority may itself make inquiries as to an applicant's status and may (and perhaps must), with special regard to the housing circumstances of the applicant, make representations to the immigration authorities. In the meantime, and of crucial importance, the housing authority may itself take the view that the person is an illegal immigrant and treat him or her accordingly. As the court points out, the consequence of this might be that the authority would take steps to evict an applicant (and his or her family) from accommodation temporarily allocated during the period of making inquiries. The legality of such a move would itself be challengeable by judicial review and, of course, a housing authority would be expected to revise its opinion of an applicant if the Home Office was eventually to give leave (or to reaffirm the original leave) to enter the country. The objection which has been taken to the decision, however, is that housing authorities are being required to act as immigration authorities of first resort—with the obligation to make intrusive inquiries, report on them to the central department and, in the meantime, deny housing facilities on the strength of their own decisions alone.

5. PROCEDURE AND ENFORCEMENT OF DUTIES

Since leaving consideration of the duty to make preliminary inquiries, the emphasis in this chapter has been upon the substantive rights and duties arising out of an authority's assessment of an applicant's position following those inquiries. This section returns to some further procedural aspects of the implementation of Part II of the Act including those concerned with the enforcement of local authority duties under the Act.

1 See eg N Dobson 'Immigration and homelessness [1993] NLJ 1436.
2 [1993] 3 All ER 439 at 444.

Section 30 of the 1987 Act requires that all applicants for assistance must be informed of the decision in their case. Each applicant has to be notified of the outcome of all aspects of the inquiry: whether homeless, whether in priority need, whether homeless intentionally, whether another housing authority is itself being notified under the transfer provisions. In addition, any decision which is in any sense adverse to the applicant (on eg priority need or intentionality) has to be accompanied by reasons. The duty to 'notify' an applicant is satisfied if the notification and reasons are made available for collection for a reasonable period at the authority's office and the assumption must be, therefore, that written notification is required. The *Code* confirms this interpretation and asks for 'a sufficient and straightforward indication of the reasons' for an authority's decision which should be made quickly.[1]

The importance of this section is that, in requiring formal notification of decisions and reasons, it should ensure that care is taken over inquiries made and that adverse decisions are not made lightly. In this, as in other forms of administrative decision-making, the imposition of a duty to give reasons for decisions is designed to produce better decisions. It may also be that, in this case, the requirement of procedural fairness of this sort is designed to compensate for the absence of any statutory right of appeal. In some other legislation affecting local authorities there is an appeal against their decisions either to the Secretary of State (as with planning appeals) or to the sheriff (as with school attendance orders or demolition and closing orders). Part II of the 1987 Act makes provision for neither sort of appeal and, subject to the limited exceptions discussed below, a person aggrieved by the interpretation a housing authority has placed upon the application of the Act to the circumstances of his or her case simply has to put up with it.

The person may, of course, apply again for assistance at a later date in the hope of a more favourable decision. We have seen that intentionality should not be considered to endure for ever and other circumstances may change. Alternatively the applicant may seek a political remedy, perhaps through a local councillor, in the hope of an improved decision. Another suggestion made in the *Code* is that, in the absence of any formal statutory appeal to another tribunal, authorities should consider the possibility of instituting internal appeals procedures of their own. Speed of handling such appeals is very important in all circumstances but detailed arrangements, including the question of whether or not to involve councillors at the

1 Paras 4.2.8–4.2.10.

appellate stage, are for authorities themselves to determine. Authorities are reminded that the institution of internal appeals does not remove from disappointed applicants the opportunity to seek judicial review (below).[1] Or, if he or she is convinced that maladministration is involved (for instance, malice) then the decision might be taken to the local ombudsman for investigation and report. The ombudsman has the power to recommend the provision of a house. Despite the Secretary of State's involvement in the working of the Act including his issue of the *Code*, he has no power to intervene to correct or reverse an individual local authority decision although, if it appeared to him that an authority was failing to discharge its duties under the Act, there would be the possibility of his commencing default proceedings under the Local Government (Scotland) Act 1973.[2]

This final option can be regarded as only a last resort; it is extremely unlikely to be deployed by the Secretary of State unless there was quite flagrant and widespread failure by a local authority; and it is, therefore, inappropriate for the individual aggrieved applicant. Much more readily available are the courts for, although there is no explicit provision for appeals under the Act, it is possible to apply to the Court of Session for judicial review of an authority's decision.

From the point of view of the aggrieved applicant, the process of judicial review carries with it three quite substantial disadvantages although the third of these has been somewhat diminished. The first disadvantage is that the grounds upon which judicial review may be sought are quite limited.[3] It is not a general appeal but requires the applicant to show that, in one way or another, the housing authority has acted outwith its statutory powers or has used its powers in an unreasonable manner or has failed to observe the rules of natural justice or otherwise behaved procedurally unfairly. It is not sufficient for the applicant simply to complain that the decision of the authority is one he or she does not like. On the other hand, as we have seen in the cases already referred to, judicial review has provided the opportunity for applicants to establish that an authority has misunderstood such central concepts in the Act as 'intentionality', 'vulnerability' and 'local connection.' The failure of an authority to take any account of the *Code of Guidance* can be challenged.[4] Where, however, an authority has not made any error of law of this sort but has exercised

---

1 *Code* para 4.2.11.
2 Section 211.
3 For full treatment of the law of judicial review of administrative action, see A W Bradley 'Administrative Law' in volume 1 of *Stair Memorial Encyclopaedia*.
4 See eg *Kelly v Monklands District Council* 1986 SLT 169.

its powers to decide against the applicant, judicial review will not normally succeed. Only if the applicant can persuade the court to accept that the authority has reached a decision no reasonable authority could reach will the court rule in his or her favour. This must be regarded as a finding which will be most infrequent in practice but it was a part of Lord Ross' reasoning in the case of *Kelly v Monklands District Council*.[1]

The general assumption that the role of judicial review is, and ought to be, very restricted was given authoritative support in an English case by the House of Lords. There the court took the view that the widespread recourse to judicial review in homelessness cases was wrong; it should not be used 'to monitor the actions of local authorities under the Act save in the exceptional case.'[2] In a more recent case in the Court of Session, Lord Clyde expressed doubts about how readily the views of the House of Lords should be applied to homelessness cases arising in Scotland but reaffirmed the general limitations of the process of judicial review. There can be no substitution of the court's views on the merits of the applicant's case. The grounds of review are restricted to 'matters of illegality, of improprieties of procedure and of improprieties in the exercise of the power.'[3]

The second limitation in the process of judicial review lies in the form of remedy available. What the applicant wants is probably a house and perhaps damages. In many cases of judicial review, however, it may be inappropriate for the court, upon finding that an authority has reached an invalid decision, to do more than reduce (quash) that decision—leaving the authority to make another.[4] On the other hand, it is clear that, in cases where it is plain that the court's reduction of the first decision (perhaps because 'vulnerability' or 'intentionality' had been misconstrued) means that the authority's obligation to provide accommodation is beyond doubt, then the court may so order. This was the outcome in *Kelly* in which it was also held that damages may be awardable in cases where the court holds that the authority has been in breach of its duties under the Act.[5] Damages were awarded in that case. Amounts of damages awarded in individual cases have however been small.

1 1986 SLT 169.
2 *Puhlhofer v Hillingdon London Borough Council* [1986] 1 All ER 467 at 474.
3 *Stewart v Monklands District Council* 1987 SLT 630 at 632–633.
4 See eg *Wincentzen v Monklands District Council* 1988 SLT 259.
5 1986 SLT 169. See also *McAlinden v Bearsden and Milngavie District Council* 1986 SLT 191.

The third restriction is that, following the decision of the House of Lords in *Brown v Hamilton District Council*,[1] judicial review can be obtained only in the Court of Session in Edinburgh. Sheriffs have no power to consider these applications and this operates as a severe limitation. On the other hand, as a consequence of the *Brown* decision, the opportunity was taken to reform and to speed up the procedure to be followed in the Court of Session. This was achieved by the introduction with effect from April 1985 of new rules of court for applications for judicial review.[2] They are not confined to homelessness cases but many homelessness applications have now been made and the experience of these shows that a procedure which might formerly have taken many months can now produce a decision within about a month. After the initial lodging of the petition and relevant papers (at which point an interim order may be made) a hearing before a single judge may follow within a couple of weeks. If it is not possible for the application to be determined at that hearing, another hearing may follow. The court may, if the application is granted, make any appropriate order (whether or not it was sought in the application itself). This includes reduction (quashing), declarator (a declaration of the respective rights of the parties), interdict (to prevent action by the authority), implement (to require action) and damages.

1 1983 SLT 397.
2 SI 1985/500 promulgating a new Rule of Court 260B.

CHAPTER 11

Sub-standard housing: powers

Housing authorities are equipped with a variety of powers designed collectively to ensure the removal by their demolition or improvement of the numbers of sub-standard houses in Scotland. They include powers directed at whole areas of houses and others directed at individual houses. Some operate as sticks to beat private householders into action; some act as carrots to encourage and assist improvement; and, of course, authorities have powers to improve their own housing stock. The powers available to local authorities have been the subject of adjustment from time to time but, despite suggestions from the Government of wider-ranging reforms,[1] have not been substantially changed since the mid-1970s. The following discussion is of existing local authority powers and, making somewhat artificial lines of division, this chapter will look at:

(1) the 'tolerable standard' which contains the central definition of officially acceptable housing standards;
(2) area procedures for the treatment of sub-standard houses whether by clearance or improvement;
(3) procedures in relation to individual properties to ensure their demolition, closure, improvement or repair; and
(4) overcrowding and houses in multiple occupation.

The next chapter deals with the system of improvement and other grants.

1. THE TOLERABLE STANDARD

The housing plans of local authorities, in addition to dealing with proposals for the provision of accommodation by new building, are also expected to refer to their intentions in relation to slum clearance and

---

1 See eg *Private Housing Renewal: The Government's Proposals for Scotland* SDD 1988.

rehabilitation. This reflects the statutory requirement contained in the 1987 Act that authorities must secure that all houses which do not meet what is called the 'tolerable standard' are closed, demolished or brought up to the tolerable standard within such period as is reasonable in all the circumstances. Authorities are under a statutory duty to survey their districts from time to time for this purpose.[1]

The concept of the 'tolerable standard' as the modern test of satisfactory housing was introduced by the Housing (Scotland) Act 1969 to replace the older, and less precise, formula of 'fitness for human habitation.' That Act introduced a list of fairly specific features required of a house before it was judged to meet the tolerable standard and, with some more recent modifications, these are now set out in section 86 of the 1987 Act. A house meets the tolerable standard if it:

(a) is structurally stable;
(b) is substantially free from rising or penetrating damp;
(c) has satisfactory provision for natural and artificial lighting, for ventilation and for heating;
(d) has an adequate piped supply of wholesome water available within the house;
(e) has a sink provided with a satisfactory supply of both hot and cold water within the house;
(f) has a water closet available for the exclusive use of the occupants of the house and suitably located within the house;
(g) has an effective system for the drainage and disposal of foul and surface water;
(h) has satisfactory facilities for the cooking of food within the house;
(i) has satisfactory access to all external doors and out-buildings.

The Secretary of State is empowered to vary, extend or amplify these criteria by order.[2] They have not, in fact, been altered in this way although, for the purpose of improvement orders, the tolerable standard is modified by legislation.[3] Otherwise, it is this tolerable standard as defined in section 86 which is the central test of housing conditions and which is incorporated into all local authority powers.

1 1987 Act, s 85.
2 Ibid, s 86(2).
3 Ibid, s 88(2) and see p 191 below.

2. AREA PROCEDURES FOR THE TREATMENT OF SUB-STANDARD HOUSING: HOUSING ACTION AREAS

We should start with a word of explanation about the distinction made in this chapter between the powers available to an authority to take action against sub-standard housing in relation to individual houses on the one hand, and, on the other hand, in relation to defined areas usually containing large numbers of houses. Later in the chapter we shall be concerned with the orders an authority can make to ensure, for example, the demolition or improvement of a single house. These orders can be made in relation to a very large number of houses in the same area but the essence of the procedure to be adopted is that action has to be directed towards each individual house affected. The essence of the area approach, on the other hand, is that a large area of housing is designated for comprehensive treatment where the effective removal or improvement of sub-standard housing so demands. Clearly such an approach has important consequences for the individual houses within the area and these have to be taken account of but underpinning the area procedures is the idea of comprehensive treatment. The current form of area procedure is the housing action area (HAA). This replaced the housing treatment area of the Housing (Scotland) Act 1969 and the old clearance area of the Housing (Scotland) Act 1966 and earlier legislation.

(a) The power to declare an HAA

There are three types of HAA. The first is the housing action area for demolition (HAAD) which may be declared where an authority is satisfied that the greater part of the houses within the area do not meet the tolerable standard and that the most effective way of dealing with the area is by securing the demolition of all buildings within it. There are two qualifications to this general statement. One is that an HAAD cannot include the site of a building unless at least a part of the building consists of a house which does not meet the tolerable standard. The other is that the resolution declaring the HAAD may provide for the exclusion from demolition of any part of a building used for commercial purposes.[1]

The second type is the housing action area for improvement (HAAI) which may be declared where the greater part of the houses in

1 Ibid, s 89.

the area lack one or more of the 'standard amenities'[1] or do not meet the tolerable standard and where the area may be dealt with by the carrying out of works of improvement sufficient to put all houses in the area up to the tolerable standard and in good repair. The authority may also insist upon the provision of standard amenities throughout the area where it is satisfied that the houses in the area have a future life of not less than 10 years.[2]

The third type is the housing action area for demolition and improvement (HAADI) where the same conditions apply as in the HAAI but where the authority believes that the remedy lies in a combination of both improvement and demolition.[3] In the case of the last two types of action area, the requirement that the greater part of the houses lack a standard amenity or do not meet the tolerable standard may be waived by the Secretary of State on the application of the authority.[4] The choice of which areas should be made the subject of HAA procedures is one for the local authority although the Secretary of State has the power to give directions as to the identification of suitable areas.[5]

Procedure

The first step to be taken by an authority is to pass a draft resolution declaring an HAA of the appropriate type. The form and content of the draft resolution are prescribed by the Secretary of State.[6] It must contain a statement of the standard of improvement specified by the authority for an HAAI or HAADI. The draft resolution must also identify buildings to be demolished; sub-standard houses requiring to be brought up to the new specified standard; and sub-standard houses forming only part of a building and requiring integration with some other part.[7]

The authority then submits the draft resolution together with an accompanying map to the Secretary of State who must acknowledge receipt.[8] Within the following 28 days the Secretary of State may direct the authority to rescind the resolution or notify it that he does

---

1 Ibid, s 244 and Sch 18. Standard amenities themselves are discussed with improvement grants. See p 201 below.
2 Ibid, s 90.
3 Ibid, s 91.
4 Ibid, s 92(2).
5 Ibid, s 92(1).
6 Ibid, s 92(3) and SI 1974/1982.
7 Ibid, s 92(4).
8 Ibid, s 94(1) and (2).

not propose to direct rescission. Alternatively he may notify the authority that he requires more time for consideration of the resolution. This is the one point in the HAA procedure at which the Secretary of State can intervene to veto or delay the local authority's plans.

If the Secretary of State notifies the authority within the 28 days that he proposes not to direct rescission or if, within the same period, the authority receives no notification at all from the Secretary of State, then the authority must give publicity to the draft resolution. This requires publication, in at least two newspapers circulating locally, of when and where a copy of the resolution and map may be inspected. Notice must also be served on every owner, lessee and occupier of affected premises which must state that the recipient may within two months make representations concerning the resolution to the local authority.[1]

The Secretary of State has laid particular emphasis upon the importance at this and succeeding stages of full explanation and discussion of the authority's proposals. Various possible procedures are suggested including contact with local groups and the holding of meetings. Specifically the Secretary of State has recommended the designation of a particular member of the authority's staff as project manager for the HAA whose responsibilities would extend from the initial consultations through to the practical implementation of the scheme.[2]

Within a further period of two months the authority must either pass a final resolution confirming its draft resolution, with or without modifications, or rescind the resolution—in either case after having regard to representations received. This must then be followed by a further process of publicity and notification of those affected. A copy of the final resolution must also be sent to the Secretary of State.[3] Although at this stage he has no power to vary the area covered by the resolution, he may do so at the time of his confirmation of any compulsory purchase order that may be required.

(b) The consequences of the declaration of an HAA

Once the HAA, of whatever type, has been declared a number of consequences follow, the more important of which are:

---

1 Ibid, s 94(5)–(7).
2 See SDD Memorandum No 68/1975.
3 1987 Act, s 95(1) and Sch 8, Pt I.

(i) Acquisition of land, compensation and the duty to rehouse

The Act confers upon the authority the power to acquire land (including land surrounded by an HAA or adjoining it) either by agreement or compulsorily in order that the authority itself may carry out the necessary works of demolition or improvement. Compulsory acquisition must be in accordance with the procedure laid down in the Acquisition of Land (Authorisation Procedure) (Scotland) Act 1947 subject to certain modifications affecting amongst other things the actual form of the compulsory purchase order. The time-limits within which a CPO must be submitted to the Secretary of State following the publication and service of the final resolution are six months in the case of an HAAD and nine months in the case of an HAAI or HAADI.[1]

Compensation payable in respect of land acquired compulsorily is assessed according to normal principles.[2] The market value is payable to owners forced to sell but in the case of a house not meeting the tolerable standard this may not exceed the 'cleared site value' save that such compensation must be supplemented if the local authority is satisfied that the house has been well-maintained and payment is to be made to an owner-occupier or to the person responsible for the maintenance and repair of the house. A local authority, when acquiring a house, must issue a notice indicating whether or not it intends to make a 'well-maintained' payment. If the authority gives notice that it does not so intend, an aggrieved person may appeal to the Secretary of State within 21 days.[3] The amount of a 'well-maintained' payment is calculated by applying a prescribed multiplier to the rateable value of the house.[4] The present multiplier is fixed at 12.7.[5] Since the abolition of rates on domestic property from 1 April 1989, the concept of a 'rateable value' for a house has become rather artificial. For these purposes, it is defined as the rateable value as at 31 March 1989 but with the possibility of adjustment if there have been 'material changes' and, indeed, the invention of a figure if the house did not exist on that date.[6] Alternatively an 'owner-occupier's supplement' may be payable to those who have occupied the house as a private

1 1987 Act, s 95(2) and Sch 8, Pt II.
2 Ibid, s 95(3) and Sch 8, Pt III.
3 Ibid, s 305.
4 Ibid, s 306.
5 SI 1983/1804. The fixing of this multiplier appears to have survived a subsequent rating revaluation.
6 Abolition of Domestic Rates, Etc (Scotland) Act 1987, s 5 (as amended by the Local Government Finance Act 1988).

dwelling for at least two years. This supplement brings the compensation payable up to the full compulsory purchase value.[1]

Other forms of compensation may include home loss payments which may be paid whether or not there are other entitlements to compensation. They are made in recognition of the attachment to their homes built up by owners or tenants who have occupied a house as their only or main residence for at least five years. Calculation of the amount used to be made by reference to the rateable value. Payments are now at a flat rate of £1500.[2]

Disturbance payments to cover removal expenses and other incidental costs of removal are payable to persons forced to leave their homes.[3] The payments are for tenants and for owners who receive only the cleared site value. Other owners are compensated for disturbance as a part of the general compensation for acquisition.

Finally, any person displaced from residential accommodation as a result of the acquisition of land in an HAA will, if suitable alternative accommodation is not otherwise available, be entitled to be rehoused and, in so far as practicable, this must be within a reasonable distance from his or her present home.[4]

(ii) Grant and loan assistance to residents in an HAA and the power of the authority to execute works itself

As will be seen, special provisions enabling the payment of improvement and repairs grants at higher percentage rates apply to applicants within HAAIs or HAADIs.[5]

Additionally the local authority is required to make loans available to residents of HAAIs or HAADIs who apply within nine months of the final resolution for assistance in bringing their properties up to the required standard and who, by virtue of the security that their properties offer, can reasonably be expected to meet the obligations arising out of the loan. The authority has a discretionary power to offer loans for a smaller amount. No loan may, in any case, exceed the total amount of expenditure to which an applicant may be liable *after* any improvement or repairs grant to which he or she may be entitled has been deducted.[6]

---

1 1987 Act, ss 308–311.
2 Land Compensation (Scotland) Act 1973, s 28 as substituted by SI 1989/47.
3 Ibid, ss 34–35.
4 1987 Act, s 98 and Land Compensation (Scotland) Act 1973, s 36.
5 See pp 205 and 208 below.
6 1987 Act, s 217.

Instead, an authority may agree with an owner to make arrangements for the execution of the necessary works at the owner's expense.[1]

(iii) *Power to retain houses for occupation*

An authority may postpone demolition of a building within an HAAD or HAADI which has been purchased by or otherwise belongs to it in circumstances where the authority considers that it must be continued in use as housing accommodation for the time being.[2]

(iv) *Control of occupation of houses in HAAs*

As soon as practicable after the Secretary of State's approval of or acquiescence in the HAA, the local authority is empowered to make an order prohibiting occupation, except by the present occupier, of houses identified as requiring demolition or integration with houses in the same building. Service of notice of the order is required following which contraventions of the order are offences which may attract a fine or imprisonment or both.[3]

(v) *The role of housing associations in HAAs*

Although not strictly a part of the HAA procedures themselves, the role of housing associations in connection with improvement of housing stock within HAAs should be briefly noted. One of the reasons for the expansion of housing associations was the priority that should be given by associations to co-operation with local authorities in improvement projects and especially those within HAAs.[4]

3. PROCEDURES IN RELATION TO INDIVIDUAL PROPERTIES

Apart from the rather special powers which are available to housing authorities to enable them to deal with multiple occupation and overcrowding,[5] the powers they have to deal with structural housing

---

1 Ibid, s 106.
2 Ibid, s 96.
3 Ibid, s 97. There is also provision for penalties for continuing offences, for revocation of orders and for the circumstances in which an order may cease to have effect.
4 For housing associations in general, see pp 32 to 37 above.
5 See pp 192 to 196 below.

conditions are the closing order, the demolition order, the improvement order, and the repair notice.[1]

(a) Closing and demolition orders

If a local authority is satisfied that a house does not meet the tolerable standard and that it ought to be demolished but, on the other hand, the affected house forms only part of a building which does not completely comprise houses which are below the tolerable standard, then the authority may make an order which prohibits human habitation from a date specified in the order (not less than 28 days from the date of the order). Such an order is known as a closing order.[2]

If, on the other hand, a building consists of one house below the tolerable standard or several houses, all of which are below the tolerable standard, then the authority may order the vacation of the building within a period of not less than 28 days, as above, and also order that the building be demolished within six weeks of the expiry of that period or within six weeks of the vacation of the building if later. Such an order is known as a demolition order.[3]

In either case, the authority may, on application by the owner, revoke the order if it is subsequently satisfied that the house or houses have been brought up to the tolerable standard.[4] Alternatively, it is possible for the operation of either type of order to be suspended following an undertaking by the owner of the house or building to bring it up to the tolerable standard.[5] Otherwise, subject to a right of appeal, the illegal use of closed premises becomes a criminal offence and the failure to demolish a building subject to a demolition order permits the authority to enter and demolish the building itself and sell its materials. The proceeds of sale, less the demolition expenses, go to the owner.[6] Additionally, if a building consists wholly of houses subject to closing orders a local authority may revoke them and replace them with a demolition order in respect of the whole building. Alternatively, it may purchase the houses either by agreement or, with the

---

1 There is also a power under ss 125–126 of the 1987 Act to take action against an 'obstructive building'—one which, by reason only of its contact with, or proximity to, other buildings, is injurious or dangerous to health.
2 1987 Act, s 114. Special provision is made in that section for the definition of the tolerable standard for underground rooms.
3 Ibid, s 115.
4 Ibid, s 116. Special provision is made by s 119 for listed buildings and houses subject to building preservation orders.
5 Ibid, s 117.
6 Ibid, ss 122–123.

authority of the Secretary of State, compulsorily.[1] Local authorities have a further power to 'determine to purchase' (compulsorily if necessary) in circumstances where they would have the power to close or demolish but consider that, having regard to the existing condition of the house or building and to the needs of the area for further housing accommodation, the house or building should be continued in use.[2] Compensation payable in the event of compulsory purchase cannot normally exceed the 'cleared site value' but the same provisions for rehousing, and the payment of home loss, disturbance, and well-maintained payments and owner-occupier's supplements apply in appropriate cases as they do in HAAs.[3]

Any person aggrieved by the making of a closing or demolition order (or by a refusal to determine such an order) or by a notice of determination to purchase or by a notice that no 'well-maintained' payment is due (on the grounds either that the house was not well-maintained or that the works of maintenance were not attributable to the person concerned) may appeal to the sheriff within 21 days. The sheriff then has the power to make such order as he thinks equitable by confirming, varying or quashing the orginal order or determination. A question of law may go by a stated case to the Court of Session but, otherwise, the sheriff's decision is final.[4]

(b) Improvement orders

In line with the general tendency to encourage the improvement rather than the demolition of sub-standard housing, a significant innovation was made by the Housing (Financial Provisions) (Scotland) Act 1978. This enabled an authority to take action to ensure the improvement and repair of a house which is not in an HAA but which does not meet the tolerable standard. The authority can make an improvement order which requires the owner of the house, within a period of 180 days, to improve the house by executing works to bring

---

1 Ibid, s 120.
2 Ibid, s 121.
3 Ibid, ss 120(3)–(6) and 121(4)–(7). For compensation in HAAs see pp 186 to 187 above.
4 Ibid, ss 129 and 324. As indicated in the text, there is an appeal against refusal to 'determine' an order. This, however, reflects a drafting error during consolidation since, at that time, 'determinations' of orders became 'revocations' at other relevant points in the Act. There must be some doubt, therefore, about whether the refusal to make a revocation is now appealable. For an interesting example of a demolition order appeal, see *McDonald v Midlothian District Council*, 27 September 1983 noted at (1983) 28 JLSS 469.

it up to the tolerable standard and to put it into a good state of repair.[1] For the purposes of these improvement orders, a house not meeting the tolerable standard includes a house lacking a fixed bath or shower and the works required may, therefore, include the installation of such a facility. In addition to requiring the tolerable standard (as modified) and a good state of repair, the authority may also require that, in the case of a house with a future life of not less than 10 years, it is provided with all the standard amenities.

In guidance issued when improvement orders were first introduced, it was stated that they might be particularly appropriate for dealing with scattered rural properties. In general, improvement orders

'should be directed to secure improvement of houses which are seriously substandard, are suitable for improvement and form a necessary part of the housing stock. Authorities are not expected to press improvement orders on the owners of houses which are not needed for general housing purposes—for example houses which are used as second homes or holiday homes.'[2]

Subject to a right of appeal to the sheriff similar to that applicable to closing and demolition orders and subject to the power of the authority to amend the order to allow more time if satisfactory progress on the works is being made, the improvement works must be completed as required. If they are not, the authority may itself carry out the works following acquisition (compulsorily if necessary) of the house. As in HAAs, however, the owner of the house is given considerable financial encouragement. The authority is obliged to award improvement grants and to offer loans to meet the cost of works not met by grant.[3]

(c) Repair notices

A power of longer standing is that of an authority to serve a repair notice. This action can be taken against a house which the authority is satisfied is in a state of serious disrepair. A house may be deemed to be in serious disrepair if, whilst not yet in such a state, it is in need of repair and likely to deteriorate rapidly or to cause material damage to another house if nothing is done to repair it. A 'house' in this context means a building which consists of either one or more houses or a

---

1 1987 Act, s 88. For the form, see SI 1980/1647.
2 SDD Memorandum No 37/1978.
3 1987 Act, s 88(7) and (8). For grants generally see chap 12 and, for loans, see p 216 below.

house or houses combined with other (non-residential) premises. Action is not confined to residential premises.[1]

An authority may serve on the person having control of the house (the person who is or would be entitled to receive the rent[2]) a notice[3] requiring him or her, within a reasonable time but not in less than 21 days, to execute works of repair necessary to rectify defects specified in the notice. Consequential powers in succeeding sections are cast in a rather more elaborate form than the corresponding provisions for improvement orders but, once again, there is the possibility of appeal to the sheriff.[4] Otherwise, failing execution of the works, the authority is empowered to execute them itself (there is no power to purchase in this case) and to recover its expenses.[5] More significantly, however, there is the duty to make repairs grants to those affected by repair notices and a duty to offer loans to assist in carrying out the required works.[6]

The repair notice does not stand alone as a means of dealing with buildings in a poor state of repair. Powers are available to district and islands councils under the Building (Scotland) Act 1959 and under the Civic Government (Scotland) Act 1982. Works required by the latter Act may, if they affect a 'house' as defined above, attract the same entitlement to loans or grants as a repairs notice.[7] Planning authorities have an additional power under the Town and Country Planning (Scotland) Act 1972 to require works on an unoccupied listed building.[8]

4. OVERCROWDING AND HOUSES IN MULTIPLE OCCUPATION

It was once the case that a principal indicator of bad housing conditions was not so much the physical state of the structure of the house but rather the extent of overcrowding. It was a major threat to public health and, in the nineteenth century, local authorities were equipped not only with powers to clear slums and to provide new accommodation but also to abate overcrowding. The successors to these powers

---

1 1987 Act, s 108.
2 Ibid, s 338(2).
3 Prescribed by SI 1980/1647.
4 1987 Act, s 111.
5 Ibid, s 109.
6 Ibid, ss 248(1) and 218. See pp 207 to 208 and 216 below.
7 1982 Act, s 87.
8 Section 97.

are now contained in Part VII of the 1987 Act and these are followed in Part VIII by related powers dealing with the control of houses in multiple occupation. Although these provisions still figure prominently in the housing code, they are relatively little used today.

(a) Overcrowding

A house[1] is defined as overcrowded when the number of persons sleeping in the house contravenes one or other of·two standards, known as the room standard and the space standard. The room standard is contravened when any two persons (over 10 years and of opposite sexes but not living together as husband and wife) must sleep in the same room. The space standard is contravened when the number of persons sleeping in a house exceeds the number statutorily prescribed by reference to the number and floor area of the rooms available as sleeping accommodation. As an example, the permitted number of persons for a house of three rooms is five, provided that two of the rooms have a floor area of more than 110 square feet and the third is over 70 square feet.[2]

If overcrowding occurs, a number of consequences follow. On the positive side, housing authorities are obliged to inspect their districts for overcrowding and report to the Secretary of State (who may himself request the inspection and report) on their proposals for a solution whether by providing accommodation or otherwise.[3] Authorities are also obliged to give preference in the allocation of council houses to applicants from overcrowded homes.[4] It should be remembered too that people living in overcrowded conditions may be homeless for the purposes of Part II of the 1987 Act and benefit from its provisions.[5]

At the same time, the occupier of a house who causes or permits it to become overcrowded commits an offence and tenants (even if protected or assured tenants) become liable to ejection.[6] It is the duty of

---

1 For these purposes, a 'house' means any premises used or intended to be used as a separate dwelling. As mentioned at p 156 above, the definition was, until amended by the Housing (Scotland) Act 1988, qualified by restriction to houses with a rateable value of less than £45.
2 1987 Act, ss 135–137.
3 Ibid, s 146.
4 Ibid, s 20(1)(a). See p 68 above.
5 Ibid, s 24(3)(d). See p 156 above.
6 Ibid, ss 139–145. The sections imposing criminal penalties apply only in localities appointed under provisions no longer operative. 1987 Act, s 157(2). There are probably no such localities.

housing authorities to enforce these provisions (including taking steps themselves to terminate tenancies of overcrowded houses) and they have the power to publish information for the assistance of landlords and occupiers as to their rights and duties relating to overcrowding.[1]

(b) Multiple occupation

The concern here is with houses which are let in lodgings or which are occupied by members of more than one family and with buildings which comprise separate dwellings two or more of which lack either a sanitary convenience accessible only to those living in the dwelling or personal washing facilities similarly accessible or both. In relation to such houses and buildings in its district (or a part of it) a local authority has the power to make a scheme for their registration, which has to be confirmed by the Secretary of State.[2] Publicity has to be given of an authority's intention to submit a scheme to the Secretary of State and, if it is confirmed, the scheme has to be published and to be available for inspection. Once it is confirmed, duties are imposed upon people affected by the scheme to supply information about houses and buildings to be registered.[3]

The purpose of making a scheme for registration is to enable the local authority to take steps to ensure the maintenance of satisfactory conditions within the affected houses. The authority can, in the first place, extend to a house which is in an unsatisfactory state as a result of a failure to maintain proper standards of management the provisions of a code prescribed by the Secretary of State which is designed to impose upon managers of houses (normally the landlord) standards of repair, maintenance, cleansing and good order. A failure to observe the code is a criminal offence.[4]

The authority also has separate powers to require compliance with the code; and to require the execution of works including the provision of fire escapes.[5] There is an appeal to the sheriff against these requirements but, if no appeal is brought or if it is unsuccessful, then the authority has the power to carry out the required works itself. Failure to execute works is also an offence.[6] One way in which the power to require the carrying out of works has been strengthened has

1 Ibid, ss 145(b), 149 and 150.
2 Ibid, s 152.
3 Ibid, ss 152–155.
4 Ibid, ss 156–159 and SI 1964/1371.
5 Ibid, ss 160–162.
6 Ibid, ss 163–164.

been in relation to the provision of fire escapes. The Local Government and Planning (Scotland) Act 1982 did two things.[1] On the one hand, it enabled the Secretary of State to specify the circumstances in which authorities must take action to require fire escapes.[2] This power has not yet been exercised. More importantly, it obliged authorities which have served notices requiring the provision of fire escapes to make grants to assist with the works required.[3] The amount of the grant is 20%[4] (or up to 90% in cases of financial hardship) of the total approved expense. Maximum levels of expenditure on which grant will be paid are currently fixed at £9,315 for the works specified in the notice and £3,340 for associated works.[5] Most of the procedural requirements relevant to improvement grants apply also to fire escape grants.[6]

An authority also has the power to give directions to prevent overcrowding in houses in multiple occupation,[7] and, most drastically of all, an authority has the power, in addition to or in lieu of the power to require execution of works, to make what is called a 'control order' if it appears that living conditions in a house are such that it is necessary in order to protect the safety, welfare or health of people living in the house.[8] If such a control order is made (and again there is an appeal to the sheriff[9]) and is in force, the authority becomes entitled to take possession of the premises and to exercise all rights of ownership. Tenancies continue with the authority substituted as landlord and the authority becomes fully responsible for the maintenance of proper standards of management with power to supply necessary furniture, fittings and conveniences.[10] The dispossessed proprietor retains only a power of inspection and a right to periodic payments by way of compensation.[11] A control order expires at the end of five years or upon an earlier date if the authority revokes it. Such earlier revocation may be requested by a person with an interest in the house with an appeal to the sheriff if the authority refuses.[12]

1 Section 52.
2 See now 1987 Act, s 162(2).
3 See now 1987 Act, s 249 as amended by the Housing (Scotland) Act 1988.
4 Reduced from 75% by SI 1990/2242.
5 1987 Act, s 249 and SI 1987/2269.
6 See pp 199 to 209 below.
7 1987 Act, ss 166–170.
8 Ibid, s 178.
9 Ibid, s 186.
10 Ibid, ss 179–182.
11 Ibid, ss 182(5)–183.
12 Ibid, s 188.

All these powers referred to derive from the 1987 Act consolidating earlier legislation but an important additional power of control was introduced when the licensing provisions in the Civic Government (Scotland) Act 1982 were applied to houses in multiple occupation. The Act requires local authorities (at present district and islands councils) to license certain activities and premises (eg public houses) and permits them to license other activities covered by the Act or to which the Act may be extended by the Secretary of State.[1] In 1991, the use of premises as a house in multiple occupation was designated as such an activity.[2] A house in multiple occupation is defined as a house (other than one subject to a control order) which is the only or principal residence of more than four persons who are not all members of the same family or of one or other of two families.[3] The need for a license in a particular area depends on the passing of a resolution to that effect by the relevant authority. Once that has been done, the sophisticated procedural code (covering applications, consultation, publicity, the consideration and disposal of applications, the giving of reasons, and appeal to the sheriff) contained in the Act applies.[4] Also important in some circumstances may be the controls imposed by the Town and Country Planning (Scotland) Act 1972. Under that Act, it is a form of development for which planning permission is required to use a building, previously used as a single dwelling-house, as two or more houses.[5] There are also older powers under the Public Health (Scotland) Act 1897 for the regulation (including by the making of bye-laws) of houses let in lodgings and of common lodging houses.[6]

---

1 The general provisions are contained in Pts I and II of the Act. The Secretary of State's power to designate further activities is contained in s 44.
2 The Civic Government (Scotland) Act 1982 (Licensing of Houses in Multiple Occupation) Order 1991, SI 1991/1253.
3 Ibid, art 2(1).
4 See especially Sch I.
5 Section 19(3).
6 Section 72 and Pt V.

CHAPTER 12

Sub-standard housing: grants

1. INTRODUCTION

Retaining the distinction introduced at the beginning of the last chapter, we can turn now from the 'sticks' of housing stock improvement in the shape of HAAs, closing, demolition and improvement orders and repair notices to the 'carrots' of house improvement—the system of financial assistance by means of grants to the occupiers of (principally) sub-standard houses. These take various forms. In many cases, they may be seen as directly related to or consequential upon other housing authority action such as the implementation of an HAA—grants may be available to those already subject to the authority's 'stick' to assist them to comply with the requirements of a resolution or order. In other cases, grants may be made to occupiers wholly unaffected by any other housing authority action. Some grants an authority is obliged to make once an application has been made in appropriate form. Other grants may be made or withheld at the discretion of the authority. Altogether, the law in this area is quite complex not least because of its adjustment in detail by successive pieces of housing legislation.

Some of the complexity which had built up in this area was removed with the consolidation of the law in Part XIII of the Housing (Scotland) Act 1987. However, an important change was made in 1988 and a much more radical reform of the law was anticipated. The powers to make improvement grants which are discussed in this chapter have in the past been (and continue to be) exercised by local authorities—the district and islands councils. The statutory change already made, however, conferred the same powers on Scottish Homes.[1] The possibility of duplication of grant-making activity was foreseen in a related power given to the

---

1 1988 Act, s 2(9) inserting a new s 256A into the 1987 Act.

Secretary of State to give directions to a local authority, local authorities generally, and to Scottish Homes as to the circumstances in which one or more of them may exercise their powers.[1]

Major reform of the substantive law of improvement grants was heralded first in the 1987 Green Paper, *Housing: the Government's Proposals for Scotland*[2] and then in a consultation paper issued by the SDD in May 1988, *Private Housing Renewal: the Government's Proposals for Scotland*. The proposals contained in that paper never reached the statute book and they need not be set out in detail here. Their main effect, however, would have been to replace existing grants with a single 'rehabilitation grant.' There would also have been an 'adaptation grant' to assist the adaptation of houses for disabled people. The rehabilitation grant would have been 'targetted' by making it subject to a means test and tied to the achievement of two new housing standards—an adapted version of the existing 'tolerable standard' and a new 'higher standard.' In general, grants to bring a house up to the 'tolerable standard' would, subject to the test of financial eligibility, have been mandatory while grants for works to the 'higher standard' would have been discretionary. In addition to these changes, the paper on *Private Housing Renewal* contained proposals for new powers to give grant assistance to developers, for the repair of tenements and other 'blocks' and for powers to replace the existing compulsory house improvement measures and housing action areas.[3]

The 1988 proposals were eventually shelved but radical reform was again mooted in a ministerial speech in November 1993.[4] No details were announced. They were to follow in a consultation paper to be published in the spring of 1994 but public expenditure restraint seemed likely to dictate adherence to the means tested approach of the earlier proposals.

Most of this chapter is devoted to the basic improvement and repairs grants which are at the heart of the existing system. Short notes at the end deal with thermal insulation grants and the assistance an authority can give towards the provision of 'professional, technical and administrative services' and towards environmental improvement in residential areas.

1 1988 Act, s 2(8) inserting a new s 239A into the 1987 Act.
2 Cm 242, paras 3.12–3.18. Yet earlier proposals in *Home Improvement in Scotland—A New Approach* (1985) Cmnd 9677 were never implemented.
3 See Chap 11.
4 See *Scotsman* 26 November 1993.

2. IMPROVEMENT AND REPAIRS GRANTS

Although there are considerable overlaps between them in both their practical application and the relevant rules of law, it is useful to imagine that there are three distinct types of grant (all made under Part XIII of the 1987 Act)[1] that a housing authority may make to assist with the improvement of sub-standard housing:

(i) Mandatory improvement grants

These are the grants made under section 244 of the 1987 Act and which are 'mandatory' in the sense that, as we shall see, an authority has no discretion to refuse an application made in appropriate form. Although not a 'repairs grant' as such, a grant of this type may include an element for associated works of repair.

(ii) Discretionary improvement grants

These are 'discretionary' in the sense that an authority may normally allow or refuse an application for grant at its discretion. Details will follow but, again, such grants may include an element for associated works of repair.

(iii) Repairs grants

Grants under section 248 of the 1987 Act are made in relation to works of repair alone.

These are the types of grant (meaningless so far in terms of their scope and application) with whose rules we are concerned. Having made the distinction, however, between these types of grant we find that much of Part XIII of the Act is common to them all. Our treatment, therefore, resembles a sandwich. In the first place, we deal with a bottom layer of preliminary rules common to all types of improvement and repairs grant. These principally concern who can apply and how. Then, in the middle, we have to provide separate descriptions of the grants where their rules diverge. These concern the type of works which may attract grant, the circumstances in which an authority may or must make grants, and the amounts of grant payable. The top layer of the sandwich then consists of more rules common to all types of grant and which concern the procedure for the approval or refusal of grants, conditions which may be attached to awards of grant, and the actual payment (and repayment) of grants.

---

1 Grants for fire escapes for houses in multiple occupation are dealt with separately at p 195 above.

(a) Common rules (preliminary)

1. In the first place, an application for improvement or repairs grants has to be made on a standard form prescribed by the Secretary of State and available from housing authorities.[1]
2. Secondly, we have to note who it is that can make an application for a grant. Until the passing of the Tenants' Rights, Etc (Scotland) Act 1980, this question had to be answered rather restrictively. Only the owner (defined to mean the person entitled to receive the rent of the house, or who, if the house were let would be so entitled or a 'tenant at will') or the lessee under a lease with at least five years unexpired could apply for a grant.[2] This restriction excluded virtually all tenants of houses in the public or private sector but the 1980 Act threw open the categories of occupier to whom grants are available. To assist them in works of improvement or repair all may apply for grants. The 'owner' of the house cannot, however, be totally disregarded. The owner's written consent to an application for grant has to be obtained and, because he or she may be bound by conditions attached to an award of grant, the consent to be so bound has also to be forthcoming at the time of application.[3]
3. No grant is payable if the relevant works have already been begun at the time when application is made—unless the authority is satisfied that there were good reasons for such a start being made.[4]
4. The Secretary of State may direct a local authority or authorities generally not to approve an application (or class of application) for grant except with his consent and subject to any conditions he may impose.[5]

(b) Separate rules (according to type of grant)

(i) Mandatory improvement grants

These are the grants an authority has no discretion to refuse provided that applicants satisfy the conditions laid down in the Act. In appropriate

1 1987 Act, s 237 and SI 1980/1647.
2 Housing (Scotland) Act 1974, ss 2(3) and 49.
3 1987 Act, s 240(1)(a).
4 Ibid, s 240(1)(b).
5 Ibid, s 239.

cases, the authority is obliged to award a grant of 50% of the 'approved expense' involved in the installation of any of the 'standard amenities' in a house which previously lacked such amenities.[1] Certain conditions attach to this duty, but first the terms 'standard amenities' and 'approved expense' require explanation.

The 'standard amenities' which must be for the exclusive use of the occupants of the house are defined in the Act as the following: a fixed bath or shower; a hot and cold water supply at a fixed bath or shower; a wash-hand basin; a sink; a hot and cold water supply at a sink; and a water closet.[2] The 'approved expense', on which grant is payable, is computed by reference to the maximum eligible amount specified for each amenity and these are respectively:

	£
Fixed bath or shower	450
Hot and cold water supply at a fixed bath or shower	570
Wash-hand basin	170
Hot and cold water supply at a wash-hand basin	305
Sink	450
Hot and cold water supply at a sink	385
Water closet	680[3]

It is permissible for an authority to allow the maximum eligible amount (and thus 'approved expense') for an amenity to be exceeded if the authority is satisfied that an increased estimate is justifiable.[4] No grant, however, can normally be made for more than one amenity of the same description. There is an exception to this general rule in the case of an application for grant for a standard amenity to meet the needs of a disabled occupant. If the authority is of the opinion that an additional standard amenity (perhaps an extra bath or shower) is essential to the needs of a disabled occupant, a further grant must be made.[5]

Two general conditions which must be satisfied before an authority is obliged to make a grant are, first, that the authority must be of the opinion that, on completion of the works, the house will meet the tolerable standard.[6] Secondly, no grant can be made in respect of a house in a building containing other houses unless the local authority

1 Ibid, s 244. For applications made to local authorities before 1 April 1984 the rate of grant was 90%. See SIs 1982/569 and 1810.
2 Ibid, s 244(6) and Pt I of Sch 18.
3 Ibid, and SI 1987/2269.
4 Ibid, Sch 18, Pt II, para 3.
5 Ibid, para 4 and s 244(3).
6 Ibid, s 244(1).

is satisfied that the works to be carried out will not prevent the improvement of any other house.[1] Until the 1980 Act, two further conditions had to be satisfied. The authority had to be of the opinion that, with the works completed, the affected house would be likely to be available for use as a house for a period of at least 10 years and that it would (in addition to meeting the tolerable standard) be provided with all the standard amenities for the exclusive use of its occupants.[2] In line, however, with a policy of making grants available to improve properties having an expectation of only a short further life, these conditions were changed by the 1980 Act. The 'ten-year' requirement was completely deleted and, at the same time, the requirement that the house possess all standard amenities following the improvement works ceased to apply to those houses unlikely to be available for use as a house for a further 10 years. Single amenities may, therefore, be added to short-life property without the need to provide all other amenities.[3]

This distinction between short- and long-life property was also introduced into the rules regulating associated works of repair and replacement which may attract grant on a discretionary basis when they are needed to enable a house (for which standard amenities are being provided) to attain a good state of repair. Thus, where an application for grant relates wholly or partly to the provision of any or all of the standard amenities then, if the house is likely to be available for at least 10 years, an additional maximum approved expense of £3,450 (or 50% of the actual approved expense of executing the improvement works, whichever is the greater) towards which grant may be paid is allowable. If the house is likely to be available for less than 10 years, the additional maximum approved expense is £345 per amenity provided—subject to a maximum of £1,380.[4]

(ii) Discretionary improvement grants

Where the improvement in respect of which a grant is sought does not involve the provision of standard amenities, the authority may approve or refuse to approve the grant application.[5] If it is refused, the applicant must be notified in writing of the grounds of the refusal.[6] Improvement grants may be made in respect of the provision of

---

1 Ibid, s 244(2).
2 1974 Act, s 7(1).
3 1987 Act, s 244(4).
4 Ibid, s 242(3)(a) and SI 1987/2269.
5 Ibid, s 238.
6 Ibid, s 241(3).

houses by conversion or for the improvement of houses. 'Improvement' here is defined to include alteration and enlargement and any 'works required for the provision or improvement of a house' which may include works of replacement needed in order for the property to attain a good state of repair.[1] Thus it appears to follow that improvement cannot consist of repairs alone but may include works of repair which are incidental to the works of improvement proper. An important modification of the definition of 'improvement' extends it to include the doing of works required for making the house of a disabled person suitable for his or her accommodation, welfare or employment.[2]

The exercise of a local authority's discretion in deciding whether or not a grant application should be approved is subject to a number of statutory guidelines. In the first place, there is an obligation (and to this extent the award of a grant becomes mandatory rather than discretionary) to make an improvement grant to the owner of a house to enable the house in an HAA to be brought up to the requisite standard.[3] The same applies to houses subject to an improvement order.[4]

There are, on the other hand, some situations in which an authority must not approve an application for a discretionary grant:

(a) If the house was constructed after 15 June 1964 then (subject to the power of the Secretary of State to waive this provision) no grant can be approved.[5] The restriction has been waived in relation to works consisting of or including adaptation to meet the particular needs of a disabled occupant.[6]

(b) There can be no approval in the case of a house in a building containing other houses if the improvement of any other such house would be prevented.[7]

(c) The authority must normally be satisfied that, when the works are complete, the house will be brought up to a standard specified by the Secretary of State and capable of providing accommodation for a period also to be specified by him. This period has been set at 30 years or exceptionally as little as 10 years. The specified standard is determined by reference to the provision of specified services such as WC,

---

1 Ibid, s 236(1)–(2).
2 Ibid, s 236(2)(a)(i) and (3).
3 Ibid, s 250(6).
4 Ibid, s 88(7).
5 Ibid, s 240(2)(b).
6 Direction annexed to SDD Circular No 36/1982.
7 1987 Act, s 240(2)(a).

sink, running water etc. and more general conditions such as adequate space and lighting and good internal planning of the house.[1]

If these conditions are not satisfied then an application must be refused although it is permissible for an authority to disregard (with the consent of the Secretary of State) any of the requirements if, in the opinion of the authority, conformity would not be practicable at reasonable expense.[2]

(d) A further restriction relates to the rateable value of the house at the date of the application and the Secretary of State has established at varying levels for the whole country two sets of 'prescribed limits' of rateable value.[3] One limit applies where a single house is to be improved or where a number of houses are to be converted into a lesser number. The other (twice the first) applies where a single house is to be converted into two or more houses. Examples are (lowest) £585 and £1,170 for Orkney; (highest) £1,255 and £2,510 for Bearsden; £940 and £1,880 for Stirling and Glasgow; £1,135 and £2,270 for Edinburgh. If the house concerned has a rateable value higher than the prescribed limit and if the application for grant is made by the owner (or a member of his family) and the house (or part) is to be occupied by the owner (or a member of his family) then (unless that occupation is to be of a self-contained part of the house and the application is made for another) the application must be refused. This rule is designed to prevent the award of improvement grants to the owner-occupiers of highly rated properties. It is also, however, aimed to encourage the conversion and sub-division of such large houses. The restrictions on applications by owner-occupiers do not apply where the house is either in an HAA declared under section 90 (but not apparently section 91) of the Act and listed as a house requiring improvement or integration; subject to an improvement order under section 88 of the Act; or a house occupied by a disabled person in so far as the application relates to works made necessary by the disability.[4]

These rules restricting the making of improvement grants by reference to limits of rateable value have, since 1 April

1 Ibid, s 240(2)(a) and SDD Circular No 72/1975.
2 Ibid, s 240(6).
3 Ibid, s 240(2)(c) and SI 1985/297.
4 Ibid, s 240(3).

1989, had to be read subject to the Abolition of Domestic Rates Etc (Scotland) Act 1987. That Act abolished the rating of domestic subjects but preserved, subject to some qualifications, the rateable values recorded as at 31 March 1989.[1]

If an application for a grant is not disallowed under any of the above restrictions and if the authority is disposed, in the exercise of its discretion, to make an award, the amount of the grant is subject to specific statutory maxima. These are determined, as with the mandatory grants, by reference to a prescribed percentage of the approved expense of the improvement works up to a prescribed maximum. Thus, at present, the standard maximum percentage is 50% and the prescribed maximum approved expense is £12,600[2] which means that, in 'normal' circumstances, the highest grant payable is £6,300 where the approved expense of the works to be undertaken is £12,600 or above. Apart, however, from a power (see below) which the Secretary of State has to vary the basic 50% maximum, he also has the power to permit a local authority to pay a larger grant in a particular case either where the expense of the works is materially enhanced by measures taken to preserve the architectural or historic interest of the house or where there are other good reasons for fixing a higher amount.[3] In this latter case, the Secretary of State can give a general authority to pay higher grants in particular classes of case and he has done this by indicating that the sum of £17,100 (or £19,700 if the work is to be carried out by a housing association) may be acceptable as the maximum approved expense applicable in the case of older tenement buildings in HAAs where it can be shown that expenditure in excess of £12,600 is necessary.[4]

More importantly, by the substitution of higher maximum percentage grants, the awards permissible in certain categories of application are generally higher. If the application concerns a house to be improved in an HAA or if it concerns a house subject to an improvement order, then the percentage level of grant is not a maximum of 50% but becomes fixed at 75% of the approved expense (subject normally to the £12,600 maximum).[5] If an application of either of these types is made by the *owner of the house* (this is not a benefit available to all applicants) and it appears to the authority that the applicant will not without due hardship be able to finance the cost of so much of

1 Section 5.
2 1987 Act, s 242(1) and SI 1987/2269.
3 Ibid, s 242(4).
4 SDD Circular No 3/1988.
5 1987 Act, s 250(2).

the improvement works as is not met by the grant, the percentage grant may be further increased up to a maximum of 90%.[1] A similar general adjustment has also been made affecting houses which are not in an HAA but which either fail to meet the tolerable standard or which lack (within the house) a fixed bath or shower provided with an adequate supply of both hot and cold water. In these cases, the prescribed maximum level of grant is adjusted up from 50% to 75%.[2]

Another adjustment to the maximum percentage rate of grant has been made for disabled people. If the grant is made for works consisting of or including works needed to meet a requirement arising from the particular disability of a disabled occupant, the maximum rate of grant is 75%.[3]

Three further details about amounts of improvement grants generally need to be noted:

(a) An authority does have the power to allow the later substitution of an increased approved expense of improvement works (up to the prescribed maximum) in place of the estimate in the original application in cases where the applicant can show that circumstances beyond his or her control will result in the estimate being exceeded.[4]

(b) As indicated above, works of improvement can include works of repair and replacement. For this, in cases not involving the provision of standard amenities, the authority may allow a maximum approved expense not exceeding 50% of the approved expense of the improvement works themselves—but the overall maximum approved expense remains at the fixed sum of £12,600.[5]

(c) If an application for grant is made in relation to a house in respect of which an improvement grant under the 1987 Act (or previous or related legislation) has been paid within the last 10 years, then the amount of grant payable must, *after the addition* of any unrepaid amount of the original grant, not exceed the amount normally payable under the ordinary rules. This is not a restriction which applies to the payment of mandatory grants for standard amenities nor does it apply in respect of discretionary grants for works for the benefit of a disabled occupant.[6]

1 Ibid, s 250(5).
2 SI 1980/2029.
3 SI 1982/1809.
4 1987 Act, s 242(2).
5 Ibid, s 242(3)(b).
6 Ibid, s 242(5).

(iii) Repairs grants

As indicated above, improvement grants cannot be made in respect of works of repair alone. The Housing (Scotland) Act 1974 did, however, make provision for the award of grants (repairs grants) for works of repair within an HAAI or HAADI but this power was considerably extended by the Housing (Financial Provisions) (Scotland) Act 1978 which introduced a new general repairs grant. The making of a grant, subject to the satisfaction of procedural requirements similar to those applicable to improvement grants, was made mandatory (assuming an application in proper form and satisfaction of the conditions below) if the works of repair were (1) in relation to houses within an HAAI or HAADI and (2) where they were required by a repair notice.[1] In this last case, grants (for repairs only) were also to be paid on the same mandatory basis in relation to 'premises other than a house' (ie nonresidential properties) provided that the premises form part of a building containing houses and that those houses will all provide the standard of accommodation referred to below. In relation to houses outside an HAA or unaffected by a repair notice, the making of a grant was discretionary. The provisions contained in the Acts of 1974 and 1978 were consolidated in the 1987 Act but with an interesting variation of terminology. Instead of the local authority's being required to 'make a grant' in the two situations described above as mandatory, the authority is required to 'approve the application.'[2] It might be thought that this would not have had any substantial effect on the actual obligation imposed on authorities but it has been held that the provisions now confer a discretionary power on the authorities rather than a mandatory obligation.[3] It will, however, be a more constrained discretion than that available to an authority in the case of applications for repairs grants at large.

The authority must be satisfied that outside HAAs the house concerned will provide satisfactory accommodation for such period as it considers reasonable. Inside HAAs the authority must be satisfied that the house will attain the standard specified in the HAA resolution. The authority must in all cases normally have regard to the question whether the applicant would, without undue hardship, be able to finance the expense of the works without a grant but the Secretary of

1 1978 Act, s 8 inserting s 10A into the 1974 Act, and see pp 183 and 191 above.
2 1987 Act, ss 248(1) and 250(7).
3 *Milner v City of Glasgow District Council* 1990 SLT 361. The case also raised interesting issues arising from the transitional provisions of the 1987 Act itself.

State is empowered to disapply this requirement in cases prescribed by him. The power has been exercised in relation to applications to replace lead plumbing (but later revoked) and in respect of 'works which in the opinion of the local authority are of a substantial and structural character.'[1] These last terms are not further defined. No grant is payable where the rateable value limits (referred to above) are exceeded but this restriction does not apply in relation to works concerning lead plumbing.[2] The same restriction on grants for new houses (post 15 June 1964) applies to discretionary repairs grants as to discretionary improvement grants.

The amount of a repairs grant may not exceed 50% of the approved expense which itself cannot exceed £5,500.[3] As with improvement grants the figure of 50% is increased to 75% in HAAs (with the further possibility of 90% for owners in the case of financial hardship).[4] In relation to applications made (but not necessarily approved) during the period to 1 April 1984 there was a general raising of repairs grant levels to 90% of approved expense.[5] A higher level of approved expense (£7,800) applies to repairs grants for pre-1914 tenement houses subject to common repairs schemes.[6]

Special provisions concerning lead plumbing make it clear that repairs grants can be made 'in respect of the replacement in a different material of such pipes, tanks, cisterns, taps or other equipment used for the supply of water to a house as are wholly or partly made of lead' to encourage the uptake of grants for this purpose. The rateable value limits do not apply.[7] The financial hardship provision does not apply; nor does the restriction on post-1964 houses.[8] Lead plumbing grants are payable at 75% provided the application relates exclusively to lead plumbing.[9] The Secretary of State has issued general guidance about the identification of the need for replacement of lead plumbing and the extent of works required.[10]

---

1 1987 Act, s 248(3) and SI 1982/1154 (replaced by SI 1992/1328).
2 Ibid, s 248(5).
3 Ibid, s 248(4) and SI 1987/2269.
4 Ibid, s 250(5) and (7).
5 Some applications made prior to 1 April 1984 have taken many years to be processed.
6 SDD Circular 3/1988.
7 Ibid, s 248(5) proviso. The same applies to works to reduce exposure to radon gas, since the amendment of sub-s (5) by the 1993 Act.
8 SI 1982/1154 and the Direction appended to SDD Circular No 10/1982.
9 SI 1992/1598 (which also applies to measures against radon gas).
10 SDD Circular No 109/1982.

(c) Further rules common to the three types of grants

Having dealt with the obvious points at which the provisions applicable to the different types of grant diverge, we now return to the final layer of the 'sandwich' containing further rules of substance and procedure which are, in the main, common to all and apply after the approval of a grant application.[1]

(i) Payment of grants

Payment of improvement or repairs grants is normally to be made within one month of the date on which, in the opinion of the authority, the house first becomes fit for occupation after the completion of the works. There is, however, provision for the payment of grant partly by instalments with full payment again being made within a month of completion of the works. If such instalment payments in advance are made, however, they are made conditional upon eventual satisfactory completion of the works and may be demanded back (with interest) if the works are not completed within a period of 12 months from the date of the first instalment. At no stage may the aggregate of instalments paid exceed 50% (75% for improvement grants or repairs grants in HAAs) of the aggregate approved expense of the works so far executed.[2]

Grants are payable to applicants themselves or, in the event of death, to personal representatives.[3]

(ii) Conditions attaching to improvement and repairs grants

For a period of five years from the date on which a house, in respect of which a grant has been paid, becomes fit for occupation after completion of the works certain conditions are required to be observed and, where appropriate, are deemed to be part of any lease or tenancy.[4]

The house must not be used within the five-year period as anything but a private dwelling-house (although use of a part as a shop or office or for business purposes is permissible). On the other hand the house must not be occupied by its owner or a member of his or her family

---

1 For problems with an 'approval in principle', see *Margrie Holdings Ltd v City of Edinburgh District Council* 1987 GWD 6–187.
2 1987 Act, ss 243 and 250(3).
3 Ibid, s 245.
4 Ibid, s 246(1).

unless as his or her only or main residence. All such steps as are practicable must be taken to secure the maintenance of the house in a good state of repair.

Enforcement of the conditions required to be observed for the statutory five-year period is achieved firstly by the recording of the conditions in the General Register of Sasines (or Land Register)[1] and, thereafter, through the duty of the authority to demand, in the event of breach, repayment of the grant (with interest) from the owner of the house for the time being—although the authority has some discretion to waive its right to payment. Observance of conditions may further be enforced by interdict and by charging order.[2] Repayment of the grant, whether in response to enforcement action or on a voluntary basis removes the need for observance of the conditions originally imposed.[3]

(d) The financing of improvement and repairs grants

Grants to successful applicants are paid, in the first instance, by the local authorities concerned. Authorities finance the grants from capital included in their non-HRA blocks.[4] Until 1988–89, the Secretary of State made contributions in the form of a specific grant towards the loan charges referable to the capital borrowed for improvement grant purposes. Pursuant to changes made by the 1988 Act, however, that system was brought to an end by the capitalisation of such loan charges and transfer of the debt to the Secretary of State.[5] Since 1989–90 improvement grant expenditure by local authorities has been subsidised out of revenue support grant.[6]

3. PROFESSIONAL, TECHNICAL AND ADMINISTRATIVE SERVICES

A more recently enacted power to assist with works of improvement is that conferred by section 170 of the 1989 Act. Brought into effect by

---

1 Ibid, s 246(7).
2 Ibid, s 246(5) and Sch 19.
3 Ibid, s 247.
4 For the system of capital consents, see p 9 above. In theory, improvement grants can be made to council tenants. These would be financed from the HRA block.
5 1988 Act, s 67.
6 Local Government Finance Act 1992, s 108 and Sch 12.

the making of regulations in 1992,[1] this enables any regional, islands or district council to provide 'professional, technical and administrative services for owners or occupiers of houses in connection with their arranging or carrying out relevant works or to encourage or facilitate the carrying out of such works, whether or not on payment of such charges as the authority may determine.' The 'relevant works' have been defined by the regulations to include the provision of standard amenities, bringing a house up to the tolerable standard, the improvement of a house and repairing a house in a state of serious repair. In addition, authorities may give financial assistance to housing associations and charities towards the cost of works of maintenance, repair and improvement.

4. THERMAL INSULATION GRANTS

A limited and rather specialised additional form of 'improvement grant' was introduced in 1978 when, as part of a programme of energy conservation, the Homes Insulation Act was passed.[2] Local (housing) authorities were required to make grants out of funds allocated to them by the Secretary of State to persons eligible, and in respect of works of thermal insulation permitted, under schemes made under the Act. However, whilst a similar scheme of grants is retained, under powers now contained in section 15 of the Social Security Act 1990, responsibility for its administration was removed from local authorities and given to an administering agency nominated by the Government and operating on a national (Great Britain) basis. Since January 1991 the Energy Action Grants Agency, whose headquarters are in Newcastle-upon-Tyne, has operated the scheme under the Home Energy Efficiency Grants Regulations.[3]

(i) Applicants

Any person who is the householder (whether as owner or as tenant) of and resident in a dwelling may apply for a grant, provided that the person (or his or her spouse) is, at the time of making the application,

---

1 The Housing (Relevant Works) (Scotland) Regulations 1992, SI 1992/1653.
2 The provisions in the 1978 Act were, for Scotland, consolidated in ss 252–253 of the 1987 Act. These are to be repealed by s 15(11) of the Social Security Act 1990, although that subsection has yet to be brought into effect.
3 These are now contained in SI 1992/483.

in receipt of income support, housing benefit, family credit, council tax benefit or disability working allowance.[1]

(ii) Eligible dwellings

Any dwelling is eligible for a grant, except a dwelling in which there is or has been at any time, during the period of the applicant's residence in it, insulation (of more than 50 mm) in all or any part of the roof space (unless it is either insulating a water tank or pipe or is in additional roof space.[2])

(iii) Eligible works

Works eligible for grant may fall into any of four categories: (a) insulation in roof space including tanks and pipes (and, if necessary, the provision of a means of access to roof space); (b) draughtproofing of external and internal doors and windows (excluding kitchens and bathrooms) and insulation of hot water tanks and cylinders; (c) a combination of both (a) and (b); and (d) energy advice. Any works must comply with standards laid down by the Agency with the approval of the Secretary of State.[3]

(iv) Scale of grant available

The amounts of grant available vary according to whether the work is carried out by the applicant him or herself or by an 'eligible contractor.' These may be either a registered 'network installer' for the locality or a person listed for the locality by the Agency.[4] If the applicant is carrying out the works, the grant is the lesser of (a) the cost of materials minus a personal contribution of £16 and (b) £235 (for works combining insulation and draughtproofing). If the work is carried out by an eligible contractor, the equivalent maximum is

1 SI 1992/483, reg 3.
2 Ibid, reg 6. The exception does not apply in cases where the works involved are confined to draughtproofing, water tank insulation and energy advice. 'Insulated additional roof space' is defined as 'roof space which has been added to the dwelling or building in multiple occupation and in all or any part of which there is insulation material of a thickness of more than 50 mm' (reg 2).
3 Ibid, reg 5.
4 Which one is involved affects the method of application. See below.

£289.[1] No grant can be paid for works for which a grant has already been paid.[2]

(v) Procedure

Application is made direct to the Agency or, if appropriate, via a network installer on a form laid down by the Agency.[3] If the application is made to a network installer, the installer must consider whether the works are eligible for grant and, if not so satisfied, inform the applicant of this and of his or her right to a determination of the question by the Agency. If the installer is satisfied about eligibility, the application must be sent to the Agency for determination but the installer may offer to undertake the necessary works even in advance of a final decision—subject to agreement with the applicant as to payment.[4] When an application reaches the Agency, whether or not by way of a network installer, its decision on whether it should be approved depends not only on the general criteria for eligibility already mentioned but also, very importantly, upon whether the Agency still has unallocated funds available. Allocations (made to the Agency by the Secretary of State)[5] are cash limited. If an application is refused, the applicant must be given reasons.[6] If the application is approved and the works are undertaken, a claim for payment of the grant has to be made in accordance with the regulations.[7]

(vi) Buildings in multiple occupation

Plainly there is a problem about extending the general rules on grant to tenemental buildings and other buildings in multiple occupation—buildings occupied by persons who do not form a single household.[8] A parallel scheme is, however, established for grants to be made to the 'person in control' (owner or tenant) of such a building in

1 SI 1992/483 reg 9.
2 Ibid, reg 4(d).
3 Ibid, reg 4.
4 Ibid, reg 7. There is provision in reg 16 for the notification in advance to network installers by the Agency of amounts of grant payable to them.
5 Ibid, reg 17(2).
6 Ibid, reg 8.
7 Ibid, reg 10.
8 Social Security Act 1990, s 15(4).

circumstances where grants have already been made in respect of at least half of the separate (single household) dwellings in the building.[1]

5. ENVIRONMENTAL IMPROVEMENT

A power related to others involving financial assistance for the improvement of housing is that contained in section 251 of the 1987 Act[2] under which a local authority may, for the purpose of securing the improvement of the amenities of a predominantly residential area, carry out works on land owned by it or assist financially in the carrying out of works not so owned. The sort of works which receive support are, for instance, the provision of new or improved drying greens, car parking space, children's play areas and landscaping.

1 Ibid, regs 11–14.
2 See also s 23 (as substituted by the Housing (Scotland) Act 1988) for an equivalent power of new towns. See p 40 above.

CHAPTER 13

Financial assistance for housing

1. INTRODUCTION

Part XII of the Housing (Scotland) Act 1987 is entitled 'House Loans and Other Financial Assistance.' Although it concentrates in the main upon loans, a number of other miscellaneous statutory forms of assistance are included. The remit of this final chapter is similar, but the net is cast rather wider than the contents of Part XII.

We have, of course, already encountered many references to forms of financial assistance available from local authorities for housing purposes. Local authorities are bound to be the main focus of attention because they are the bodies most widely and most closely concerned with the provision of housing services. Apart from his statutory contributions to the housing operations of local authorities, Scottish Homes, the new towns and also to voluntary organisations,[1] the Secretary of State has few powers to make direct financial payments to members of the public. We have, however, noted his power to contribute to the cost of transfers and exchanges and to assist tenants in 'right to buy' proceedings.[2] A form of loan assistance by the Secretary of State is discussed below. Scottish Homes, in addition to its financing of housing associations, has the power to make other forms of financial contribution. In particular, its power to make improvement and repairs grants was noted.[3]

In addition to the scheme of improvement grants (including improvement of amenity grants),[4] other local authority powers involving a financial contribution of one sort or another have included the duty to offer discounts when tenants exercise the right to buy;[5] assistance by way of reinstatement grant for those who have

---

1 See pp 9, 31 and 40 above and, in relation to voluntary organisations, the 1987 Act, s 197.
2 See pp 87 and 133 above.
3 See p 197 above.
4 See Chap 12.
5 See p 111 above.

purchased 'defective houses';[1] compensation payments made when land and houses are purchased;[2] and rent rebates under the housing benefit scheme.[3] Some attention has also been given to the power or duty to make loans. In the next section, there is further discussion of loans and other home purchase assistance. The final section refers to one other form of financial assistance.

2. HOUSE LOANS AND OTHER HOME PURCHASE ASSISTANCE

We have already seen that local authorities and other landlords selling houses to tenants with the right to buy may be obliged to make loans to assist with the purchase.[4] Similar obligations arise in relation to those affected by housing action areas, improvement orders and repair notices.[5]

In addition, however, authorities have a wider permissive power to make loans and many of the rules which apply to them apply also to the mandatory loans. The general power is conferred by section 214 of the 1987 Act which permits housing authorities to make loans for the purpose *inter alia* of acquiring, constructing, converting or improving houses. It also permits loans to facilitate the repayment of an outstanding previous loan provided that the authority is satisfied that the primary effect of an advance would be to meet the housing needs of the applicant by enabling him or her either to retain an interest in the house concerned or to carry out works of improvement or conversion which would be eligible for loan assistance as above. A loan under the section may be made in addition to other forms of assistance.

The power to make loans is, however, subject to a number of limitations. In particular the local authority must be satisfied that the house concerned either does or will, following conversion or improvement, meet the tolerable standard.[6] The Act also provides that, in determining whether to make a loan, an authority must have regard to any advice which may be given from time to time by the Secretary of State.[7] Such advice was given in SDD Circular No 29/1980 where the

---

1 See p 133 above.
2 See p 186 above.
3 See p 96 above.
4 See p 114 above.
5 See pp 187, 191 and 192 above.
6 1987 Act, s 215.
7 Ibid, s 214(3).

Secretary of State 'asked that authorities should restrict their lending to cases which, while acceptable to them, do not satisfy the normal conditions imposed by the building societies or other lending agencies, and not to seek to compete with these bodies.' In particular authorities were requested by the Secretary of State to concentrate their lending on the following categories of applicant:

(a) tenants of local authority homes and persons on an authority's waiting list wishing to become owner-occupiers;
(b) homeless applicants and those at present living in substandard or overcrowded accommodation, or who are likely to be displaced by redevelopment or slum clearance operations;
(c) those coming into the local authority's area to work, particularly employees required by new or expanding industries;
(d) those desiring to purchase older houses for improvement, though loans should not be given for the purchase of substandard houses unless the purchaser is prepared to submit suitable proposals for improvement; and
(e) individual members of self-build groups when they are about to enter the premises as individual borrowers.

If a loan is to be made under section 214, it is governed by the terms of that section and by Schedule 17 to the 1987 Act which together regulate the maximum loan permitted; security for it; its repayment; and the interest to be charged on the outstanding debt. The loan cannot exceed the value (or estimated eventual value) of the affected lands secured by a heritable security to the authority. Repayment of the principal may be either by instalments (of equal or unequal amounts) during the period of the loan or by a single payment at the end of the period. Interest is payable by instalments over the loan period. All loans entered into since 3 October 1980 are 'variable interest home loans' and so are sums secured by a standard security on the sale of a dwelling-house by a housing authority and loans made pursuant to housing action areas or improvement orders or repair notices.[1] These terms do not, however, extend to loans made under the 'home purchase assistance scheme' (nor to loans which may be made to persons acquiring houses in need of repair or improvement under homesteading schemes).[2]

---

1 Ibid, s 219(1)–(2).
2 Ibid, ss 219(8), 230. Nor do the rules apply when financial assistance is given under the Local Government Act 1988. See p 220 below.

Thus, authorities do not offer fixed interest loans but must normally charge instead the variable rate determined for the period of the loan. This in turn is required to be the higher of (a) the standard rate declared by the Secretary of State from time to time and (b) a locally determined rate. In determining the standard rate, the Secretary of State takes into account current building society rates and movement in those rates. The locally determined rate is that (fixed by local authorities for successive periods of six months) necessary to service loan charges on money applied to home loans plus one quarter per cent to cover administrative costs.[1] The principle underlying the rule requiring the higher of these two rates to be charged is that local authorities should, in general, be lenders of last resort and should not compete with building societies.

Where a variable rate of interest is required local authorities must, within two months of the declaration by them or by the Secretary of State of a new rate affecting that required to be charged, give notice to borrowers of the new rate which will become payable from a date one month thereafter. If the Secretary of State considers that an authority is not charging an interest rate which satisfies the statutory requirements he may direct the authority to charge a new rate.[2] The mere power of housing authorities to make loans to assist with home purchase does not, of course, guarantee that loans will be made. One important constraint is the availability to the local authority of loan finance. This depends upon authority from the Secretary of State to incur the capital expenditure involved and consent has not always been readily available. Since they both draw on the non-HRA block of capital allocations, house purchase loans compete with home improvement grants.[3]

The other constraint is the individual house owner's ability to finance a loan which may be made available. The size of the necessary loan and the rate of interest chargeable may place a loan out of reach of those on low incomes and there have been different responses to this problem. One was the facility made available by Part II of the Housing Subsidies Act 1967 under which the borrower could opt (hence 'option mortgage') for reduced payments of a home loan (the difference being reimbursed to the lending authority by the Secretary of State) in return for giving up any income tax relief which might have been available in relation to the mortgage interest. However, the

---

1 Ibid, s 220.
2 Ibid, s 221.
3 See p 9 above. Loans for the purchase of an authority's own houses do not count against the non-HRA block.

arrangements for mortgage interest relief introduced by the Finance Act 1982 led to the repeal of Part II of the 1967 Act.[1]

Another response, this time specifically in favour of first-time purchasers, was the home purchase assistance scheme. This allowed a first-time buyer (of a house intended to be the buyer's home) special (but very limited) borrowing facilities from the Secretary of State. A number of conditions attached to the availability of these facilities[2] and, for some years, the limits on the assistance available were frozen at unrealistically low levels prior to the eventual winding up of the scheme as a whole.[3]

A different power to assist house purchase is that of acting as guarantor of a loan made by a building society. A local housing authority may, with the approval of the Secretary of State (which may be given on a general basis), enter into an agreement with a building society under which the authority binds itself to indemnify the society in respect of the whole or part of any outstanding indebtedness of the borrower and any loss to the society resulting from the borrower's failure to perform the obligations imposed under the loan agreement.[4] The purpose of this statutory indemnity scheme is to enable building societies to lend lower down the housing market and to borrowers who may appear to be a little more risky than usual. Although this and some other local authority powers of assistance remain on the statute book, the role of local authorities is declining in favour of Scottish Homes.[5]

A more recent innovation was, however, made by the Housing (Scotland) Act 1988 which enabled local authorities to draw up schemes for making grants to qualifying tenants to assist them to obtain other accommodation ie not as a tenant of their landlord authority.[6] The assistance to be given under a scheme is to be towards either the acquisition by the qualifying tenant of an interest in a house or the carrying out of works to provide additional accommodation or both. Authorities are not obliged to draw up schemes but, before implementation, any scheme must be approved by the Secretary of State. The Act provides that a scheme may provide, *inter alia* for the determination of qualifying tenants, the interests which may be acquired or works assisted and the amount and number of grants to be made. The Secretary of State has issued guidance on the use of the

1 Finance Act 1982, s 27.
2 1987 Act, ss 222–227.
3 1989 Act, s 171 and SI 1990/374.
4 1987 Act, s 229.
5 For discussion of the powers of Scottish Homes see p 28 above.
6 Section 66.

powers and has indicated that one of the main purposes of the schemes is to be 'a new approach to helping to relieve the problems of homelessness.'[1] The Secretary of State will, therefore, have regard, when considering whether or not to approve a scheme, to the level of homelessness in an area and the value for money to be obtained from any payment made by the authority.

3. FINANCIAL ASSISTANCE FOR PRIVATELY LET HOUSING ACCOMMODATION

Another relative newcomer to the statute book has been the power contained in the Local Government Act 1988 under which housing authorities may provide financial assistance for privately let housing accommodation.[2] The forms of financial assistance (grants, loans, guarantees, indemnities or, where relevant, the acquisition of share or loan capital) are spelled out and so too are the objects of assistance ie the acquisition, construction, improvement, maintenance or management of property. The Secretary of State's consent is required and local authorities (of any description, ie including regional councils) are specifically forbidden to give financial assistance of the sort permitted under the Act without that consent.[3]

1 SDD Circular No 31/1988.
2 Section 24.
3 Ibid, s 25.

Index